PASSAMAQUODDY CEREMONIAL SONGS

A volume in the series

NATIVE AMERICANS OF THE NORTHEAST:
History, Culture, and the Contemporary

Edited by Barry O'Connell, Colin Calloway,
and Jean M. O'Brien-Kehoe

PASSAMAQUODDY CEREMONIAL SONGS

Aethetics and Survival

ANN MORRISON SPINNEY

University of Massachusetts Press

Amherst and Boston

LC 2009048710
ISBN 978-1-55849-718-4

Designed by Dennis Anderson
Set in Times Roman by House of Equations, Inc.
Printed and bound by Thomson-Shore, Inc.

Library of Congress Cataloging-in-Publication Data

Spinney, Ann Morrison, 1962–
Passamaquoddy ceremonial songs : aesthetics and survival /
Ann Morrison Spinney.
p. cm. — (Native Americans of the northeast : history, culture, and the contemporary)
Includes bibliographical references and index.
ISBN 978-1-55849-718-4 (cloth : alk. paper)
1. Passamaquoddy Indians—Maine—Songs and music—History and criticism.
2. Passamaquoddy Indians—Maine—Rites and ceremonies.   I. Title.
E99.P27S68 2010
974.1004′9734—dc22
2009048710

British Library Cataloguing in Publication data are available.

Publication of this book was aided by a grant from the
Donna Cardamone Jackson Publication Endowment Fund of the American Musicological Society.

Dedicated to the memory of Joseph A. Nicholas
And to David A. Francis

Nil oc ntoliyan, nenuhkuwiyin, nmoshunokc, ntiwak wapanakiyik

[I will go if you lead me; I will hold in my heart the Wabanaki people]

Contents

Preface

This is a study of a group of Native American ceremonies, written by a musicologist whose cultural identity is Euro-American. It reflects centuries of relations between Europeans, including my direct ancestors, and Native people in northeastern North America. The ceremonies under consideration are part of the alliance protocols of the Wabanaki Confederacy, and I imagine that some of my forebears may have experienced something like them before I did. I know that my father, Alvin H. Morrison, has, for I followed him into research in the same area of study and under the guidance of some of the same teachers.

I was introduced to Wabanaki culture, part of the Maritimes region and Algonquian language group, when I was too young to remember. Salient recollections are of being miserable on a foggy shell midden, visiting Abenaki Elder Stephen Laurent in Intervale, New Hampshire, tramping around countless sites of importance in the intercolonial wars, and always admiring the sweetgrass and ash baskets that were used around our house. My sister and I were research subjects one year when my father investigated how Wabanaki people were presented in children's literature. When his analysis of the political systems and adaptive diasporas of northeastern First Nations was used in land claims and federal recognition cases, I saw applied anthropology at work.

I had no special interest in Native American music until a graduate class with Bruno Nettl at Harvard University prompted me to investigate Wabanaki songs and dances. I discovered that although well defined culturally, this was too large a research area. My father suggested that I present my seminar paper on sources for such a study to the Algonquian conference in 1990, and it was here that a Mi'kmaq Elder impressed on me the value that such sources could have for Native communities, and also that having access to Harvard University's libraries put me in a unique position to find them. Passamaquoddy educator Wayne A. Newell, a Harvard alumnus, was also encouraging; and he showed me the file that he keeps on outside researchers, which impressed me as a reversal of the usual anthropological relationship.

Accepting the challenge of finding a research topic within Wabanaki studies, I attended the Sipayik Indian Days first in 1993, after being invited during a previous trip to the Waponahki Museum. The gracious welcome I received there from Joseph A. Nicholas and David A. Francis, and their dedication to promoting language and cultural traditions inspired me. Similarly moving was the frank interest of young people, and the hospitality of Denise Altvater, Margaret Apt, Barbara and Louis Paul, and others. I spent a year in Eastport, Maine, studying Passamaquoddy language, songs, history, and culture under the guidance of the museum staff and Robert M. Leavitt. There I met other researchers working with and within the Passamaquoddy Tribe. I also spent time observing the youth programs and talking with the staff, and having a great deal of time on my hands, attending Mass almost daily at St. Ann's Sipayik (an excellent way to get to know older people). I made almost weekly visits to Indian Township, driving my friends from Sipayik to visit their friends there, to observe the school programs, and consult with individuals and families. During the next two years I returned several times to visit various consultants in both communities. My engagement and marriage to an Eastport man has facilitated continual contacts, with my helpful and well-connected in-laws passing along oral communications.

When I first arrived at Sipayik and Indian Township, I found that the various tribal cultural offices had received repatriated materials including recordings, artifacts, and the bones of Ancestors; people were well aware of written sources on their culture, as well, even if they did not have access to copies. Attitudes toward these materials differ among individuals, but I did not find that helping people to access these resources would in any way upset a cultural process that was well under way when I arrived on the scene. I have therefore always shared my sources and assisted with requests for access where I could. Subsequently, much of my work has been collaboratively investigating historical sources. The uses to which these have been put by the Passamaquoddy community itself are many, ranging from publications to classroom teaching tools to private ceremonies and artistic creations.

In 1995 the Wabanaki Confederacy meeting was held at Sipayik, hosted by the youth council. Invited to observe the meeting, I attended all the public events and the workshops that I was particularly interested in, always asking first if my presence would be acceptable. It was obvious that the presence of people not of Native heritage, or of mixed heritage, caused friction among some of the Elders. The priest then in residence at Sipayik was dismissed from

1. Singers Joseph A. Nicholas and Blanche Sockabasin, June 2002, Photograph by Ann Morrison Spinney.

2. Singers Joseph A. Nicholas and Wayne A. Newell, 2001. Photograph courtesy of the *Quoddy Tides*.

one event, even though traditions indicate that historically the local priest had offered a blessing on such proceedings. That event, since many of the enrolled Natives attending the Confederacy meeting were of mixed heritage (including the master of ceremonies of the dances, who confided that he shared my surname, Morrison) led to some illuminating revelations of Native identity politics. I also experienced "passing" for the first time when, despite my careful self-presentation, I was mistaken for a Native person by a stranger who later castigated me for "sneaking into" a ceremony to which I had in fact been invited by a friend. The lessons I learned during those few days profoundly deepened my understanding of present-day Native American life and encouraged me to explore my own ethnic heritage, which has become my second field: the music of Ireland and Scotland. The challenges that field presents for American researchers have surprising resonances within my experience of Native American cultures.

This study is concerned with the alliance ceremonies of the Confederacy, preserved in oral tradition by Elders, who used to recite the protocols regularly with the aid of mnemonic wampum strings and belts. The traditional laws thus preserved became known as the Wampum Records, among which the Passamoquoddy versions were the best documented. My argument, that Passamaquoddy techniques of song composition and performance parallel the structure of the Passamaquoddy language and the political organization that these ceremonies support, is based on a variety of sources: written documents, sound and video recordings, oral communications, and my own field experiences. I have gathered information from all these (though no doubt I have overlooked others), and the bulk of this work is an interpretation of that information, parts of which conflict with or plainly contradict each other. I have had many teachers, among them academics and Native people, and I am very grateful to all who gave me insights. I hope that I have learned the lessons that everyone attempted to teach me, but the interpretation presented here is ultimately my own synthesis, and none of those who helped me should be held responsible for any errors.

In order to keep this presentation focused, I have had to minimize discussion in several areas where much more could be said. Two issues stand out in particular and were duly noted by readers of my manuscript. First, the wampum protocols show clear relationships to religious practices—both indigenous and European-influenced. Religion, particularly as a site of cultural syncretism, has been much discussed in Algonquian studies; several analyses treating the Passamaquoddy situation have been published, including my own recent work on indigenized Catholic songs and liturgy. I have chosen simply to reference this research here rather than expand upon the details.

Second, consideration of gender roles in the Wabanaki Confederacy, in its protocols, and in its constituent communities could have become a separate study. Much work has been done in this area—including analyses of the lives of individual Native women in the history of the Maritimes and autobiographies and essays by contemporary women—but much more remains to be done to understand Native women's experiences in the wake of centuries of male-biased documentation. I have limited my discussion to some basic ideas that I hope will be expanded upon and critiqued in future work. In this as in so many areas of my research I confronted the reality that my subject is a living culture and that its situation is changing on the ground, every day, sometimes in small ways that may lead to upheavals.

Passamaquoddy songs and dances related to the Confederacy ceremonies are my topic, although throughout this book there are references to other eastern First Nations, especially Penobscot, Maliseet, Abenaki, and Mi'kmaq. This is because the Confederacy was a diplomatic instrument, created out of older alliances among two or more groups. Thus historical sources even for individual communities are inclusive. I have tried to reconcile this essential feature of the ceremonies with recognition of the inherent differences between communities. I would not wish to feed the tendency both in popular culture and in some academic models to lump North American cultures together, erasing the significant differences between them.

By the same token, what I observed and describe of Passamaquoddy ways of doing things should not be understood as applying to all the Confederacy members; nor should my emphasis on correspondences between present and past practices be taken as promoting ideal ways of doing them. The modern Confederacy meetings follow some specific protocols, but in other respects each member nation or tribe has its own ways of fulfilling traditional functions.

No better example of the Wabanaki Confederacy's adaptation to contemporary circumstances could be given than to note that as I write, the sixteenth annual meeting has just concluded. Hosted by the Penobscot Indian Nation at Indian Island, Maine, attendees included a representative from the French Consulate—building on contacts reaffirmed in 2004 at the 400th anniversary celebration of the French colony on Ste. Croix Island—and also representatives from the Venezuelan government, with whom the Penobscot Indian Nation has an agreement for petroleum fuel supplies. Elders as well as elected officials of the Passamaquoddy, Abenaki, Maliseet, and Mi'kmaq Nations, and also of the Wampanoag and Nipmuc, were present; according to newspaper accounts, over forty First Nations were represented. At the meeting of these leaders, a resolution was passed affirming the UN Declaration of Indigenous Rights, which includes the right to self-governance. The federal governments of the United States and Canada have refused to sign this declaration. Just one month prior to this meeting the Penobscot Nation led Maine's other recognized tribes in presenting a similar resolution to the United Southern and Eastern Tribes semiannual meeting in Cherokee, North Carolina, where it was also affirmed. Clearly, the work of the Confederacy within larger networks of alliance, shifting and extending to reflect the needs of the people of the dawn, continues. It is my hope that this study contributes to wider knowledge of the Wabanki Confederacy and the traditions of the maritimes First Nations.

It should be clear that I have not attempted to write a definitive study of the Wampum Records protocols or of Passamaquoddy songs. For a person who is not Native, that would be absurd; it is my personal view that definitive studies are a mirage in any case. Yet though the social sciences moved beyond such notions decades ago, academic language still retains inflections of authority, which I have tried to keep to a minimum (but have not entirely succeeded). Further, some parts of my analysis rely on the elegance of terms that will appear to be jargon even to my colleagues who are not musicologists or are not anthropologists or are unfamiliar with Native American studies.

Throughout the text I have used terms carrying different associations to different groups of people. Most obviously, I have used indigenous words, primarily the proper names of places, groups of people, and social roles. A glossary is included for quick reference while reading. Some English words appear capitalized to indicate a special Native usage: "Elder," for example, designates not merely a person of great age but someone of great experience; "Teaching" in Native contexts is used as a noun, analogous to "lesson" in that it means not merely facts but the wisdom of how to apply them properly. Following standard ethnomusicological practice, names of dances that have proper titles are capitalized for clarity (as in, "he danced the Crow Hop"), which here also distinguishes them as ceremonies (as explained in Chapter 3).

My academic discipline owes an enormous debt to Native Americans. Without their cooperation and patience over several generations, ethnomusicology would never have developed as it has. An even greater debt is owed to those who, in the face of oppression, kept traditional ceremonies in practice, among them the singers who contributed to this book. Passamaquoddy singing features soloists and song leaders, and thus in addition to the Drum groups and others who participated in the events documented here, four individuals stand out. Most of my insights into Passamaquoddy songs and singing come from them, and they graciously permitted me to transcribe their songs.

Joseph A. Nicholas lived most of his life at Sipayik, Pleasant Point Reservation, in Maine. He was raised speaking Passamaquoddy, despite being discouraged from using it in school, and was fluently bilingual after learning to speak English. Joe was a gifted speaker, a talented singer with a keen rhythmic sense, and an inveterate joke teller. After serving in World War II, he returned to finish high school in neighboring Eastport and then trained as a barber. He used to joke that he was "the only Indian licensed to scalp white men." After living for a time away, he returned to the reservation with his wife, Alice, and their young family; he explained that he was disturbed by seeing his children root for the cowboys on TV and wanted to give them a sense of their heritage. At the time, making a living was not easy, as the Passamaquoddy communities are located in the most economically challenged area of Maine. In addition to barbering, Joe worked for the Catholic Diocese of Portland as a coordinator of pastoral programs, through which he encouraged traditional basketmakers and other artisans and out of which also came his concern with reviving traditional public dances; by working with Elders he developed the program that became the Indian Day. As outside interest in Native culture and language grew during the 1960s and '70s, Joe became a public figure, working to develop a bilingual program for the Passamaquoddy schools, founding the Waponahki Museum and Resource Center at Sipayik (Pleasant Point Reservation), and contributing to countless other efforts promoting his community and culture. He served as the Passamaquoddy Representative in Maine's state legislature and in tribal government. Joe was a generous and patient teacher to generations of students, both Native and non-Native, and made use of every available resource and technology—including computers, which enormously frustrated him.

David A. Francis has lived through profound changes as the Passamaquoddy Tribe transformed from a relatively isolated, tightly knit community with close ties to the Catholic Church to one that works directly with federal agencies and utilizes global connections. David has lived most of his life at Sipayik and was raised speaking Passamaquoddy, which remains his first language, though he became fluent in English to the point of working with Morse code during his military service. He returned to Sipayik after World War II, eventually raising fourteen children with his wife, Marion. He worked locally, including as a groundskeeper, while continuing to absorb traditional knowledge from Elders. Over his life David has served his community in various positions in tribal government, including *Sakom* (governor) and director of the Housing Authority. His careful, studious nature and linguistic talents distinguished him as an assistant for academic researchers and he became involved with efforts to produce a writing system, the Wabanaki Bilingual Education program, and the Waponahki Museum. David has contributed to preserving Passamaquoddy song traditions by translating words from historical transcriptions and recordings, including the wax cylinders made in 1890 by Jesse Walter Fewkes with Noel Josephs and Peter Selmore. David has also translated songs into Passamaquoddy for ceremonial and liturgical church use.

Blanche Sockabasin is Joseph A. Nicholas's cousin, and was raised by their grandmother at Sipayik, speaking Passamaquoddy. She is also fluently bilingual and, as a prominent singer of traditional Passamaquoddy songs, is much in demand for public events. She juggled such appearances with her job as a cook at the elementary school in Indian Township until retiring in 2003. Blanche's singing and performance talent—she accompanies herself on a hand drum and is expert at extemporizing text in the traditional way—has been recognized by state and federal artist apprenticeship grants. She knows many of the young people from her work at the school, and her irrepressible personality—which keeps her up late at night with the youth during powwows (despite having had open heart surgery!)—surely plays a part in her success as a cultural teacher. Blanche has been a guest artist at Brown University.

Wayne A. Newell's generation bridges traditional Passamaquoddy singing and drumming style and the intertribal styles that became popular during the 1970s. At public events he can be found singing with older people and then joining a youth Drum group for a powwow-style song. He possesses a stellar vocal tone and is a gifted extemporizer in performance, with a wide knowledge of traditional songs and stories. Wayne was raised at Sipayik, speaking Passamaquoddy at home and English at school, before embarking on an academic career in education which took him to the University of Maine, Harvard, and Boston College. After receiving his masters of education degree, he worked to create the Wabanaki Bilingual Education programs and settled at Motahkomihkuk with his wife, Sandy, and their four children. Wayne worked as a disc jockey in college, and when portable recording devices became available, he was one of the first in the community to use them to collect traditional knowledge from Elders. In addition to the administrative duties of his job in the local school system, Wayne has assisted an enormous amount of research and cultural outreach. He has been invited to speak, to sing, and to MC events at many museums and universities in the Northeast. He has served in various positions in tribal government and currently is on the Board of Trustees of the University of Maine.

Many more people than I can name have helped my work on this project: my father, who has been my longest-serving teacher in Native studies and perhaps the most patient, as it is really only through this project that I have gained a full appreciation of his work; Wayne and Sandy Newell, who have provided continual hospitality as well as teaching; Donald Soctomah, who has supplied encouragement and resources for Passamaquoddy cultural arts; the people of

Sipayik, most especially my language teachers, David A. Francis and Joseph A. Nicholas, and their families; Blanche Sockabasin and the Dana family at Motahkomikuk; everyone whom I interviewed, formally or informally (many are anonymous within these pages); all the participants in events I observed at Sipayik, Motahkomikuk, Indian Island, Big Cove, and elsewhere; and participants in the Algonquian Conferences. Professors who encouraged my work include especially Bruno Nettl, Kay Kaufman Shelemay, Philip Bohlman, Robert M. Leavitt, Anne Dhu MacLucas, Graeme M. Boone, Reinhold Brinkmann, and William Porter. I thank colleagues and predecessors in my research area, especially Nicholas N. Smith, Bruce Bourque, Harald Prins, Colin Calloway, and Pauleena MacDougall. I am grateful to Edward French, editor of the *Quoddy Tides* newspaper in Eastport, Maine, who has documented the Sipayik Indian Days in photographs for several decades. I owe a special debt to the readers for the press of this book in manuscript, Victoria Lindsay Levine and "Reader A," who made many helpful comments and suggestions both detailed and broad. My editors at the press, Clark Dougan, Carol Betsch, and copyeditor Patricia Sterling, have been tremendously helpful with details large and small, and I am especially grateful for their patience with me.

My initial field research was funded by grants from Harvard University and Radcliffe College. Further support for writing and manuscript production has come from Boston College, and my colleagues there have been generous in sharing ideas and the workload of an undergraduate department. Richard Parmentier and Peter Conrad of Brandeis University encouraged me to return to my work and provided a stimulating collegial atmosphere in which to do so. Last but not least I thank my extended Morrison and Spinney families, who have supported this ongoing study in countless ways.

The death of Joseph A. Nicholas in July 2008 only intensifies my admiration for him and for David A. Francis as teachers, leaders, and bearers of Passamaquoddy tradition. I am just one among many who strive to follow their example.

Versions of examples, 1, 4, and 12 were previously published in *Algonquian Spirit: Contemporary Translations of the Algonquian Literatures of North America*, edited by Brian Swann. Used with permission of the University of Nebraska Press. © 2005 by the Board of Regents of the University of Nebraska.

An earlier version of my analysis of the Snake Dance appearing here in chapter 7 was previously published in *Papers of the Thirtieth Algonquian Conference*, edited by David Pentland (Winnipeg: University of Manitoba, 1999).

Photographs of Joseph A. Nicholas with Wayne A. Newell, the Welcome Dance, offering the Peace Pipe, War Club Dance, Tuhtuwas Dance, and Snake Dance are copyright The Quoddy Tides. Used with permission.

Transcriptions from the Speck Collection are published with permission of the University of Pennsylvania Museum and the Archives of Traditional Music, Indiana University.

Transcriptions from the Mechling Collection are published with permission of the Canadian Museum of Civilization.

Glossary

Capitalization is used to show respect for certain elements in ceremonial context, such as the powwow dance Drum, Peace Pipe, Regalia, and names of ceremonies. Specific song genres are capitalized for ease of reading (Greeting Dance).

Kahnawá:ke: Mohawk community, now a First Nation reserve in Canada

Motahkomikuk: Peter Dana's Point, Indian Township

Penawahpskek: Penobscot River area

Penawahpskewi: Penobscot Indian Nation, Penobscot people (lit., "the people living in the Penobscot River area")

Peskotomuhkatik: Passamaquoddy Bay area (lit., "place where there are plenty of pollock fish")

Peskotomuhkatiyik: Passamaquoddy Tribe, Passamaquoddy people (lit., "the people living in the Passamaquoddy Bay area")

Qanute: archaic word used in welcome chants

Sakom, pl. *sakomak*: elected tribal governor, leader, "chief"

Sipayik: Pleasant Point reservation (lit., "shore")

Skicin, pl. *skicinuwok*: Native Americans; human beings; men (lit., "surface dweller")

Waponahkik: the Northeast (lit., "dawn land")

Waponahkiyik, Waponahkewiyik: Wabanaki peoples (lit., "the people living in the dawn land")

Wolastokuk: St. John River area (lit., "beautiful river place")

Wolastoqewiyik: Maliseet First Nations, Maliseet people (lit., "the people living in the beautiful river place")

PASSAMAQUODDY
CEREMONIAL
SONGS

ONE

Identity, History, Tradition

Identity of the Passamaquoddy People

Peskotomuhkatiyik are the people living in *Peskotomuhkatik*, the region where there are plenty of pollock fish, now called Passamaquoddy Bay.[1] This area of deep bays, high tides, and many small islands—only one part of their traditional homelands—is shared between the United States and Canada. The bay itself is fed by several rivers, along which the people traveled in small bands to their inland hunting grounds in the winter, returning for fishing in the spring and fall, and gathering on the coast in the summer. *Peskotomuhkatiyik* are one regional group of a people who identified themselves as *wskicin*,[2] a word that the first Europeans who encountered them heard as "Etchemin."[3]

Peskotomuhkatiyik have selected the term "tribe" to designate their local government, and presently there are three, each centered in a section of their traditional territory. *Sipayik* (Pleasant Point) is a point of land located along a river between two coves on the U.S. side of the coast. This reservation lies between what is now the town of Perry and the city of Eastport, Maine. Inland along the Schoodic Lakes that empty into the St. Croix River is Indian Township, within which *Motahkomikuk* (Peter Dana's Point) is situated on Big Lake. Across Passamaquoddy Bay from Sipayik is St. Andrews, New Brunswick; the third tribe has its headquarters here, but does not have Canadian federal recognition.

Also on the Canadian side of the border in the province of New Brunswick are several Maliseet reserves, and inland to the north are the Houlton Band of Maliseets in Maine and another reserve in Quebec. The people living in these communities, known as *Wolastoqewiyik* (people of the beautiful river), after the territory in the St. John River watershed where they still reside, are also descended from the Etchemin. Maliseet was an epithet meaning "speak differently" or "poor speech" given by their Mi'kmaq neighbors.[4] Maliseets are recognized by the federal governments of both Canada and the United States.

1

The political entity known as the tribe consists of registered members whose eligibility is based on descent as found in census rolls. As of this writing, there are 2,005 Passamaquoddy enrolled at Sipayik and 1,364 at Indian Township (see the websites of each government for updated details).[5] A *Sakom* (governor) and *Leptenant* (lieutenant governor), tribal council, and school board are elected at each community and work together in the Joint Tribal Council of the Passamaquoddy Tribe. All tribal members together elect a representative to the Maine state legislature, with the candidates alternating from each reservation.

Elections were introduced at Sipayik and Indian Township when Maine became a state in 1820. Before that date the *Sakom* and *Leptenant* were appointed following protocols codified in the Wampum Records, laws based on tradition. These required that delegates from allied nations be present to confirm the choice.

The Wabanaki Confederacy

The Wampum Records are the protocols of an alliance known as the Wabanaki Confederacy, named after *Waponahkiyik* (the people of the dawnland), who constituted it along with neighboring nations to the west. Although ethnologists have used the name Wabanaki to designate the Mi'kmaq, Maliseet, Passamaquoddy, Penobscot, and Abenaki nations as a group, it accords with colloquial usage of the "ethnonym" Abenaki for all the people of Acadia, a usage Bruce Bourque found in missionary documents beginning in the mid-seventeenth century (1989:271). The area the French designated Acadia does not exactly correspond to *Waponahkik*—the territory of Waponahkiyik.

The Wabanaki Confederacy as constituted around 1700 was part of larger networks of alliance and continued to function within them during the eighteenth century.[6] It was formally invoked in the political affairs of its constituent nations until about 1870, but the division of territories between the United States and Canada made it increasingly impractical. In 1978 the Wabanaki Confederacy was reconstituted during the course of the Maine Indian land claims case, which made unification once more of primary importance (Prins 1996:212).[7] Different claims are made regarding when and where the first formal meeting of the reconstituted body was held, but it has met annually in the summer since 1992.

Ceremonies of the Confederacy

The ceremonial protocols of the historical Wabanaki Confederacy, based on traditions older than the Confederacy itself, were codified as a result of confederation. The protocols were memorized and mnemonic symbols of them woven into wampum bands; other wampum was exchanged during the proceedings. First published in written narrative form by Passamaquoddy leader Louis Mitchell and linguist John Dynely Prince, the protocols are still practiced today, and their contemporary forms are the focus of this study. How these wampum ceremonies were developed, their deep significance, multiple meanings, and survival are a remarkable story. It is one example, perhaps a microcosm, of the survival of the Passamaquoddy people.

Persistent political practice is a requirement for recognition as a tribe in the United States. Peskotomuhkatiyik have accomplished this in part through ceremonies of song and dance signifying alliance. My central finding is that the aesthetic principles making it possible to keep these ceremonies viable have parallels in the political organization and ultimately the Passamaquoddy language and thus may represent a core cultural theme. This possibility has been overlooked in studies that focused on the techniques of improvisation rather than on the underlying principles of organization.

Political organization is crucial to understanding these ceremonies and the lives of the people who continue to perform them. Historically, Peskotomuhkatiyik were organized into families, which formed the basis of the bands that traveled seasonally inland to fish and hunt and to the coast in summer. Bands fluctuated in size as living conditions permitted and came together in alliances around charismatic leaders. In historical records these alliances were sometimes referred to as tribes. Alliance sometimes was based on language affinity and sometimes crossed the boundary of language difference. Over the seventeenth and eighteenth centuries, alliance structures shifted constantly, and bands moved hundreds of miles within short periods to avoid conflict.

The Wabanaki Confederacy was the largest alliance in the history of this area before the constitution of the United States was ratified. It brought together Etchemin, Mi'kmaq, Abenaki, and Mohawk nations allied with the French as part of a great peace made around 1700. This treaty, signed in Montreal in 1701, bound First Nations[8] from the Maritimes to the Great Lakes together with the French colonial government. Elements of the original Wabanaki Confederacy lasted until the 1870s (Bourque 2001:243–44). After ties were finally broken, the protocols for appointing leaders, greeting allies, and celebrating marriage were left up to the constituent communities. Peskotomuhkatiyik continued to observe them with Maliseet and Penobscot communities, their closest neighbors. Since the Wabanaki Confederacy was reconstituted in 1978 delegations from all the member nations have continued to meet regularly at a different reservation each time in order to spread knowledge of its protocols.

Ceremonies of the wampum protocols are performed today for two principal purposes. The first is, most obviously, to fulfill their traditional functions

3

(described later). The second is to educate the public about Wabanaki traditions. Over time, adaptations have been made to the procedures recorded in
the Wampum Records, but many Elders today can recall past ceremonies viv-
idly. Historical records and accounts by ethnographers and journalists help to
document the continuing practice of these traditions.

Cultural and Regional Designations

Anthropologists recognize Waponahkiyik as a culture group, a subset of the
Northeast culture area (older models include the Northeast as part of the
Eastern Woodlands culture area). The culture-area concept is based on the
ecological features that have shaped the economic possibilities in a given region. Complete cultural homogeneity does not exist within any area of the
model; in the Northeast the lifeways of Wabanaki communities are distinct
from those of neighboring Iroquoian peoples. The culture-area model can give
a false impression of stasis, but life in the Northeast was affected by changing
maritime conditions and human migrations.

Residing in the northeastern Maritimes region of this area, Waponahkiyik
historically subsisted by combining fishing, hunting, and gathering; where
possible, some people grew maize but often did not settle to cultivate the
fields. Before Europeans came among them, they were active participants in
trade networks that linked the Maritimes to the Great Lakes and the rivers
leading to the Mississippi. These networks were the basis of later fur-trading
activity and political alliance after the Europeans arrived.

All the Wabanaki tribes and First Nations speak Algonquian languages.
Algonquian is a very large language group, ranging across North America
and including peoples with very different cultures. Language affinity has been
used to make arguments about ancient migrations of people and technologies.
Relevant to this study, similarities in root words and grammatical forms can
facilitate trading and alliance.

The Europeans who first traded along the Maritime peninsula distinguished
Native people in part by their language. They identified four main groups: from
east to west these were the Souriquois, Etchemin, Abenaki, and Almouchiquois (Bourque 2001:106–7).[9] The Souriquois (and Gaspesians, named after
the Gaspé Peninsula, where they lived) were ancestors of the Mi'kmaq, speaking a language from which modern Mi'kmaq descends. Their territories included what is now Nova Scotia and New Brunswick, down the coast to the
St. John River watershed. The Etchemin, as already noted, were the ancestors
of Peskotomuhkatiyik and Wolastoqewiyik. When the French first allied with
them and wrote about them, they ranged from the Kennebec River in Maine to

the St. John River watershed, where Souriquois territory began. The historical evidence, backed up by place names, is that the Etchemin consolidated
in the eastern part of their territories as a result of Governor Dummer's War
(1721–26).[10]

Given the political structure of various sized bands, from family-based to
larger groups, coming together in alliance, the people speaking Abenaki became known to the Europeans also by the specific areas where they lived:
Norridgewock, Penacook, and the like.[11] When the French and English first
encountered them, their territories ranged from the Kennebec River south to
the Saco River watershed. Pushed by English settlements both northeast and
northwest, they eventually divided into the Western Abenaki and the Penobscot nations of today.

In the early seventeenth century another group to whom the French were
introduced as *Almouchiquois* were living westward of the Kennebec River to
Cape Cod. Their language was so different from Souriquois and Etchemin that
they could not converse (Lescarbot [1618a] 1914(3):113). Their lifestyle also
differed from that of the Souriquois and Etchemin in that they were seden-
tary agriculturalists (Eckstorm 1939:211–12). These people were at war with
the Souriquois and Etchemin in the early seventeenth century. Devastated by
disease and warfare, they did not survive as an identifiable group whose descendants can be traced (Bourque 2001:107). It is probable that the remnants
merged with neighboring groups.

Other groups also operated on the Maritime peninsula as allies of the people
resident there. Mohawks figure prominently in historical sources and in oral
tradition—first as terrifying enemies but later as allies who tried to mediate
conflicts between Native people and Europeans. This shift was the result of a
divide within the Mohawk group: some communities split from the Iroquois
Confederacy and allied with the French colonial government. Of these, the
community at *Kahnawá:ke* were the keepers of the council fire at the center
of the Wabanaki Confederacy. Mahicans also appear in the historical record,
sometimes called *Amalingan* (Rale 1886(67):182–95; Bourque 1989:276 n6).

Identity and Alliance Structures

Even this thumbnail sketch cannot help but indicate the fluidity of the territorial situation in the Northeast. Both Native and European communities
were in motion for over two centuries. European contact wrought profound
changes on the political, economic, and social life of this region. Trade in furs
put pressure on the subsistence economy of First Nations. Europeans brought
epidemic diseases that decimated American populations, and as they began

to settle, their uses of land conflicted with traditional Native uses. Warfare between Native groups resulted from competition for trade, territory, and resources, and the Europeans exported their own conflicts to the American theater. Missionaries brought to Native people new spiritual practices that conflicted and competed with traditional ones, even as healing was desperately sought in the face of mounting confusion.

Since the 1990s, scholars have probed the complexity of these changes, seeking a perspective that combines what we know of Native worldviews with the historical record. Much work has been done to illuminate the processes of alliance that were the backdrop to the formation of the Wabanaki Confederacy. Richard White's study of alliance and warfare in the Great Lakes region illuminates the profound social fragmentation there, beginning with the destruction of Huronia in the mid-seventeenth century, which alliances sought to heal (White 1991). James Drake's reconsideration of the 1675–76 King Philip's War in New England probes the complex social networks that implicated both Native and English participants in conflict and alliance (Drake 1999); treating this same topic, Jill Lepore (1998) gives new attention to multiple sources for reconstructing the past.

In his study of the "Great Peace" treaty concluded at Montreal in 1701, Gilles Havard (2001) argues that it reflected the larger framework, comprising over forty different First Nations, of which the Wabanaki Confederacy formed part. Crucially for my purposes, the descriptions of the Montreal process reveal how protocols and signifiers of alliance from many cultural traditions were combined. The same processes of accommodation are apparent in the wampum ceremonies of the Wabanaki Confederacy. This study advances these arguments, finding evidence that the Wabanaki Confederacy historically was linked to these larger alliances in the songs and dances of its protocols. The Mohawk nations allied with the French were the link. Traditionally, the Mohawk were the "eastern door" of the Iroquois league, which was conceptualized as a metaphorical longhouse.[12] The French-allied Mohawk at Kahnewá:ke became the westernmost nation of the Wabanaki Confederacy, in which they were keepers of its great council fire.

There are significant similarities between the ceremonies of the Iroquois Confederacy, codified in various versions of what is called the Great Law, and those of the Wabanaki Confederacy, codified in the Wampum Records. Both oral codes of traditional law take as their structural focus the death of a leader, a time of potential social instability, and provide protocols for the arrival of allies to mourn and to affirm the selection of a new leader (Fenton 1998; Leavitt and Francis 1990). Similarities also emerge in the details of the protocols.

6

Archaeological evidence indicates that the nations of the Great Lakes had been connected to those on the Maritime peninsula by trade networks for centuries before European contact; the trade in European goods increased these (Bourque 2001:92–94). Both Passamaquoddy and Ojibwe oral traditions tell of closer affinities, and many Native people today assert that they were once one people. This is a Teaching known in both communities as the Seven Fires Prophecy.[13]

These connections are not just historical but are lived concepts in Waponahkik (Wabanaki lands). There is currently much sharing between *Anishena'abeg* and Peskotomuhkatiyik,[14] with members of each group attending spiritual and cultural events of the other. Similarities in the Ojibwe and Passamaquoddy languages facilitate the exchange.

Contemporary Context of Wampum Protocols

The term "Wabanaki" is used with some flexibility by contemporary Native people, who may include Wampanoag, Nipmuc, and other northeastern Algonquian First Nations under this designation. Representatives from these nations are often present at the formal meetings of the Confederacy (AMS 18–25Jun.95, AMS 21Jun.08). The context for the wampum protocols is thus contemporary as well as historical, and their meaning must be understood in these terms too. Waponahkiyik today emphasize connections across Native America, making use of all available technologies to do so. These contacts are particularly evident in political activity and in ceremonies, song, and dance. Powwows are a primary site of such engagement, and even some traditional Passamaquoddy cultural events are listed on powwow websites and draw visitors from other First Nations. Ceremonies created for contemporary purposes likewise draw visitors, such as the intertribal Sacred Hoop ceremony held at Sipayik in 1995. Sipayik has also hosted Kateri Gatherings, in honor of the seventeenth-century Mohawk woman who has long been a candidate for sainthood, which celebrate Native forms of Catholicism.

Political and Cultural Accommodations

The legal demands of maintaining sovereignty continue to force accommodations in Native concepts and practices. A certain blood quantum is required to qualify for tribal membership and to claim Native identity.[15] To remain a recognized political entity, a tribal government must meet certain legal requirements, such as holding elections to a tribal council. Maintaining a government requires a resident population, no longer easy to sustain in many areas where reservations are located. Washington County—which includes

7

Passamaquoddy territories in the United States—is one of the most economically depressed regions of Maine. Since financing is required to maintain the government infrastructure, as of this writing the Passamaquoddy government is pursuing plans to locate a liquefied natural gas (LNG) terminal on traditional territory in order to generate jobs and revenues. But these plans have divided the Tribe and are supported by a slim majority. Those opposed believe that the idea goes against all traditional principles; those in favor point to the need to provide economic support for their community. The location of such a facility on tribal land will alter the people's relationship to the land irrevocably.

The LNG debate is the latest of several issues that have challenged Passamaquoddy traditions. Broadly speaking, these have been the result of external cultural pressures. Such challenges have proved divisive in the past. Repeatedly, Peskotomuhkatiyik have met these challenges with sophisticated forms of accommodation.

In his study of the Native peoples of Maine, Bruce Bourque (2001) proposed that cultural dynamism is a feature of the cultures that developed on the Maritime peninsula, arguing that it derives from the constantly changing environment. Harald Prins (1996) invoked the model of accommodation to explain how Mi'kmaq people have retained their cultural distinction since European invasion. My study of Passamaquoddy ceremonial practices reveals an overarching aesthetic of flexibility that allows traditions to be kept viable and vital, even in the face of internal community divisions.

Cultural Pressures and Responses

European alliances led to missionization and pressured Native communities to choose sides in the intercolonial wars. In the nineteenth century, schooling and other issues surrounding assimilation led to disagreements within communities. The land claims case that the Passamaquoddy Tribe brought against Maine in the late 1960s alienated some Peskotomuhkatiyik because of the nontraditional way that it was prosecuted and resolved.

Traditionally, issues that affected a whole community were decided in councils. Leaders sought to persuade others that their ideas were the best. The Jesuit missionary Paul LeJeune, working along the St. Lawrence River, wrote of Native leaders in 1634: "They have reproached me a hundred times because we fear our Captains, while they laugh at and make sport of theirs. All the authority of their chief is in his tongue's end; for he is powerful insofar as he is eloquent; and even if he kills himself talking and haranguing, he will not be obeyed unless he pleases [them]" ([1634] 1896(6):243).

In the nineteenth century, several questions surrounding the tribe's relations with the state and the church came to a head in a struggle led by a few powerful men who had influence in both Passamaquoddy and Penobscot communities. This debate took place within each group nearly simultaneously and is referred to in various historical and traditional sources as the "Old Party–New Party" split. It was resolved in Peskotomuhkatik by a large faction of the community removing to Motahkomikuk (Peter Dana's Point) in their winter hunting territories.

The debate was complex.[16] The state was offering schooling in English, but those schools were run by Protestant missionaries who attempted to gain converts. Psalm singing and Bible recitation were compulsory parts of education. Despite this pressure, many parents thought that schooling in English would be a good opportunity for their children. The Catholic priests who served Wabanaki communities were already offering catechism classes, in which they taught at least some students to read and write in Latin, French, and Penobscot or Passamaquoddy;[17] these services were expanded in the face of the Protestant threat. Some leaders supported accepting the state's offer for full education; others feared that doing so would result in a political capitulation and loss of their independence.

THE MULTIPLE ROLES OF MISSIONARIES

The premier example of a great change affecting an entire community was the adoption of Christianity. In 1610 the Mi'kmaq *Sakom* and regional leader Membertou decided to be baptized in the Catholic faith; his whole family and most of his band were baptized as well. This was not a personal decision; Kenneth Morrison (1974) argues that it was part of his alliance with the French and thus should not be interpreted in purely spiritual terms.[18]

Membertou's decision opened the door to Catholic missionaries throughout Waponahkik. The cleric who baptized him and his band was a *prêtre seculaire*, the equivalent of a diocesan priest. Several orders competed for the missions to New France; the next to arrive in Waponahkik were Jesuits, under private sponsorship. The religious orders were part of political life in Europe, and like the conflicts between the European powers that pursued alliance with the First Nations in America, their struggles in Europe affected their presence in the Americas. The suppression of the Jesuits in Europe during the middle of the eighteenth century meant the withdrawal of their American missionaries and a break in the documentation of Native cultures that they had provided.[19]

In addition to producing written descriptions of Native North American cultures, the missionary priests were a pivotal structural factor in the relationship between Americans and Europeans. Priests often served in diplomatic roles and even as leaders of Native communities. Their acceptance was eased by parallels between their social function and that of traditional spiritual specialists, although at the same time these similarities brought priests into direct conflict with shamans. Still, seventeenth-century French Catholic practice had many features in common with Wabanaki practice—both societies had spiritual specialists; both used chanting to invoke spiritual help; both used ritual objects in curing—which led both to ease of syncretization and to conflict stemming from competition as well as from the differences in content between the two practices. Both French and Waponahkiyik preferred to keep a spiritual specialist in their company to advise them on how to proceed. As European contact spread European diseases to which Native people had no immunity, priests were accepted into their communities to replace traditional shamans.

The missionaries' letters to their superiors in France were published to proseletyze for the missions and for the religious orders carrying them out. Surviving letters reveal that although the missionaries believed they were bringing the Gospel to North America and transforming Native people's lives, from another point of view they were fulfilling the traditional functions of shamans. The parallels between the two systems of practice were close enough that the significance of ritual actions and roles could never be entirely controlled. (On the basis of my experience worshiping with Waponahkiyik, I have argued that this liminal situation still obtains in Wabanaki Catholic practice today.)[20] Thus, as the practice of Catholicism or Protestantism became part of alliances binding Native communities to one or another of the colonial powers, priests and Christian liturgical elements were incorporated into Native ceremonial practices. The Wampum Records of the protocols of the Wabanaki Confederacy mention certain ritual actions performed by the priest and also certain points where participants in the ceremonies go to church. Historical accounts of actual ceremonies also confirm this practice (Williamson 1832(1):495–98; Brown 1892).

Some priests took on the shaman's role as war leader. They often were called upon by other Europeans, as well as their own mission charges, to mediate in treaties, but a few priests also took up arms and functioned as a *kinap*, a warrior with spiritual power that could affect the outcome of a confrontation. Although such a role seems at odds with that of a Christian minister of the Gospel, some of the missionaries reported directly to the French cabinet. The Missions Étrangères was an administrative unit that functioned in this way.[21] The Abbé Maillard is the most celebrated example of a priest fulfilling this complex role; he was in Acadia from 1735 to 1762, during the final phase of the intercolonial conflict.

TENSION BETWEEN CHURCH AND STATE

After the French ceded their colonial control of Waponahkik to Britain in 1763, the practice of Catholicism became a way of keeping the state at a distance and maintaining community autonomy and traditions. Native leaders seem almost to have played church and state against each other.

In 1775 and 1776 as British colonists contemplated rebellion and pursued alliance with Waponahkiyik, their representatives asked that in return, their communities be supplied with a priest (Leger 1929:125).[22] The constant warfare of the eighteenth century disrupted their access to the sacraments, which had become necessary to them. After the Revolution, John Carroll, the first Catholic bishop in the United States, sent John Cheverus as his delegate to Peskotomuhkatik. The Passamaquoddy congregation's maintenance of liturgical practice greatly impressed him; he noted that without any notation, they performed the Requiem Mass in the very same manner as French Catholics "with the correct singing of the Kyrie and the responses at the Preface" (Leger 1929:138). The American bishop then made arrangements with the bishop in Quebec to assign French-speaking priests to the Penobscot and Passamaquoddy communities (Leger 1929:142–43). These are the oldest Catholic congregations in the state of Maine.

CULTURAL RENEWAL

The Catholic Church has recognized the contribution Native communities made to its establishment in Maine through diocesan support. When St. Ann's at Sipayik burned down at Christmas 1927, a special appeal was made to all the Catholic congregations in Maine for funds to rebuild it (Lucey 1957:338–39).[23] Many Elders from Sipayik and *Motahkomikuk* recall that in the mid-twentieth century, the church would charter a bus to take basketmakers to Boston to sell their wares. When Joseph A. Nicholas wanted to bring attention to Passamaquoddy traditions with a public performance of ceremonies, the church helped sponsor the event that became Sipayik's Annual Indian Day. Similar sponsorship was provided to the Penobscot community at Indian Island for its Indian Day (Davenport 1977).

On the other hand, the Catholic Church was entangled in Euro-American projects to assimilate Waponahkiyik forcibly. During the twentieth century, church attendance was required to get aid vouchers from the Indian agent. English-only language policies were enforced at the Passamaquoddy reservation schools run by the Sisters of Mercy, supported by parents who believed that using two languages would keep their children back. Residential schools in Quebec and Nova Scotia separated children at a young age from their families and suppressed Native culture; further, many children were physically, psychologically, and sexually abused by the staff, crimes for which the churches and government of Canada have made legal restitution.[24]

Today an increasing number of younger people find that Christian practice is not relevant to their lives. This is the result of the foregoing factors, and the general drift in North American culture away from organized religion. Some of my contacts attend church only at Christmas or Easter, simply because they want to celebrate these mainstream holidays. They also attend church services that are part of traditional ceremonies such as the *Sakomawkan* (inauguration) or Indian Day. But during contemporary Confederacy meetings, priests are not always welcome to perform the duties ascribed to them in the Wampum Records (AMS 18–25Jun.95).

The land claims case, which began in the 1960s and dragged on over the next decade, blew open many of the barriers that had kept Native people in Maine hidden in plain sight. The historical moment at which it occurred was probably also responsible for the outward turn that communities have taken in the decades since. No longer relying on the church and an Indian agent, the tribe availed itself of programs instituted under the War on Poverty in the 1960s (AFSC 1989:A-27). Racial consciousness was raised by the civil rights struggle of African Americans, and Native people took notice, adapting their own strategies.

With the land claims settlement in 1980, the tribe was granted a status equal to the state of Maine in some matters, with authority over their own affairs. Even though such changes have brought administrative burdens that are foreign to the culture, Peskotomuhkatiyik use these new resources to traditional ends. One result has been a renewal of interest in Passamaquoddy culture. After the settlement, many families returned to Sipayik and Motahkomikuk, as they were now able to make a living there, and thus restored the generational and community networks so vital to the maintenance of traditions. Native language and culture are now taught in the reservation schools, and there has been a revival of old arts such as porcupine quill work. At the same time, there has been a growing interest in intertribal culture, the "pan-Indian" culture fostered by the American Indian Movement and powwows—which ironically sometimes conflicts with older Passamaquoddy traditions (as shown later in the discussion of song style). It can be difficult to sort out retrieved traditions, such as elements of sweat lodge practice as noted by seventeenth- and eighteenth-century Europeans in Peskotomuhkatik, from such adopted traditions as the songs sung in sweat lodges, which my contacts report were taught by outsiders.[25]

Women's Changing Status

The changing status of women in the domain of music, as singers, dancers, and teachers, is a theme sounded throughout this study. Some of these changes are the result of external influences such as powwow dances and popular feminism. Some are the result of internal developments such as the economic migration of young families to industrial cities in the early twentieth century and the creation of teaching positions in the schools in the later twentieth century.

Historically, gender roles were very clear in Passamaquoddy society. Women had important roles in transmitting songs, historical knowledge, and dance steps, as was emphasized by many of my consultants (see chapter 8). Within memory, several women have been prominent singers and teachers, roles that have acquired more public recognition recently. In the past their teaching was most often done informally, even privately, but since the 1960s, cultural classes have been incorporated in school and youth programs. Current questions about women's involvement with music include changing styles of dance and the use of drums—the latter relating to larger questions in the culture about women's unconscious power as menstruants and the bearers of children.

English law and custom limiting women's social and economic power were imposed in New England and the Maritimes during the colonial period (Plane 1996). Thus it is not surprising that no woman has been elected Passamaquoddy *Sakom* since the state-mandated elections began, though several have been elected to the state legislature and have directed various tribal government offices such as the Passamaquoddy Housing Authority.[26] Women did not serve on the tribal councils until the 1970s, despite being community leaders whose opinions were sought and heeded. Their traditional roles were complementary to men's roles of hunting and warfare, as described by ethnohistorians in neighboring First Nations. Men's exploits in these activities were sung about at the feasts that celebrated political gatherings of Waponahkiyik, but women were asked to confirm leaders in office, and probably also to sanction war parties, by dancing and singing.[27] The assumption that women were or are "powerless" in Native societies is often due to the "silence of familiarity" surrounding their roles (Klein and Ackerman 1995:4, 245). Passamaquoddy women today are thus caught between two traditions: though accredited exceptional spiritual power and acknowledged as singers and teachers, they do not yet have equitable political power within the accommodated social system.

Tourism

The new institutional support for traditional arts is evident in Sipayik's Annual Indian Day, held the second Sunday of August. The centerpiece of this event is a presentation of the protocols of the Wabanaki Confederacy. While similar to the Wampum Records, which historically were recited at least once a year to the community, this program is specifically adapted for tourists. Indian Day is now the culmination of several days of events both traditional and contemporary and is administered much like any ethnic festival in North America today: there is a planning committee with subcommittees devoted to specifics such as children's activities; donations are solicited from local businesses; and the events are advertised in local media, Native media, and online. In addition to tourists, many members of the tribe who have moved away treat the festival like "Old Home Week" and return to visit and reconnect with their heritage. The public presentation of traditional arts is specifically designed for outsiders and meets many of the criteria of touristic culture, such as conscious enactment, but (as detailed in the concluding chapter) these adaptations also fulfill specifically Passamaquoddy needs. Despite historical changes, cultural continuity is readily apparent. The ceremonies of the wampum protocols are central in maintaining continuity with the past.

Methodology of this Study

For an understanding of the dynamic nature of these connections, I have combined the methods of ethnohistory and ethnomusicology, thus drawing on three disciplines: anthropology, history, and musicology. My approach is never strictly chronological but moves between descriptions of present-day practices and historical accounts in order to interpret the multiple significances of the wampum protocols.

History and traditional practice can be approached as parallel records of Passamaquoddy culture. Both are equally valuable but not equivalent in function, and their differences demand different treatment.[28] The methods of ethnohistory and ethnomusicology allow me to compare them, while recognizing and respecting their essential differences.

The majority of historical documents referenced here were written by outsiders, who had their own agendas to advance: missionization, colonization, political enfranchisement, even ethnological method and scholarship. Traditional practice is a record only metaphorically. "Tradition" is maintained in the consciousness of living individuals whose "practice" is in living as Passamaquoddy people. Cultural knowledge was shared with the first European settlers in Peskotomuhkatik, some of whom tried to document it. In the nineteenth century, traditions were shared with ethnographers in a mutual effort to stop the loss of this knowledge.

Respecting the actions, statements, and beliefs of Passamaquoddy people as parallel to the historical record is not the same as judging them against the record of history or turning friends and colleagues into museum mannequins. Rather, it is a way of accounting for what is known but cannot be written down. It sets up a dialogue between streams of data that could be construed as conflicting.

"We Have Our Own Kind of History"

The skepticism with which Native people have learned to approach history was often manifested during my fieldwork. "We have our own kind of history, and it's not found in any of your books," a visiting Elder declared to me at the 1993 Sipayik Native Gathering, on hearing that I was an observer from a university. At this event held just before that year's Indian Day, he gave Teachings on the Wabanaki Confederacy, handed out to the assembled people copies of the new constitution, and reverently displayed a beaded Pipe dating from the historical Confederacy. Asked by a local Elder to explain the ceremonial Pipe, the visitor took her hand and guided it along the stem. That the local Elder understood this wordless Teaching was evidenced by her ability to instruct others immediately afterward in the Teachings of the treaty the Pipe represented (AMS 6Aug.93).

This Sipayik Gathering was held shortly after the Wabanaki Confederacy meeting at Listiguj (Restigouche), Quebec. Many of the participants felt then, and many Waponahkiyik maintain, that the Confederacy today is a continuation of the historical Confederacy. In important ways it is: Abenaki, Penobscot, Passamaquoddy, Maliseet, and Mi'kmaq nations are joined once again to advance common political goals and work for one another's welfare. There are some important differences as well: the international border between Canada and the United States means that these nations live under different legal codes and maintain different relations with their respective federal governments. No external body now recognizes the Confederacy. Some scholars point out that the historical Confederacy was dissolved in the nineteenth century and argue that the break of over one hundred years should not be glossed over.

The conflict between the scholarly view of the Confederacy and the lived sense of connection to the past has broad implications. Obviously, as the ceremonies under consideration here are substantive components of the Confederacy, these differences of interpretation shape different understandings of them. Further, the sense of connection to the past is manifested in general attitudes toward historical sources and their uses by many of my consultants. Some treat these sources as Teachings from their Ancestors and have altered their own practices as a result—for example, by changing the style of their dance regalia, or learning a song recorded a century ago but not sung in their own memory. Historical recordings in particular are respected by many consultants as though the sound brings listeners into the presence of the Ancestors who made them. Although many Westerners personally share this sense, the science-based academic belief system militates against incorporating it into a scholarly interpretation. Instead, scholars focus on documenting instances of cultural contact, on repatriation, and on analyzing different mechanisms in the maintenance of tradition.

In his seminal book *God Is Red*, Vine Deloria homes in on differences between Western and Native conceptions of time as crucial to understanding the respective cultural systems. Arguing that Christianity underlies the system of Western European thought, Deloria highlights its dependence on history.[29] He demonstrates that Native religious systems emphasize place: "No one can say when the creation story of the Navajo happened, but everyone is fairly certain where the emergence took place." A crucial point in his overall argument is that one of the consequences of the Christian emphasis on time is that experience is interpreted through the lens of dogma rather than being important in itself: "Events become symbolic teaching devices, and the actual sequence of physical action which could indicate a divine intervention becomes unimportant; what is important are the moral lessons and ethical choices the legend illustrates" (2003:121, 120) Deloria believes that the Western concept of history has led to the alienation of mankind from the world of experience, from other creatures, and from the forces of nature. He finds in doctrines such as Manifest Destiny evidence of the Western will to impose history on nature.

In Native religious systems, Deloria argues, experience itself is what is important: that is, the ceremonies and power that result from it. Obviously, when experience rather than dogma is used to structure belief and practice, there is opportunity for almost endless adaptation to circumstances. It is this flexibility in practice that many outsiders find confusing and that in some cases has given rise to debates over tradition and factionalism within Native communities.[30] The fascination that Native adaptations have held for anthropologists is evident in the theories devised to explain them, notably nativism and revitalization. The typology of "invented traditions" was first published without reference to Native North Americans (Hobsbawm and Ranger 1983), but ideas similar to this theoretical formulation were circulating concurrently among scholars working on Algonquian topics (A. H. Morrison 1982), and the model has been applied widely in Native American studies (e.g., Clifton 1990).

Ethnohistory

Scholars are concerned with reconciling the claims of history and practice, as recent shifts in the paradigms of anthropology, sociology, and history evidence. Ethnohistory is a methodology rather than a discipline, combining the methods of history and ethnology. Reading historical records as ethnographic data, ethnohistorians apply ethnological models of the cultures involved in order to interpret the recorded actions. A principal contribution of ethnohistory thus has been to make explicit the agency of individuals and of groups in colonial encounters.

Another important contribution of the ethnohistorical method is its focus on problems of sociocultural change. In his articles on methodology, William N. Fenton warned ethnohistorians not to be "taken in by the fallacy of assumed acculturation," declaring that "major patterns of culture tend to be stable" (quoted in Axtell 1979:5). James Axtell pointed out that the combination of historical and ethnological methods allows us to "detail specific changing variables" in a culture by moving back and forth in time, as well as to "control our comparison of variables" (1979:3). Charlotte Heth (1982) was an early proponent of ethnohistory in ethnomusicological studies, finding that its methods exposed stability in Cherokee musical practice over two centuries and despite their removal to Oklahoma.

Ethnohistorians rely on the concept of a cultural system, but because their data are historical, the dimension of time is undeniable, and therefore the picture they compose cannot be static. Recent work on the northeastern First Nations has been concerned with improvisation and strategy by Native leaders. The similarities between ethnohistorical explanations and Pierre Bourdieu's (1977) theories of *habitus*, *praxis*, and *body hexis* are striking, if little recognized—specifically, his conception of the *habitus* as the dispositions generating practice, including principles with which individuals improvise in their social interactions. *Praxis* is Bourdieu's rubric for what is called practice here; *body hexis* is his rubric for embodied knowledge. Ann Marie Plane's discussion of embodiment in explaining the changing position of Native women in New England during the seventeenth century is exemplary (Plane 1996:154). Bourdieu's work has provided a larger theoretical framework for the analysis of Passamaquoddy ceremonial singing presented here.

Ethnomusicology

Ethnomusicologists also struggle to reconcile history, culture, and practice. Their field is generally defined as the study of music as a component of a cultural system (Nettl et al. 2001:15; Titon et al. 2002:4). While participating in anthropology's critique of culture as a concept, ethnomusicology exhibits structuralist tendencies in several important regards.

First, many studies, including this one, posit a "music theory" to explain the compositional, performance, and listening choices of subjects in the cultural group being studied. Even when such a theory is not explicit among the group's members, this is done because not to offer a theoretical analysis and interpretation risks consigning an ethnomusicological study to mere description, "show and tell." Further, the way that any listener hears sounds (and songs) is already structured by an implicit music theory inculcated in him by his own culture and from which he approaches other musics. The very details that an ethnomusicologist notices will be structured either by her own enculturated music theory or by ideas that she learns from her subjects.

The second tendency is a legacy of the discipline's close connection to historical musicology: ethnomusicologists rely on historical accounts, when available, to formulate descriptions of musical systems. Because music is a creative activity, however, ethnomusicologists have generally acknowledged the presence and parameters of innovation and change within musical style systems. Musicology, developed in territories of German influence which were subject to great political upheavals, has always operated with the understanding that history is a construction of data, and writers may not have all the facts from which to theorize.

In interpreting musical sounds, ethnomusicologists are forced to turn to other symbolic systems (Seeger 1977:16). As the (anonymous) colloquial saying goes, "Writing about music is like dancing about architecture"[31]—but the problem is not merely that of translation. Even hermeneutic interpretations of music must model the sounds somehow, because they are not fixed but passing through time: we can not gaze at sound.[32] The goal of ethnomusicology is not usually hermeneutic; rather, it is to model musical sound in terms of its social or cultural context. To do so requires theoretical constructs, even if temporary. The following overview introduces theories that underlie my work here.

SONG AND DANCE STYLE

The concept of style is used both colloquially and academically to evaluate the products of expressive and material culture. Just as one talks about the "styles of dress" appropriate to an era or a social group, one can also refer to styles of music. Musicologists analyze the elements of sound and discern style features such as rhythm patterns in performances, recordings, and written records.

There is no equivalent word for "music" in the Passamaquoddy language, a conceptual difference from English (see chapter 3). Since most of the material discussed here is vocal music, song style is a useful rubric under which to group a description of the general features of music used in the Confederacy ceremonies. The elements of Passamaquoddy song style must be analyzed in order to evaluate historical continuity and changes. These include pitch, rhythm, vocal tone color, phrase relationships, form, and texture. I use historical descriptions, recordings, and my own experiences of contemporary performances as source materials for analysis.

Dances also adhere to parameters of style, colloquially discussed as "moves" or "steps." As with songs, the elements of dance movement can be analyzed, those from different sources compared, and features discerned that can then be correlated with other domains of culture. An aesthetic of mimesis or iconicity is characteristic of Passamaquoddy dances in all genres.[33] The choreography of a dance enacts its function, symbolizing it by resemblance. This is especially evident in dances associated with the Confederacy ceremonies but is found as well in social dances such as *Tuhtuwas* (Little Pine Tufts) and the Snake Dance, and in men's solo dances such as the Flight of the Wounded Eagle and the Hunter's Dance.

The choreography, the song texts, mnemonic symbols woven into wampum belts, and the ceremonial context all combine to convey meaning on several levels at once, which allows both overcoding and slippage for the use of poetic techniques, irony, and multiple meanings. The outwardly visible movements of the body in dance are arguably extensions of the movements of internal muscles (tongue, throat) in song. A similar idea is expressed in the Native idea of the drumbeat as a heartbeat. Thus the goal of this study is to present Passamaquoddy songs and dances from different perspectives, in an attempt to understand them as fully as possible. They are analyzed as musical sound in chapters 3–4, and as constitutive components of ceremonies in chapters 5–7. Chapter 8 focuses on the expressive function of songs and dances. Analogies to features of the cultural system as it is collectively understood at present are made throughout the analysis.

AESTHETICS

The philosophical principles that generate and explain musical style features are part of aesthetics. I use the term "aesthetic" in the well-established sense of "philosophy of taste" rather than its equally common sense of "philosophy of art," since art is not a concept expressed in the Passamaquoddy language. This European concept developed in the eighteenth century to distinguish the fine arts from other technologies, and it implicated style features in a moral system: the beautiful was judged good and understood to have social significance.[34] These eighteenth-century European ideas may be closer to Passamaquoddy conceptions of the power of song and dance than is some contemporary Euro-American usage of the concept of aesthetics,[35] although in Passamaquoddy philosophy what is good is not neccessarily beautiful but efficacious—an inversion of the European system. To use aesthetics as a cross-cultural "translation term" (Clifford 1990) we must only uncouple it from its European association with beauty. It is by now a truism that the judgments of taste are culturally determined, even where there are individual variations. In his analysis of French tastes, Pierre Bourdieu argued that all systems of aesthetics have an ethical basis ([1979] 1984:5). My argument is based on the similar conclusion that aesthetic principles may carry implications beyond the parameters of the medium in which a song, dance, or speech is constructed and reveal interrelationships between the expressive and social domains of a culture.[36] Earlier generations of anthropologists sought to account for this relationship with terms such as *ethos* (Benedict 1932, 1934) and *eidos* (Bateson 1936).[37] In struggling to represent the different domains of the wampum protocols—expressive and social—for a general audience, I find "aesthetics" to be at once the most specific and the most generally applicable term for their configurational principles.

My coupling of aesthetics with survival may have the additional benefit of startling readers out of the West European assumption that traditional music is not a particularly crucial place to do analysis but is useful only in reinforcing findings made in other aspects of a culture. I believe that in the Passamaquoddy case the songs are "a key into" understanding, to paraphrase Roger Williams ([1643] 1973). Many Native people have applied the term "sacred" to their songs for the similar purpose of underscoring how central they are to traditional life.

The crucial function of songs and dances as part of Passamaquoddy practice—of living life as Peskotomuhkatiyik—is the reason they have been maintained. All the description and analysis offered here should never obscure this essential fact but help to illuminate it.

Practice and Performance Theory

I employ the term "practice" with acknowledgment of its uses in sociology, religious studies, and performance studies. Its appearance in the preceding paragraph follows current anthropological thought in using it as a replacement for the term "culture" (Kemper 2001). Whereas "culture" carries connotations of a system of lifeways often theorized external to the people who live it, and misunderstood as static or hegemonic, "practice" forces the recognition that

lifeways are lived by individuals who constantly make choices as they inter-
act with others and with their environment. Pierre Bourdieu's seminal ideas
about practice include that it is generated by habitus—individual repertories
of behavior in social situations, allowing for improvisation within limits set by
social agreement—and that behavior becomes embodied experience, falling
under his rubric of body hexis. In religious theory, practice is the living out of
ideological principles. In this, too, improvisation is necessary. Practice also
carries a particular connotation for musicians that is not extraneous to its use
here: the repetition of a repertoire until mastery is achieved. Even improvisation must be practiced until perfect, as the saying goes.

Linked to the concept of practice is the idea of performance. This concept
too places individuals rather than systems in the foreground. If culture is lived,
its principles are performed in ceremonies, myths, and "social dramas." The
word "performance" expresses an important anthropological concept: carrying out actions. The connotations of these actions are often multivalent, with
meanings that are symbolic as well as practical. No other word is expansive
enough to enclose the many layers of meaning that actions may carry, and so
I have decided to use it throughout in this sense.

I am acutely aware that this word has unfortunate associations for many
Native people, whose cultural praxis has been belittled in Wild West shows,
world's fairs, and other tourist attractions. It is certainly not my intention
to give offense by using this term. I believe that the good work it does in
conveying the complexity of meaningful action redeems it. (Given that I am
writing for multiple audiences, I suspect that other terms will be problematic
as well—"tribe," for example.)

Several aspects of the ceremonies of the Wabanaki Confederacy suggest
that performance theory can usefully explain their multiple meanings. They
are rituals from an anthropological perspective. Presented in an exhibition
format at the annual Sipayik Indian Day, these ceremonies, both in exhibition
and in more traditional tribal contexts, are the site of the negotiation of power
relationships between older and younger generations in the Passamaquoddy
(and larger Wabanaki) community.

In this they are similar to Victor Turner's idea of a social drama. Turner's
influential model of performance distinguishes three different fields: ritual
process, which separates and marks off certain actions and states of being,
revealing significant aspects of the social structure that ritual serves; *com-
munitas*, in which the symbols worked with in ritual are seen extending
into an expressive process beyond specific ritual events; and social drama,
in which situations function like rituals to reveal the structural features of a

society (1986:33–34, 39, 44–45; Hughes-Freeland 2001). In social dramas the principles of a culture are made manifest. These principles are at other times "liminal," meaning always awaiting instantiation.[38]

Turner's notion of the liminal parallels the way music is composed and performed, particularly in oral traditions such as the Passamaquoddy repertories that are the focus of this book. An important subconcept here is that each instantiation is also an interpretation, and subject to social approval. Change may be introduced in these situations. It is the essential dynamism of the wampum ceremonies, their continued relevance and capacity to express being Passamaquoddy, that my analysis ultimately seeks to honor.

TWO

Sources

Native Practice: Traditions, Songs, and Dances

Written sources constitute the materials for historical study, which may employ a variety of interpretive tools (chapter 1). Tradition, conventionally contrasted with history because it is not written, may reside in orally transmitted repertories or in the practices of living as a member of a group. Other methods, principally those of ethnography, help observers to understand and analyze tradition. When data from written documents, orally transmitted repertories, and lived traditions are combined, as they are in ethnohistory and ethnomusicology, the differences among these sources are obvious. But even though tradition and history are constructed differently and accomplish different purposes, they are parallel tracings of the past into the present, and both are valuable resources.

The concept of Native practice as a kind of record paralleling what is found in written historical sources is well illustrated by the ceremonies of the Wabanaki Confederacy. As presented at current Indian Day programs, these consist of the Welcome Dance, Greeting Dance, Peace Pipe Ceremony Dance, War Club Dance, and Marriage Dance. These protocols are used today as they were historically: for welcoming allies, greeting leaders, confirming a new *Sakom* or a marriage. They are also performed to signify to outsiders the continuity of Passamaquoddy traditions.

Similar ceremonies were observed and described by Europeans who visited *Waponahkik* from the sixteenth century on. Once codified by the Wabanaki Confederacy, wampum belts woven with mnemonic symbols kept these protocols in memory and the history of why they were needed.

The protocols were first written down in narrative form at the end of the nineteenth century, after the historical Wabanaki Confederacy had broken down (Prince 1898).[1] Versions also survived in oral traditions, occasionally shared with ethnographers. The ceremonies for installing the *Sakom* were still performed throughout the twentieth century, however, and delegates attended these events in each other's communities. Ceremonies for greeting leaders were recalled by Elders with whom I consulted, and sporadic documentation exists.

Ceremonies were maintained in Native communities by performing them. Performance encodes experiential knowledge, and participants embody the meaning of the ceremonies they perform, reinscribing these valences from generation to generation through practice. In other words, by participating in the wampum ceremonies, people learn the protocols and come to understand the symbolism of various ritual actions. They also learn and maintain a sense of what it means to be *Waponahkiyik*, knowledge that may sound nebulous when translated into words but, according to the testimonies of my consultants, is perhaps most powerful of all.

The Wampum Records Ceremonies as a Core Repertory

Passamaquoddy Elder Joseph A. Nicholas believed that the Confederacy protocols and the songs and dances they comprise are a core Passamaquoddy repertory. They have a similar position in Penobscot and Abenaki traditions. Nicholas's assessment is supported by the fact that Greeting Chants and Wedding Dances are prominent among the musical examples recorded by researchers throughout Waponahkik over the twentieth century. I believe that their central position is an extension of the importance of the Confederacy in the lives of Waponahkiyik.

Confederation did not immediately bring stability. Rather, it set up expectations and patterns of alliance. As explained in chapter 1, the political upheavals in the Northeast during the seventeenth and eighteenth centuries required constant social adjustment. Bands moved to take advantage of trade opportunities and protection, coming together in larger composite communities, many of which survive to the present day, with families now intermarried. The Abenaki community at St. Francis, Quebec, is an example; and many Maliseet families became residents of the Penobscot community at Old Town, Maine.[2]

The Reading of the Wampum

The importance of the Wabanaki Confederacy as bedrock fundamental to the maintenance of cultural traditions is reflected in the ceremony of Reading the Wampum to the entire community. Each band, tribe, or nation had a Wampum Keeper who held the belts that symbolized the protocols. These he knew by heart, and needed only the mnemonic symbols woven into the belts as prompts to recite them. Sopiel Selmore is remembered among Peskotomuhkatiyik for this role. When Frank Speck, William Mechling, and Wilson and Ruth Wallis did their fieldwork with Penobscot, Maliseet, and Mi'kmaq communities, Elders still recalled these occasions. Each summer, often at the St. Anne's Day gatherings that served as homecomings, the Wampum Keeper would bring out the beautiful old belts and "read" them to the assembled community.

Annual Indian Day: A Contemporary Reading of the Wampum

When Joseph A. Nicholas and Mary Moore wanted to give the youth of Sipayik a firm foundation in their traditions, they chose the wampum protocols as the focus of their teaching. They prepared a group of young people to perform the dances, also teaching them the values associated with the traditions. Many of my female contacts remember Mary Moore as their most important teacher of Passamaquoddy culture. Regalia were prepared for the dancers and older people recruited to perform the pivotal roles in the Greeting Dance, War Club Dance, and Marriage Dance with the young troupe. These dances were still maintained by some members of the community, but the dance group seems to have become a focal point for transmitting traditions.

At the time, Joseph Nicholas was employed by the Catholic Diocese of Maine to coordinate pastoral programs in the community. The church sponsored a bus that would take basketmakers and other traditional artisans down to Boston to sell their pieces. Joseph got the church to sponsor also a public program at Sipayik where the dance group would perform the dances and artisans could sell work. It was held on Sunday and opened with a Mass; a public supper closed the day. His purpose was dual: to inculcate a sense of pride in Passamaquoddy youth but also to educate outsiders about the traditions and to show that they were being maintained. He developed short explanations to accompany the program of dances, a practice continued by the subsequent masters of ceremony John Francis and Wayne Newell.

The similarities to the older tradition of Reading the Wampum are striking, although wampum is not usually displayed in the public version of the ceremonies.[3] The year that the dance group was founded, 1964, coincided with the start of the dispute over land in Indian Township which developed into the celebrated Maine Indian land claims case. As noted in chapter 1, during the course of this lengthy legal case the need to reconstitute the Wabanaki Confederacy was recognized.

The Historical Record

Outsiders have documented Wabanaki ceremonies for various purposes, from getting diplomatic advantage to understanding human diversity. Native people have found such documents useful for proving political sovereignty and for reconstructing their traditions. Some of these written records have acquired more authority than the knowledge encoded in practice.

This overview of the historical record is not an exhaustive catalogue of all sources that include a mention of Passamaquoddy—or even Wabanaki—music, singing, or dancing, since until the development of folklore studies in the late nineteenth century, music, singing, and dancing styles were not the focus but only adjunct to the larger purpose of the documentation. Instead, the following survey is arranged by the function of the document and the role of the writer, with an eye to chronological placement. It is not strictly chronological, however, because the details in the documents are dictated by function, and because the different enterprises these documents served do not divide conveniently into centuries or decades; missions, for example, were continued despite warfare and the treaties that ought to have ended it. Europeans began focused exploration of the Maritime peninsula in the late fifteenth century and continued into the early seventeenth. Missions began in the early seventeenth century and continued into the nineteenth, as Protestants sought to convert Peskotomuhkatiyik and their neighbors from Catholicism. The Catholic church at Peter Dana's Point today is still named St. Ann's Mission. Traders continued to have access to daily details of Native life into the twentieth century, as Fannie Hardy Eckstorm's familiarity with her father's customers shows.

Not all the writers surveyed here are European or Euro-American, though the majority are. Native people assisted Europeans in translating and notating texts, in devising writing systems, and in making sound recordings. Several Waponahkiyik published their own accounts of Native lifeways. Among them are Peter Paul (Piel Pol) Wzokhilain, a schoolmaster at St. Francis and Old Town who published an Abenaki language grammar and prayerbook (1830); and Joseph Nicolar, a Penobscot who published a collection of oral traditions ([1893] 2007). In the present day the Bilingual Program at Motahkomikuk has published works documenting Passamaquoddy life in the Passamaquoddy language (Socobasin 1979), and the Passamaquoddy historic preservation officer, Donald Soctomah, has written a multivolume history of the tribe. Allen Sockabasin, a former *Sakom* at Motahkomikuk, published his autobiography in 2008.

Early Contacts

The earliest accounts by European visitors to northeastern North America were written primarily to stake claims for trade and colonization. They are neither detailed nor systematic but are valuable sources because they are the closest to descriptions of precolonial musical practices that we have. On the other hand, their shortcomings reflect some of the issues that have persisted in the interaction of Wabanaki and European cultures.

Contact events affected how European and Native peoples perceived each other, and directly influenced the tenor and content of later European accounts. Although the focus of this study is not history per se, a summary of influential contacts is required in order to understand the different relationships of later writers with Native communities.[4]

It is difficult to place exactly when contacts between Europeans and Americans began. The mythohistorical oral traditions of both American and northern European peoples speak of contacts between the two groups.[5] In *Handbook of North American Indians*, Theodore Brasser wrote: "The first relevant contacts are difficult to determine....Recorded early contacts...[were] possibly preceded and certainly interrupted by a number of others that remained unrecorded apart from indications in the behavior of the Indians noted in the recorded contacts" (1978:78).

The first extended contacts between European and Native American peoples that can be documented began in the eleventh century. Norse expeditions were able to reach northeastern North America by sea, and the natural resources of the area, particularly fish and timber, enticed them to return. But as Bruce Bourque explains, "The Norse seem to have confined their activities to the Gulf of St. Lawrence, mainly Newfoundland...and Labrador" (Bourque 2001:93). They did not have direct contact with Wabanaki communities; the Norse artifacts that have been recovered in Waponahkik most likely came through trade with other First Nations.[6]

The late fifteenth-century voyages of discovery were sent out from several European kingdoms with a primary goal of establishing trade routes; colonies and missions would follow. These voyages set up rival claims to areas of Waponahkik that took several centuries to resolve. In 1497 the Italian seaman John Cabot (Giovanni Caboto) was sponsored by King Henry VII of England in a voyage of discovery across the northwest Atlantic. He "discovered" Newfoundland, and his voyage was a basis for English claims to the Maritime peninsula, but there is no evidence that he made contact with Native people. Three years later, Gaspar Corte-Real explored the Newfoundland coast under sponsorship of the King of Portugal; on his second visit in 1501 he captured fifty-seven native people (probably Beothuks) and took them back to Europe, where they were enslaved (Brasser 1978:79). Later captives were exhibited in the cities and courts of Europe, along with other "primitives" from colonial areas such as Ireland and the Scottish islands.

Such treatment of Americans by Europeans established a foundation of mistrust for further relations, however, it did raise awareness that the American peoples were human beings, a question decided affirmatively by Pope Paul III in 1537.[7] His decision led to a concern with bringing Christian missionary efforts to the Americas, a major focus of European efforts in the seventeenth century, and a primary site of cultural contestation.

Giovanni da Verrazzano explored the Atlantic coast of North America for King Francis I of France in 1524. His unfavorable impression of the people he encountered in Maine, who scorned his trade, is jokingly referenced in the Native community today as "the invention of mooning":

> If we wanted to trade with them for some of their things, they would come to the seashore on some rocks where the breakers were most violent, while we remained in the little boat, and they sent us what they wanted to give on a rope, continually shouting to us not to approach the land; they gave us the barter quickly, and would take in exchange only knives, hooks for fishing, and sharp metal. We found no courtesy in them, and when we had nothing more to exchange and left them, the men made all the signs of scorn and shame that any brute creature would make (such as showing their buttocks and laughing). (Wroth 1970:140–41)[8]

Brasser interprets their gesture as a clear indication of previous contact (1978:80). From Verrazzano's account it is clear that the Native men wanted only metal from the Europeans and had preconceived standards of quality.

Jacques Cartier's account of his 1534 voyage provides further evidence that sixteenth-century Gaspesian nations were acquainted with European goods, and would go to great lengths to secure trade. His description of an encounter in Chaleur Bay, probably with a group of Souriquois people, includes dancing and singing protocols:

> We caught sight of two fleets of canoes that were crossing [Chaleur Bay]. . . . Upon one of the fleets reaching this point [on land], there sprang out and landed a large number of men, who set up a great clamor and made frequent signs to us to come on shore. . . . But as we were only one boat we did not care to go. . . . All came after our long-boat, dancing and showing many signs of joy, and of their desire to be friends. . . . Seeing that no matter how much we signed to them, they would not go back, we shot off over their heads two small cannon. . . . They set up a marvelously loud shout, and came on again. . . . The next day some of these *sauvages* came in nine canoes to the point . . . where we lay anchored. . . . As soon as they saw us they began . . . making signs to us that they had come to barter with us; and held up some furs of small value. . . . We likewise made signs to them that we wished them no harm, and sent two men on shore to offer them some knives and other iron goods, and a red cap to give to their captain. . . . They showed a marvelously great pleasure in possessing and obtaining these iron wares and other commodities, dancing and going through many ceremonies. (Cartier 1924:49–53)

Such ceremonies were the precursor to those codified in the Wampum Records to signify alliance between First Nations in this region and those inland.

It was obvious to Europeans that their feudal colonial model of realizing profits from agriculture, applied in southern regions, would not work in northeastern North America. Because of the climate of the region (a short growing season, poor soil), the Native peoples of the Maritime peninsula practiced only limited agriculture and pursued instead a modified hunting-gathering lifestyle. Thus trade, especially in furs, was early established as the means for Europeans to reap benefits from their contacts with Native peoples. Political alliance became important, and in general the Europeans were forced to treat the peoples of the Northeast as human beings if not as equals.

The Europeans' focus on trading and alliance structured their descriptions of Native ceremonies. In the seventeenth century, as European nations began to compete for trade with the American nations of the Northeast, and for possession of their territories, descriptive sources became more important. An explorer's claims were best established by publishing documentary evidence of his expeditions, so the sources themselves became more systematic. Maps were produced and reproduced, and disputes about accuracy hinged on claims of empirical observation—of actually having been there. Accurate maps and good contacts were crucial assets in the struggles between European nations for control of trade with the American nations.

With the spread of less expensive printing, the market for descriptive sources among educated classes multiplied rapidly. Many accounts of early English and French voyages were excerpted by Richard Hakluyt and Samuel Purchas in English-language publications.[9] As accounts were translated, some writers began to omit navigational information to protect their claims. Information also got corrupted, and musical notation—which was expensive and rare—suffered misplacement.

Explorers whose accounts contain information about music include the English voyagers Martin Pring and George Weymouth. They were preceded by Bartholemew Gosnold who in 1602 came into the Gulf of Maine along the coast between the York and Mousam Rivers. Hakluyt obtained the narrative of Martin Pring's 1603 voyage from Bristol to the lands north of Virginia. At what is now Plymouth Harbor in Massachusetts he traded with the local people, who especially favored a youth in the crew who played the "gitterne" (lute): "In [his] music they took great delight, and would give him many things, as Tobacco, Tobacco-pipes, Snakes skinnes of six foot long, which they use for Girdles, Fawnes skinnes, and such like, and danced twentie in a ring, and the Gitterne in the middest of them, using many Savage gestures, singing lo, la, lo, la, la, lo: him that first brake the ring, the rest would knocke and cry out upon" (Burrage 1906:347). These people were the southwestern neighbors of the nations who later formed the Wabanaki Confederacy. The population in this area was devastated by epidemics and later decimated in King Philip's War.

Pring's anecdote indicates the fondness for exuberant social dancing shared by the lower classes who worked on ships and Native people alike. In subsequent centuries this contributed to a vibrant tradition of back-country dancing, including round dances and contra dancing.[10]

George Weymouth's voyage to the Maine coast in 1605 was for the purpose of finding sites to establish colonies. One of the sponsors was Lord Thomas Arundell, a Catholic who was interested in the prospect of a colony for Catholics, who were then being persecuted in England. Arundel sent James Rosier as his representative. In addition to Weymouth's own records, the voyage was documented by Rosier, whose narrative Hakluyt published. A servant, who had been sent as a goodwill hostage to stay overnight with a party of Native men encountered in the Muscongus Bay area, reported to Rosier of ceremonies that included drumming and dancing. Rosier's account, analyzed in chapter 4, is the source of the adaptation to English of the word "powwow" to mean a ceremonial gathering.

So jealous was Rosier of the fine place where they landed in Muscongus Bay that he left out the latitude measures from his account, and the names of the local leaders. However, he gives "Bashabes" as these people's word for "leader," revealing that this area was under the control of a *Sakom* by that name (Rosier 1605:[19]). Bessabez was a regional leader whose alliances included Etchemin and Abenaki bands (Eckstorm [1945] 1980:76); the people Weymouth's party encountered were one of these. The English group kidnapped five of the Native men and took them back to England, ostensibly to question them about the geography of the area and to use them as pilots for future voyages. Not all were returned, however, and this treacherous act was remembered in Waponahkik.[11]

Samuel de Champlain, who was apparently trained as a cartographer as well as a navigator, published extensive accounts of his voyages up the St. Lawrence River and along the Maritime coasts. His involvement in New France began in 1603 as an observer and culminated in his appointment as Commander in 1629 (Trudel, 2000.) In 1603 he participated in great feasts celebrating the successful campaigns of the Montagnais, Hurons, and Algonquians, under the leader Anadabijou, against the Iroquois ([1603] 1992:101–3). These wars were carried out along the St. Lawrence, and did not involve Waponahkiyik directly. Champlain overwintered with the de Monts company first at Ile Ste. Croix (Dochet Island at the mouth of the St. Croix River) in Etchemin territory and then at Port Royal (Annapolis Royal, Nova Scotia) in Souriquois territory before returning to the St. Lawrence River. In all places he drew excellent maps and interacted with Native leaders. His descriptions include accounts of their daily life, as well as of ceremonies associated with alliance, warfare, and peace. At the time of the French arrival in the Bay of Fundy, the Souriquois and eastern Etchemin peoples were allied and had a contentious relationship with the "Almouchiquois" residing in the vicinity of Saco, Maine.

European Trading Colonies

England and France had a long history of conflict that they brought to their activities in North America. In addition, during the seventeenth century the West European nations were bitterly divided along religious lines, stoking their rivalry. In northeastern North America, the Netherlands, and later the American colonies contributed to hostilities in the region. The struggle for influence was carried out not only by warfare but also by granting, withholding, or disrupting trade and in the work of missionaries.

The first French trading colonies in North America were at Sable Island (1598), Tadoussac on the St. Lawrence (1601), and St. Croix Island (1604). The St. Croix crew—members of a trading company headed by Pierre du Gua, Sieur de Monts—moved to Port Royal (Annapolis), Nova Scotia, after one winter, where they remained until their license was revoked in 1607. At St. Croix Island they were helped by Etchemin people to survive that first brutal winter. Samuel de Champlain was among that party, and his account thus provides more details about the Etchemins and Souriquois than of other Nations whom he met only briefly.

The English followed on their sponsorship of Giovanni Caboto's 1497 voyage with a tentative settlement on the Kennebec in 1607–8, contemporary with a permanent colony in Jamestown, Virginia. They also attacked the French posts in Acadia in 1613, seeking to control the disputed region. (Acadia was the French name; English sources typically referred to it as "the north part of Virginia.")

At the opening of the seventeenth century, many Native Americans who appeared to be meeting Europeans face to face for the first time had already acquired European implements through trade with other Natives (Brasser 1978:81). In 1607, Marc Lescarbot was observing that there had been many changes in the lifeways of the Etchemin and Souriquois, especially in relation to the procuration of food. He described the bands coming down to the coasts in spring with pelts and waiting for the European cod-fishing ships to arrive with extra flour, biscuits, and dried peas and beans to exchange (Lescarbot [1618] 1914:168).

The French and English approached the northeastern First Nations differently, for reasons that were ideological and based on political experience. The English brought ideas and technologies honed in Scotland and Ireland to their dealings with Americans. Their religious practice was independent of the Catholic hierarchy and bound to their sense of nationalism. English settlers tended to live apart from Native people in their own communities, one reason being that their laws granted specific rights to certain classes and denied them to outsiders (Fischer 1989:199–201). The French settlements were more closely integrated with Native communities and intermarried, especially with Catholic converts. Thus French and English accounts of Native life differ in some fundamental aspects that Bruce Bourque has summarized: "French accounts of Indian culture...are more accurate than those of the English for the French routinely interacted with and married into Indian populations....The English, on the other hand, often recorded individual actions and events in greater detail through documents such as deeds, treaties, and official reports" (2001:105).

Another difference is their use of the term "savages." As Harald Prins has noted, the English term carries pejorative connotations (1996:5 n2). The Old French word *sauvage* meant "in a state of nature," connoting forest dwellers. Samuel de Champlain, who provided some of the first details of Maritime people's lives, by using this term was careful to distinguish them from the "Indiennes" whom he had met in his Caribbean voyage.[12]

The best descriptions we have of Etchemin lifeways in the early seventeenth century were penned by the Parisian lawyer Marc Lescarbot. He accompanied his friend Charles Biencourt de Poutrincourt (Pierre du Gua de Monts's partner) to the Port Royal colony in 1606 and stayed nearly a year. Situated on the northwest edge of what is now Nova Scotia, Port Royal was in the territory of the Souriquois leader Membertou, and the colony was under his protection. Membertou was a very powerful man who organized trading and alliance, and was visited by other Native leaders from around the region.

Lescarbot's major work was his *History of New France*, first published in 1609; he also wrote a letter on the "Conversion of the Sauvages," ironically included in the *Jesuit Relations* (1896) with those of Father Pierre Biard, whom Lescarbot accused of treachery and treason. Lescarbot called his poems *The Muses of New France* "literary confection," yet his epic *La Défaite des Sauvages Armouchiquois* (1607) contains ethnographic data on war ceremonies.

Although equally systematic accounts with more data were provided by some of the Jesuit missionaries who arrived in the following years, Lescarbot had an intellectual's interest in aesthetics and was alert to the different philosophies underlying the differing ways of life of different peoples. He was a relativist and often in his writings compared Native people favorably with Europeans, whose vices he excoriated. He was also interested in religion from a philosophical perspective and had much to say about religious concepts.

Lescarbot's *History* was the first comprehensive survey of Waponahkik and the lifeways of the people who lived there. Following the method popular among European writers on foreign cultures at the time (Hodgen 1964), Lescarbot combined his own observations with those of others on the Americas and on ancient Greek, Hebrew, Roman, and northern European cultures.[13] He first compared Etchemins and Souriquois with other American peoples in contrast to Europeans. Second, he strove to educe universal human traits from the customs and behaviors observed among peoples all over the world, from classical times to the present. He revised his *History* twice and republished it in 1611 and 1618. An English edition by Pierre Erondelle appeared immediately after the first French edition, also in 1609. Lescarbot's work on the book overlapped with the first publications by missionaries on the Etchemin and Souriquois peoples and their culture.

Lescarbot went further than his missionary colleagues in his treatment of music as an aspect of culture. In the third edition he devoted a chapter to the dances and songs of the Souriquois and Etchemin in several social and religious contexts ([1618] 1914:179–84). He gave four principal uses of dancing among the Etchemins and Souriquois: "Either to please their gods (let who will call them devils, it is all one to me)...or to cheer up somebody, or to rejoice at some victory, or to prevent sicknesses"; he also stated that in all instances dancing was accompanied by singing ([1618] 1914:181). There were many more occasions on which dancing was employed, as evidenced by Lescarbot's own accounts. In retelling the history of the de Monts Company's expeditions he never failed to note the ceremonies with which the traders were welcomed. Preparations for war were another important Wabanaki ceremonial complex personally observed by Lescarbot at the Etchemin village of Ouigoudi. He described them in some detail in his *Défaite des Sauvages Armouchiquois*, which recounts the raid led by the Souriquois *Sakom* Membertou on the Almouchiquois at Chouacouet (Saco, Maine).

In discussing shamanism, Lescarbot provided examples of songs, and these are the first musical notations from North America. He claimed to have overheard them sung by an assembly of men undergoing a sweat in the cabin of the *Sakom* Membertou. By all accounts, Membertou was a powerful leader because he was a shaman. The three songs are given in *solfège* in the text of his third edition, published in 1618:

> I drew near to Membertou's cabin, and wrote in my tables part of what I heard, which is written there yet, in these terms: haloet ho ho he he ha ha haloet ho ho he, which they repeated divers times. The tune is also in my said tables in these notes: *re fa sol sol re sol sol fa fa re re sol sol fa fa*. One song being ended, they all made a great exclamation, saying, *He-e-e-e*! Then they began another song, saying: *egrigna hau egrigna he he hu hu ho ho egrigna hau hau hau*; the tune of this was: *fa fa fa sol sol fa fa re re sol sol fa fa re fa fa sol sol fa*. Having made the usual exclamation, they began yet another in these words: *Tameja alleluyah tameja douveni hau hau he he*. The tune whereof was: *sol sol sol fa fa re re re fa fa sol fa sol fa fa re re*. (Lescarbot [1618] 1914:106–9)

The authenticity of these melodies has not been questioned, but it would be difficult to prove. They consist of repeated melodic phrases with a high degree of pitch repetition and constitute an anhemitonic pentatonic collection. They are not unlike Wabanaki songs recorded in the last century but are much shorter than is typical—each is only one phrase. Lescarbot's examples might be melodic outlines (we can infer from his description that he wrote them down in a single hearing); they might be fragments; or they might be fakes, made up to impress his readers. In any case, his transcriptions were the first music from North America ever recorded for European audiences. Lescarbot may have been influenced to add the melodies to his third edition by the account published by the Protestant missionary Jean de Léry of his voyage to Brazil. Léry's third edition included five notated melodies sung by Tupinamba Indians ([1585] 1941).

Lescarbot included two of Léry's melodies in the third edition of his *History* for comparative purposes, rendering the Tupinamba songs as he did the Souriquois songs—in solmization rather than staff notation (1618] 1914:106–7). He may have chosen syllable renditions because they were easier and less expensive to print. Léry's staff notations were corrupted, but Lescarbot gives them in their correct form, using *re* for the note D. This means that if Lescarbot's own song notations are not fakes, they could be accurate even as to pitch, because the fixed-*do* solmization system was in use in France at this time.[14] Judgment of Lescarbot's transcriptions is hampered, however, by the absence of any other sweat lodge songs from the Wabanaki past. The sweat lodge was disapproved of by the Catholic Church and has been reintroduced to Wabanaki communities only recently (Prins 1994); my Wabanaki contacts indicated also that the songs used were introduced from other First Nations (AMS 13Aug.93).

Native American song notations fascinated Europeans and were reprinted and arranged; however, no evidence has appeared that they were performed in any of the court masques and ballets that imitated American cultures. The ballets were like parades, displaying royal power and influence around the globe. The masques were more dramatic works, which often contrasted the godlike glory of the court with comical colonial subjects in an "anti-masque."[15] Robert Stevenson has traced the corruption of Lescarbot's melodies as they appeared in various French sources (1973:14–18). The Franciscan missionary-chronicler Gabriel Sagard included examples from Lescarbot and Jean de Léry's description of Brazil, in his *Histoire du Canada* (1636), along with a Huron song from Sagard's own experience. Sagard was the first to harmonize Lescarbot's version of Membertou's songs.[16]

Lescarbot was not alone in his concern with ritual as an area of cross-cultural comparison; rituals and ceremonies were a focus of contemporaneous missionary efforts. His particular concern with music was perhaps not only the result of personal affinity but also a reflection of seventeenth-century French Catholic attitudes about its function as a crucial element of ritual. His attempt to go beyond mere description and provide concrete representation of his "field data," however, is extraordinary. In translating the songs he overheard into the contemporary French system of oral transmission, he was making an interpretive leap between cultures that was well ahead of his time.

The account of Mi'kmaq lifeways written by the trader Nicholas Denys (1672) 1908) is already concerned with changes in Native culture brought about by contact with the Europeans. Denys wrote his *Description and Natural History of the Coasts of North America* after several decades of residence on the Gaspé Peninsula. He was one of the first French settlers and sometime governor in the Port Royal area. Despite his colonial involvement, Denys makes plain that he thought European contact was corrupting Native people, ruining their lives and culture rather than uplifting them. He takes particular aim at sailors on fishing vessels, who plied Natives with liquor and instigated licentiousness. As one of the principal licensed traders in the area, Denys's livelihood was threatened by such behavior. This illicit trade caused the Jesuits to abandon their missions: "There was nothing more to be done with these people, whom the frequentation of the ships kept in perpetual drunkenness" (Denys [1672] 1908:446).

Denys's descriptions of Native marriage and healing ceremonies are substantially the same as those of other seventeenth-century writers, including missionaries. His description of burial rites is circumspect; he states that before contact with the French, the Gaspesians "had no worship." His account is relatively rich with data about their everyday lives, however, because he had extended daily contact with them. He discussed how they procured their food, traveled, clothed and housed themselves; their manners and customs (including healing, how menstruants were treated, the protocols of intertribal visits); and their festivals, noting the importance of recited histories.

Denys devoted an entire chapter to describing the many changes that had taken place since contact with Europeans: "thirty-seven to thirty-eight years ago when I was first in that country...they had as yet changed their customs little, but they were already making use of kettles, axes, knives and iron for their arrowheads." Their festivals, he noted, "they make...as they did formerly...they always make speeches there, and dances; but the outcome is not the same. Since they have taken to drinking wine and brandy they are subject to fighting" ([1672] 1908:399, 443–44).

Missionaries

French Catholic missionaries to the Northeast wrote disciplined cultural descriptions of the peoples they worked among. The *Relations* (reports) of the Jesuit fathers are the most consistent corpus of sources. Their accounts focus on the customs of the Native peoples and efforts to "civilize" them (i.e., enforce seventeenth-century French customs) and convert them to Catholicism. These reports are valuable because they are in some cases the only written record of precolonial practices that the missionaries were eventually successful in eradicating or driving underground. This is especially true of music for ceremonial and shamanic purposes.

In addition to the obvious prejudices of the European missionaries toward Native American culture, their accounts are skewed by their intent—which was to report successful conversions to their superiors in France. Many of the *Relations* were published in France after being received, to encourage application for the missions and to raise church officials' esteem for the rival orders who competed for these assignments (Cadieux 1973). They also encouraged the public to view Catholicism as an adjunct to French nationalism rather than as a threat to national sovereignty during the turbulent politics of early seventeenth-century Europe.

Despite these biases, the first Jesuit missionaries carried on a tradition of scholarship inherited from the Middle Ages but infused with new humanist concerns for phenomenological evidence. Their comprehensive approach may have been spurred by competition between the various Catholic orders. The Jesuits are known for their systematic accounts of Native cultures, covering a predictable repertory of topics including morals and the life cycle. Franciscan accounts in this period are also thorough and cover the same topics. In any case, missionaries' accounts constitute the principal primary sources for study of Wabanaki ancestral lifeways in the early colonial period and today are used by Native cultural programs as well as by scholars.

Margaret Hodgen (1964) demonstrated that these missionaries covered aspects of culture singled out by European ethnographers since the Middle Ages.[17] They include physical description, manner of dress, subsistence, social protocols (including manners of interaction and morals), language, and religion. Also included (usually with an emphasis on descriptive color) are ceremonies, rituals, and many other occasions that involved chanting, singing, or musicmaking. From the missionaries' accounts it is clear that music was an integral part of tribal political and social life and had an efficacious function in medical and religious rites. Thus descriptions of Native music in their functional contexts are integral parts of the reports.

Most of the accounts do not deal directly with the substance of the musical sound, however, nor include attempts at transcription, as these would have been peripheral to the missionaries' purpose in writing the reports. They were not merely documenting Native culture, but defining it in order more effectively to propound their own. Discussions of music thus emphasize the contexts of musical performance and its function within them.

Events in Europe influenced the missions to the Americas, Asia, and Africa. The Protestant Reformation set in motion competition for souls in heaven and political power on earth. Protestantism had taken souls from the Catholic Church, but the missions could replace them. Political alliances formed between nations that did not follow Rome in ecclesiastical matters, and those that did. Catholic and Protestant intellectual currents such as Jansenism complicated the internal politics of European nations. Shifts on all levels subjected the direction of the first American missions to some radical policy changes.

Some of the instability began within the Catholic Church, where the different religious orders competed for mission assignments. In France, the Recollects staked a claim based on a priest who had accompanied Cartier's 1534 voyage (Koren 1962). Jesuits were first sent to Port Royal with the de Monts company in 1611 under private funding; the Recollects were given a North American mission in 1615; and the powerful Cardinal Richelieu supported the Franciscans.[18] The suppression of the Jesuit order from 1750 to 1783 caused a rupture: a dispute in Portugal over American missions spread to France, Spain, and the Italian city-states and culminated in a proclamation issued by Pope Clement XIV in 1773. Jesuits were rounded up and taken prisoner, in some cases deported to prison camps; some of the Fathers were executed, and many of their documents were destroyed.

Chapter 1 noted examples of missionaries who were able to gain influence over Wabanaki communities because their spiritual role was understood in

Native terms. French Catholic missionaries lived with Native people, either residing in villages set up for converts or accompanying them on seasonal migrations. In the seminomadic bands, priests fulfilled the traditional functions of a shaman but substituted Catholic practices. Thus the level of detail in the Catholic mission accounts extends to daily concerns. In pursuing conversion, missionaries were also looking for details of Native lifeways that could be turned to European Christian purposes, either through congruence or through confrontation and substitution. This process, called syncretism, is still followed in Roman Catholic missions around the world.[19]

In North America, Catholic and Protestant missionaries were often on the front lines as European powers fought for influence with First Nations. In functioning as shamans, they were included in negotiations and treaties. This was the context for their inclusion in the wampum ceremonies.

The first missionary effort by a Christian in Waponahkik was undertaken by the French *prêtre seculaire* Jesse La Flesche. He was the equivalent of a diocesan priest, not a member of a religious order. It was he who baptized the Souriquois *Sakom* Membertou and his family in 1610. La Flesche had come to *Nouvelle France* to serve the trading colony at Port Royal, which he did from May 1610 to spring 1611 (Trudel 1966:460). He did not write extensive accounts of his work, but his success encouraged further missionary efforts.

Thus in 1611 Pierre Biard arrived at Port Royal, under private sponsorship separate from the trading company. A Jesuit, Biard argued that Membertou and his band had not been sufficiently catechized to understand their conversion, and La Flesche had erred in celebrating it; by this fault, Biard could establish the necessity of giving the mission to the Jesuits. In 1613, four Jesuits, including Biard, attempted to set up a mission station south of Port Royal on Mt. Desert Island. Almost immediately the missionaries were captured (and two were killed) by the English Captain Samuel Argall, who had come up from Jamestown to drive the French out of what England considered to be the north part of Virginia (Rosier 1605). Guided by information provided by either Biard or a Native informant, Argall proceeded to sack the French establishments in the Gulf of Maine.[20]

Biard sent two detailed *Relations* from the field, one in 1611 and one in 1612, both of which were published. Following his escape from Argall and his return to France, he published in 1616 a sort of "Natural History": *Relation de la Nouvelle France, de ses Terres, Naturel du Pais, & de ses Habitans*. Lescarbot (1615) challenged him on a number of points reflecting on the political situation of the de Monts colony, but in most ethnographic respects their accounts confirm each other.

Biard's letters to his superiors during his missions are full of detailed information about Waponahkiyik. He traveled along the coast of the Gulf of Maine with the Biencourt-Poutrincourt trading party, making new contacts and observing the lifestyles of the different Native peoples. He also engaged in missionary work with the Souriquois and Etchemins of the Bay of Fundy, attempting to catechize them and to change their lifeways to conform with Catholic norms. He argued with local *Sakomak* and *Kinapiyik* (community leaders and warriors) over their custom of taking as many wives as they could afford to support. His meddling in local political relations was not appreciated by the traders, although they also opposed polygamous relations.

The Recollects began missions to *Nouvelle France* in 1615; they were based at Quebec, from which they worked mainly among the Wendots (also known as Wyandots or Hurons). According to John G. Shea, the Recollects had a station on the St. John River as well (1855:135). Gabriel Sagard was the first chronicler of the Recollect presence and of the Huron missions in particular. His description of his Huron mission, the people, and their country ([1636] 1939) provides a comparative ethnographic source for use with missionary sources on Waponahkiyik. It also includes his adaptations of Lescarbot's transcriptions of Membertou's sweat lodge songs. These corrupted versions subsequently became more well known to musicologists, perhaps because Sagard set the songs into four-voice European-style harmony.

A later Recollect writer of importance for Wabanaki history is Chrétien LeClercq, who worked on the Gaspé Peninsula between 1671 and 1683. His *Nouvelle Relation de Gaspesie* ([1691] 1910) is a comprehensive account of the Gaspesians' way of life. He indicated that drastic changes had already taken place because of their increased dependence on trading from the shore with European boats. Still, some of what he observed is generally accepted to be a good indication of earlier, precolonial, layers of culture. LeClercq's account is rich with details of the indigenous ceremonial practices against which he struggled. His is also the first historical source documenting a traditional hieroglyphic writing system. He adapted it for proseletyzing and catechizing, and it is still used today by Catholic Mi'kmaqs (Kauder 1866; Schmidt and Marshall 1995).

French Catholic missions were competing with Protestant missions, chiefly undertaken by English settlers. French mission posts were not spared attacks by the English and their allies during intercolonial warfare as English and French influence in Waponahkik ebbed and flowed. Samuel Argall's raid on the first Jesuit post has already been mentioned; the English capture of Quebec in 1629 disrupted missions to western Abenakis. From the European perspective, the leadership roles that missionaries often acquired in Native bands conferred on them military status. The English made several raids on the Jesuit Sebastien Rale, finally killing and scalping him at Norridgewock in 1724; the Native people who had settled with him were also massacred.

The goal of the French missions was expanded in the 1630s to include proselytizing to New England, especially to regain Irish Catholics who had come as indentured servants to Protestant families (Kenny 2000:7–9). The Capuchins sent to North America were charged with this task, and later the Congregation for the Propagation of the Faith as well.

The Capuchin Fathers received approval for missions "to impede the progress of Puritanism" in New England in 1630, extended to Acadia in 1632. Capuchin missions were established at many forts and places of trade with Native peoples, including Port Royal; Pentagoet; St. John; La Heve, Nova Scotia; and Nepisiguit, New Brunswick (Leger 1929:33–34; Shea 1855:135). Jesuit Father Gabriel Druillettes, who established the settlement of Catholic Indians at Norridgewock as a mission station, at first worked under the beneficence of the Capuchins on the Kennebec.

Only two reports from a Capuchin describing life with Waponahkiyik in the seventeenth century are known today: both are by Ignace de Paris, written in 1653 and 1656. In the course of reporting the activities of fellow missionaries Ignace gives details of Native bands moving around Waponahkik, as they pursued seasonal occupations and responded to French and English military activities. At this time the priests lived and traveled with the bands—usually groups of related families—subjecting themselves to the same risks of starvation, exposure, and warfare. They were fulfilling the traditional role of shamans, to which they had many parallels: both performed propitiary rites for traveling, hunting, and warfare; both invoked spirits; both tried to cure illnesses.

At some point, priests associated with the Missions Étrangères became involved in missions to Nouvelle France. No source gives an exact date. According to Henry J. Koren (1962), any priest not a member of an order given permission to work in Nouvelle France who wished to work there himself had to apply to the Missions Étrangères, which provided general oversight of his work. The Spiritan Fathers (*Congrégation du Saint-Èsprit*) founded in Paris in 1703 were thus in conflict with the Missions Étrangères over missionary work until the Spiritans were granted their own mission to Nouvelle France in 1752. The Spiritans and Étrangères took orders from an official of the French Court, l'Abbé de l'Isle Dieu, from 1734 to 1779. In the intercolonial wars many Spiritans acted as leaders in Wabanaki bands, even leading war parties against the English. It is probable that the direct access of the court to these missions compromised their spiritual purpose in favor of overtly political ends.

L'Abbé Maillard is usually termed a Recollect, as he worked under the direction of that order, but Koren (1962) claims him as a Spiritan. Maillard worked for the Missions Étrangères among the Mi'kmaqs and Maliseets in New Brunswick and Nova Scotia from 1735 to 1762, making detailed descriptions of their customs. He was also involved in directing Mi'kmaq nations in warfare against the English, and was treated with the protocol of an enemy General by the English during the Fourth Intercolonial War (the "French and Indian War") of 1754–63 (Koren 1962:73–80). He accepted peace conditions from the English in 1760 and became an official in the interim Government for the last two years of his life; he died before the Treaty of Paris was signed.

Maillard's *Account of the Customs and Manners of the Mickmakis and Maricheets* (1758) is often quoted as an ethnographic source. It was first published in London, in English, purportedly from an intercepted letter dated 1755. This account is in a pamphlet that includes several other anti-Catholic, anti-French, and anti-Indian tracts and may have been published as propaganda against peace agreements with France and the Wabanaki nations. As an ethnographic source this letter must be used with caution because of its publication format.[21] In many respects, however, the data on ceremonial feasts correlate with those given by other sources, most significantly the Wampum Records. Maillard focuses on ceremonies of war and alliance, including marriage, which the Wampum Records of the Wabanaki Confederacy also address. Because the information corresponds with other sources, it may be accepted tentatively as confirmation that these protocols were in place.

Maillard wrote many letters and statements in his various roles as missionary, interpreter, and Indian agent. Another letter that contains information about music was written to his superior at the Missions Etrangères and forwarded with a cover letter to Madame de Drucourt. This letter was apparently unpublished until 1863, the anniversary of the Treaty of Paris that extinguished French claims in Acadia and Canada. Sections of this text report the speeches of Mi'kmaq Elders describing precontact lifeways, but Maillard's primary intent was to advocate for his mission work. He relates how he intervened with the Mi'kmaq people under his instruction to persuade them not to torture English prisoners, going into great detail of the agonies inflicted and reproducing his lengthy sermon against torture. He describes his role interpreting between Mi'kmaq and English military envoys, and the good impression his congregation made on the English by chanting Mass. Unfortunately, the letter as it is now available is incomplete and cannot be dated precisely, but the interactions with English officials described in it likely indicate the 1740s.[22]

The English, during the seventeenth century, were sending Protestant missionaries among the First Nations of the Northeast, and their efforts immediately came into conflict with those of the French Catholics. Although a Protestant minister had been included in de Monts's first expedition seeking to establish a year-round trading post, the claims of French Protestants to missions seem to have been ignored by the French court. Protestant missions had been undertaken in Brazil in the sixteenth century; this was the reason for protoethnographer Jean de Léry's visit.[23] The Edict of Nantes (1598) had proclaimed tolerance, but this did not translate into equality. Cardinal Richelieu's influence and later control over the French Court was insurmountable.[24]

The records of John Eliot's and Daniel Gookin's missionary efforts among the peoples of southern Massachusetts provide comparative information for a study of the French Catholic missions to Waponahkiyik. Gookin's letters provide some ethnographic information about the Massachusetts and other tribes he served.[25] Eliot's famous Bible (*Mamusse Wunneetupanatamwe Up-Biblum God,* 1663) and other texts can usefully be compared with the prayerbooks translated by Jesuits for use in the Wabanaki missions.

Roger Williams's *A Key into the Language of America* (1643) provides a philosophical basis for understanding these missionary efforts. More than a dictionary, it is a translation between Native and English ways of being in the world. Williams extended his own ideas about the primacy of the God's Word to explore the basis of competing worldviews in language. As John J. Teunissen and Evelyn J. Hinz note in their introduction, "*key* is a metaphorical term indicating the way in which the work will use vocabulary as a means to a non-linguistic end[;] . . . language will be used as an index to a culture which in turn will function as material for spiritual insights" (Williams 1973 [1643]:29).

Colonial Wars

As wars between European powers were prosecuted in the Northeast, the First Nations became involved as allies. They continued to follow their own protocols for conducting warfare, including treatment of captives. Captives were sometimes ritually tortured, which united the Europeans in censure against Native custom. Some captives were treated as slaves, while others— particularly women—were adopted and had children. Many captives who were ransomed, rescued, or escaped published narratives of their captivity, and these form a genre of American writing in the eighteenth century.

The function of captivity narratives written by English people was a complex mix of religious praise, proselytizing, and nationalism; the same can be said of the motives of the public who consumed them. Thus John Gyles, who lived for six years as a captive with an inland Etchemin band, wrote:

These private Memoirs were collected from my Minutes at the earnest Request of my Second Consort; for the Use of our Family; that we might have a Memento ever ready at Hand to excite in ourselves Gratitude & Thankfulness to GOD; and, in our Offspring, a due Sense of their Dependance on the SOVEREIGN of the Universe. . . . In this State and for this End they have laid by me for some Years: At length . . . I was pressed for a Copy for the Publick: . . . I have now determined to suffer their Publication. (Gyles 1736:[2])

The narrative seems largely concerned with describing how Gyles endured the travails of his captivity and in proving the superiority of his English culture. He had been taken captive in a raid on Pemaquid, Maine, in August 1689. He described the tests and tortures he was put through and observed other captives enduring. He conveys the sense of solidarity that French and English prisoners felt as fellow Europeans in the stress of captivity.

But the majority of his account details Etchemin life, with much important information. He calls them "Maliseet," indicating that this name was then in use. He described their seminomadic hunting lifestyle, with its frequent removals and gatherings of the bands; the roles and status of men, women, children, the elderly, and captives; hunting methods; feasts and funerals; and beliefs about the supernatural. Many details are provided of ceremonies, including those of sweat lodges, proving that men still used these ceremonially despite over a century of Catholic practice as well. Gyles accounted for all aspects of warfare except combat, in which he as a captive did not participate. After six years with Maliseet masters (1689–95), he was sold to a French master as an indentured servant, who returned him to a British ship in recompense for his good service after three years in June 1698. Thus Gyles followed his account of life among the St. John Indians with acerbic observations on the ritual practices of the Catholic French. The equation of Catholicism with Native beliefs is a common feature of English Protestant writings in this period.[26]

Gyles's account may be read as testimony of the degree to which acculturation was resisted. His captivity came at the end of a century of colonial contact in Etchemin territory (Acadia), but despite the presence and influence of priests in the region, bands still migrated seasonally, pursuing a hunting lifestyle. Gyles provides evidence that many ceremonial practices were retained. His discussion of Maliseet beliefs in the supernatural, coupled with his observations about the French colonists with whom he lived, demonstrates how aspects of Maliseet culture could exist under the rubrics of Catholicism.[27]

Europeans had used Native captives as translators, and European captives were likewise used by Native people. Those who were released after acquiring facility with Native lifeways, or who elected to remain with the Native community, often served as intermediaries. A modern term for such persons is "culture broker." John Gyles was a typical one in his later career, assisting as a translator in legal proceedings as well as in military negotiations with the Acadian Indians. He appended a summary of his career to the account of his captivity.

The French ceded Acadia to the English in 1763, but the American colonists' rebellion against England soon disrupted Etchemin and Abenaki communities. Mi'kmaq leaders declined direct involvement, which made the colonists suspicious of them. Most of the accounts from the late eighteenth century of Passamaquoddy life are focused on military affairs, to the exclusion of ceremonial life. The journals of Colonel John Allen are an example. It was during this time that the settlement at Sipayik was occupied year-round, leading to closer relations with the Anglo-American communities nearby.[28] But the region remained tense. Passamaquoddy Bay was the site of a major engagement during the War of 1812, and the city of Eastport was re-captured by British forces. The border between New Brunswick and Maine remained disputed and was not fixed until 1842; Native people assisted in resolving it.

The Nineteenth Century

Accounts of Wabanaki culture from the first half of the nineteenth century largely concern public ceremonial life. From this period come several descriptions of events in which the writers were participants or invited observers. In Maine, the change undergone by the Passamaquoddy and Penobscot nations to an elected governorship, and the ensuing Old Party New Party controversy, elicited notable accounts by William D. Williamson (1832), Henry David Thoreau (1864), and Father Eugene Vetromile (1866).

The Euro-American accounts of the Passamaquoddy (and Penobscot) people and their life at this time reveal confidence in the process of assimilation and fascination with "disappearing" Native traditions. These are evident in popular literature as well as the first scholarly studies of the culture. Perhaps the most ironic instance of this cultural conundrum is the body of work done by missionaries in the nineteenth century to document the languages and cultures of Waponahkiyik, whom they were trying to convert. What might today be called linguistic and ethnographic work had previously been left to missionaries, especially the Catholic priests who mediated for many Native groups with federal, state, and provincial governments. Some missionaries had also collected Native stories. These documentary efforts were continued and similar projects undertaken by Indian agents during the nineteenth century.

Some of these sources have proved valuable to Native communities. The Baptist missionary Silas Rand made some of the first transcriptions of Wabanaki oral traditions about Koluskap, the culture hero (Rand 1850, 1894). The writers often studied early mission materials and participated in the nascent field of folklore. Scholarly interest in Native American traditions and languages is evidenced in publications such as prayerbooks in Native languages, journals such as the *Journal of American Folk-lore*, and learned societies such as the Maine Historical Society.

Chapter 1 discussed some of the stresses introduced to the Passamaquoddy community by competing Protestant and Catholic missions, as well as state and provincial Indian agents. By present standards the missionaries' and agents' claims to scholarship are tainted by their involvement with assimilation programs. Another problem is the frequent concatenation of information from different languages, communities, and traditions, attributable to the fact that several of the priests and ministers were assigned to travel circuits.

The publications of the Rev. Eugene Vetromile, who served the Penobscot and Passamaquoddy communities in Maine from 1854 to 1881, exemplify these issues. He came to Waponahkik first as a Jesuit, and when that order was withdrawn because of a dispute with the diocese, he resigned and was immediately reassigned to the same post as a diocesan priest. Vetromile inherited several valuable manuscripts from previous Jesuit missionaries, among them Sebastian Rale, who compiled an Abenaki dictionary; Edmund Louis Demillier, who produced a manuscript prayerbook in Passamaquoddy and Penobscot; and James Romagne, whose Penobscot and Passamaquoddy prayerbook was published in 1834.[29] What remains of their material in Vetromile's publications is valuable, especially for the study of Catholic practices and for linguistic analysis. But Vetromile's own essays into linguistics are beset with errors and misinformation, and he was challenged by his contemporaries.[30] His notated representations of Passamaquoddy and Penobscot music are largely spurious, though his description of singing styles has some value.[31] Vetromile was a contributing member of the Maine Historical Society and a person of public intellectual stature. Although he misrepresented Wabanaki culture, he also maintained its profile among scholars.

At the end of the nineteenth century the wife of the Indian agent to the Passamaquoddy tribe assumed a similar role as "culture broker." Mrs. W. Wallace Brown, as she preferred to be known, contributed articles to the *Calais Advertiser* on Passamaquoddy culture during the 1880s. She read a paper on Wabanaki games before the Royal Society of Canada and contributed to the *Journal of American Folk-lore* (Brown 1888, 1892). Mrs. Brown was also recognized for assisting other scholars to make contact with the tribe, and she supplied ethnographic information.

Her description of the Passamaquoddy *Sakomawkan* ("chief-making" ceremony), published in 1892, is not only a valuable source of data but may be an early example of scholarly activism. It is possible that she was attempting to assist the tribe in reestablishing its sovereignty after it was challenged during the prosecution of a Passamaquoddy man for hunting out of season. Mrs. Brown did not transcribe the music performed on the occasion she observed, and she apparently did not make any recordings; however, her article provided transcription of the Passamaquoddy words for the ceremonies and their dances and songs (spelled phonetically), as well as elucidating the particular functions of the musical pieces through translations of important words in the texts. Her information is detailed enough to be used in reconstructing the tradition (see chapter 6).

A trend toward the popularization of Native North American cultures by rendering Native material into the idiom of Anglo-American popular culture emerged during the nineteenth century. This was part of the search for a uniquely American character in all areas of the arts and contrasts markedly with the cultural attitudes expressed in eighteenth-century captivity narratives such as that by John Gyles. Public interest in "original" sources developed as a result, demonstrated by the appearance of legends in media ranging from women's magazines to the *Journal of American Folk-lore*.[32] The collections of Wabanaki oral traditions published by Charles Leland (1884; Leland and Prince 1902), Abby Alger (1897), Mrs. W. W. Brown (1888, 1892), and Joseph Nicolar (1893) were all strongly affected by popularization, but have ethnographic value. Similarly, Henry David Thoreau's accounts of his travels in Maine with Penobscot guides, published in the *Atlantic Monthly* and other popular literary magazines, include some information about the traditions and contemporary life of Penobscot people. These trips formed the raw material for Thoreau's *The Maine Woods* (1864).

In early folklore research and the fledgling science of ethnography, the division between scholarly and popular publications appears blurred when compared with present practice. One example is the collaboration between Charles Leland, who had the bare credentials of a Harvard undergraduate degree, and the philologist J. D. Prince, who taught at Columbia University. Prince criticized not only Leland's work, but his own collaboration with Leland as "poetical and inexact" in his later publications (1921:3). Women researching Wabanaki culture at this time seem to have occupied a particularly precarious position between scholarship and popular journalism. Several women made significant contributions in their own right as well as serving male scholars as assistants. Although the standards of their work were scholarly, some of their major publications were in popular media.

Many of these writers attempted to preserve the voice of Native storytellers by using quotations, and some used dialect to approximate Native pronunciation of English. Several collectors indicated that the stories were chanted, and some tried to reproduce chant in their versions; many of the legends they collected contained songs, which they marked off in various ways in their texts. Musical notation is extremely rare, however, reflecting the bias of philologists toward collecting texts.

The invention of phonographic recording revolutionized the collection and analysis of songs and oral traditions. Two Passamaquoddy men, Noel Josephs and Peter Selmore, participated in the world's first test of field recording equipment when they collaborated with Jesse Walter Fewkes, a research assistant from Harvard. The article Fewkes published as a result of this fieldwork contains transcriptions and some minimal analysis of the music. The song texts, however, are for the most part given only idiosyncratic anglophonetic transcriptions, as Fewkes had no knowledge of the language (Fewkes 1890a). The Snake Dance Song notation contains obvious errors in its layout, with ends of phrases cut off. Fewkes was not undertaking serious study of Passamaquoddy culture but only testing the machine for potential use on a Harvard expedition to Zuni. Still, his article helped to make phonographic recording part of standard anthropological field equipment and ushered in a new subfield of anthropology focused on gathering musical repertories. As the first-generation equipment was difficult to use, requiring singers to sing into a cone, the contributions of Native Americans to this research cannot be overstated.

The Twentieth Century

Many of the studies undertaken in the first decades of the twentieth century were efforts to document Native cultural practices before they "died out." Thus, fieldwork often attempted comprehensive coverage of a culture. Three long-term studies of Waponahkiyik undertaken by researchers who started out under the auspices of the Canadian Geological Survey's Division of Anthropology included music as an area of investigation. William Hubbs Mechling pursued field research among the Maliseet and Mi'kmaq of New Brunswick beginning in 1909; Frank Speck began fieldwork in the same area about 1906 and eventually moved to comprehensive study of the Penobscot community in Maine in addition to studies of eastern Algonquian cultures in general. Wilson Wallis began with fieldwork on Mi'kmaq culture in New Brunswick and Nova Scotia, also for the Geological Survey, and continued into midcentury working in this area, assisted by his wife Ruth Sawtell Wallis, a physical anthropologist. The publications and recordings of these three researchers are primary sources for the study of continuities and changes in Wabanaki song repertories.

Frank Speck's comprehensive monograph on Penobscot culture, *Penobscot Man* (1997 [1940]) included photographs of musical instruments, descriptions of musical performance practices and contexts, and transcriptions of songs and of some dances from various genres, both group and solo. He treated music as a discrete subject of his investigations. Speck's book is particularly valuable for its coverage of private (or intimate) musical genres, which were not much discussed by earlier researchers. Speck's collection of recordings (1911) includes about 120 songs sung by Penobscot, Passamaquoddy, Abenaki, Maliseet and Micmac singers (hereafter cited as Speck Collection). He elicited performances for his recordings, describing the songs and dances in their functional contexts either from the memory of his consultants or from observed occasions. Many of the examples Speck recorded were transcribed by Jacob D. Sapir for inclusion in *Penobscot Man*, where he treats all songs as Penobscot, even though his notes to the recordings clarify that many of the singers and locations were Maliseet. Much of the information Speck presents as Penobscot is in fact duplicated in other Wabanaki communities. [33]

Speck was part Mohegan and spent seven years, from age seven to fourteen, in a Mohegan household (Feit 1991:114). Perhaps his early experiences led him to emphasize individual informants' information over the seemingly more scientific material that documentary historical sources could provide. His notions of method may be gleaned from his 1947 review of Eckstorm's book *Old John Neptune* (Eckstorm 1980 [1945]). He acknowledged her ability as a historian but faulted her for not considering ethnographic data from other Algonquian peoples. He took as a personal insult her suggestion that his principal informant could behave unreliably. In his dealings with informants Speck actively rejected Franz Boas's injunction (which few would now defend) never to trust the Natives, but occasionally he too seems to have disregarded tribal consensus and historical evidence. Frank Siebert's review (1941) of Speck's *Penobscot Man* disclosed several instances of Speck's gullibility to manipulative informants. Harvey Feit has presented further evidence that Speck allowed himself to be manipulated during fieldwork; perhaps most tellingly, it was in Speck's review of Eckstorm's *Old John Neptune* that he was forced to recant the thesis he had defended against the U.S. and Canadian governments, that the Penobscot people had inhabited their present territory since "time immemorial" (Feit 1991:123–25). Eckstorm's historical and linguistic evidence that the Penobscots were an Eastern Abenaki group who had moved eastward since the seventeenth century to their present location apparently convinced him in this instance.[34]

William Hubbs Mechling began comprehensive documentation of Maliseet and Mi'kmaq culture in 1910 for the Canadian Geological Survey. He too included music as an area of research, gathering extensive material on songs and dances from both groups. His intention of publishing a monograph on Maliseet dances and dance songs is alluded to several times in his publications, but no such monograph has never appeared. Mechling's dissertation (1917), written at Harvard between 1914 and 1917, draws heavily on the information he had obtained in his fieldwork with the Geological Survey. A version of material from his dissertation was submitted to Edward Sapir at the National Museum in Ottawa in 1916; although approved for publication in 1923, this material was not published until 1958–9.

In his yearly reports to the Geographical Survey, Mechling claimed to have made "over one hundred" recordings of songs, but the collection I obtained from the Canadian Museum of Civilization contains only forty-six songs, two of which are not recoverable. Like Speck, Mechling elicited songs for recording and observed them in context.[35] Although this was not unusual at the time, Mechling (1912, 1913) was explicitly apologetic about his need to record out of context.

Both Mechling's dissertation (1917) and the article published later (1958–59) contain only descriptions of the contexts in which music was used. These are fairly detailed, and include current material along with historical accounts. The musical data provided mostly concern general public ceremonies and the songs and dances performed there. There is no consideration given to songs sung by individuals for amusement, group game songs, love songs, work songs, or songs for religious or magical purposes. Presumably he meant to include consideration of these in his discussion devoted to music, as we know from Speck's nearly contemporary work among the Penobscot that such things existed.

Mechling described his methods of research and analysis as a combination of the ethnographic and the historical (1958–59:274). He viewed attempts to reconstruct traditional customs from the memories of older informants as less than desirable, basing this view on his assessment of Wabanaki culture at the time of his fieldwork. He advocated use of written historical material, a great deal of which was then available; hence, his work offers a valuable comparison of historical sources.

Wilson Wallis, whose initial ethnological work on the Mi'kmaq in 1911 and 1912 was funded by the University of Pennsylvania, confined his consideration of music to the contexts of its use. He complemented his original fieldwork with follow-up studies done in collaboration with his wife, Ruth Sawtell Wallis, in the 1950s. Their book, *The Micmac Indians of Eastern Canada* (1955) included descriptions of music in Mi'kmaq social life and quoted historical sources as bases for comparison. Their transcriptions of the musical repertory, while spanning various solo and group song genres, are confined to phonetic transcriptions and translations of song texts with commentary on the functions of various song types. The text transcriptions were done by Jacob Sapir from recordings Wilson Wallis made in his early work for the Geological Survey. The recordings themselves have apparently not survived, as there is no record of them.

Natalie Curtis (Burlin) was a classically trained musician, a prodigy whose later research is commonly referenced by her maiden name. Her independent work with Waponahkiyik and other First Nations was principally concerned with music. *The Indians' Book*, which she edited and published in 1907, was an attempt to help Native Americans document their own cultural traditions in order to preserve them. The book consists primarily of stories, legends and songs from the various tribal traditions. The songs were all transcribed by Curtis directly, without the aid of recording equipment, in performances elicited for the purpose in a spirit of collaboration (Curtis [1923] 1968:xxi, xxii). Not surprisingly, many Waponahkiyik whom she recorded also worked with Frank Speck and William Mechling. Her transcriptions give texts and melodies in Western staff notation, with the fluid metrical nature of the music rendered in a gross way through the use of meter signatures. The commentary provided, written from the point of view of her Native contributors, describes the functional contexts of the songs and dances and the drums and rattles used to accompany them. Although presenting a cross section of Wabanaki musical traditions, Curtis did not draw comparisons between the repertoires. The purpose of the book was to let the material speak for itself, without critical or analytical commentary.

The Wabanaki songs and stories were gathered from reservations and communities in Maine. Included are Penobscot and Passamaquoddy Greeting Songs; a Penobscot "Barter Dance" or Trading Game song; Penobscot, Passamaquoddy, and Maliseet (Round) Dance songs; a Penobscot "Medicine Song," which the notes say may be a social song; and a Maliseet love song. Although the Mi'kmaq are mentioned as a Wabanaki tribe in the chapter preface, they are not represented by a contribution. The Abenaki, by that time residing principally in communities at Bécancour (Wolinak) and St. Francis (Ôdanak) in Quebec, are not even mentioned (Curtis [1923] 1968:3).

The Passamaquoddy songs were contributed by John Salis in Eastport, Maine, next to the Sipayik Reservation; he also sang two of the Penobscot songs, but his name was not recognized either by members of the Passama-quoddy community or the senior field researchers of whom I inquired. The Penobscot material was contributed by Francis Joseph Dana in Lincoln, Maine, and by a man known as Bedagi (Big Thunder) at Old Town. Lincoln is a paper mill town, about midway between the Penobscot and Passamaquoddy Reservations on what is now State Route 6 along the Penobscot River. This route between the reservations is called "the Indian way" at Sipayik. Thoreau ([1866] 1972:290) mentioned Lincoln as "one of [the Penobscots'] homes." After the land claims case, in the 1980s and 1990s, Lee Academy in Lincoln was a popular school among the reservation communities because the curricu-lum emphasized Native perspectives. But there has long been a Native pres-ence in this town: Nicholas N. Smith remembered several Penobscot families who had been living there for several generations. Situated at the head of the lower Penobscot, Lincoln was a center for river drivers, many of whom were Penobscot.[36]

Bedagi is a controversial figure in Penobscot cultural history. Although he contributed to Speck's Penobscot ethnography, he was not Penobscot but of European descent, adopted into the tribe. He is remembered by some consultants as a "Hollywood Indian," a showman, who in later adulthood would regale visitors—particularly scholars and journalists—with ethno-graphic material that was heavily embellished. The songs he sang for Curtis have largely unintelligible texts, Penobscot-sounding "words" mixed with vocables. Nor do the melodies conform to the outlines typical of the Wabanaki traditions. Strange phrase modulations lead to the hypothesis that he was not singing the pitches clearly, misremembering common songs, or simply not carrying the tunes properly.

Some consultants expressed skepticism of Bedagi's motivates, but it is probable that within the Native community he was useful for throwing un-known researchers off the track of critical cultural information, which could not be shared without confidence (Siebert 1941). Curtis's research must have been especially problematic for the Native community in Maine, given the scope of her project and the culturally hostile climate under President Theodore Roosevelt in which she worked—as her preface to *The Indians' Book* acknowledges. An Abenaki colleague has informed me that Curtis did not distinguish "personal songs" from other (public) songs, thus flouting pro-prietary restrictions. Use of her materials thus presents problems of authority and propriety.

Recent Collaborative Projects

The founding of the Society for Ethnomusicology in 1955 was a signal of new methods distinguishing this discipline from anthropology and musicology. Audio recordings of songs and interviews became standard, as did fieldwork over extended periods of time. Nicholas N. Smith's descriptions and recordings of Penobscot, Passamaquoddy, and Abenaki songs and dances are exemplary (1955, 1962); other scholars undertook short-term studies (for example, McAllester 1952, Gilbert [Davenport] 1977). Members of the Native community began actively participating in recording and documenting musical materials and ceremonial events and practices. More recently, singers and Drum groups especially have produced recordings that are sold at powwows and gatherings and are available online at sites such as MySpace.com. Tribal historian Donald Soctomah has guided several projects to completion, including a film on the Machias Bay petroglyphs, which discusses shamanic practices, singing, and drumming (Gerber and Hedden 2004) and a CD sampler of old and new Passamaquoddy songs.

The records previously made of Passamaquoddy culture have also become resources for the maintenance of tradition. A few singers have learned songs from ethnographic collections and are using them again. Similarly, scholarly descriptions in combination with oral traditions help to reconstruct ceremonies. Different opinions are expressed about the appropriate use of outsiders' documentation, but the majority of Waponahkiyik I have consulted view historical sources and academic research as potentially helpful. Many indicated that they felt their ancestors had turned to writing and other recording media as means of transmitting traditions during periods when young people were leaving the traditional homelands for economic exile. Thus, despite different origins, methods, construction, and ostensible purposes, at the present time it is practice—lived Passamaquoddy culture—that is incorporating history. In analyses of the individual ceremonies of the wampum protocols, I explore further this process of reclamation.

THREE

Overview of
Passamaquoddy Songs

There are two way to define the music of any contemporary community: by all the music that is made and used within it, or by the style identified with that community wherever it is made and used. I have chosen the latter, because Peskotomuhkatiyik have maintained their social ties and their culture despite conditions that caused migration and dispersal throughout Native North America. The definition is predicated on the assumption that there is a Passamaquoddy musical style, and this chapter provides an outline of it. Such an enterprise is academic to those who live the culture, but it is a necessary representation to outsiders.

Walking around "the Res" today, a visitor hears many musical styles. Car radios blare the latest hits and selections from the personal collections of their drivers. The question, "What's on your iPod?" would be answered with a mix of styles found in any North American community. Among Peskotomuhkatiyik there is more interest in Native American musics generally, and people are likely to own some of the recordings made in their own community. Given the small size of this community (just under, 3,500), the number of people involved in making music is relatively high, as is the number of those involved in all the arts.

Some music and dance styles are regarded as traditionally Passamaquoddy, and they are still practiced and passed down by elder to younger people, parents to children, both in public performances and in more restricted private situations. In the close knit social structure of the reservations, there is much contact between generations. This has been essential to the maintenance of traditions.

The concept of what is traditional changes as innovations continue to affect the repertories, performance styles, and sound of Passamaquoddy music. Some changes are made by individuals; some have been the result of external styles imported into the community. Even within the ceremonial complex that is the focus of this book, historical "layers" of musical style are evident. These differences are recognized within the community, although any song that fulfills a traditional function might be called "traditional"—especially to outsiders. In ceremonies recently adopted, such as singing an Honor Song at a pow-wow, a song might be called "traditional" regardless of its style. The purpose of analyzing Passamaquoddy song elements is not to disparage innovations and adopted styles but to reveal the integrity of the tradition that underlies the contemporary musical mix.

The question "What is a song?" exposes the different conceptual schemes dividing Passamaquoddy and mainstream Euro-American culture. The terms used to talk about the realm of music, to designate meaningful bits of sound and ideas of what sounds do, are cognitive categories. They can be indicators of, and points of comparison between, different cultural systems.[1]

As suggested above, Peskotomuhkatiyik are fluent participants in mainstream North American culture. The situation with music, as with language and other forms of expressive culture, is of having something extra besides: in this case, traditional music.

Terminology

The ways my contacts used musical terms reveals their ability to function in both Passamaquoddy and European musical systems. Many used English language terms when talking about the field I call Passamaquoddy music but employed them in culturally specific ways that reflect traditional Passamaquoddy concepts. There is no word for "music" in the Passamaquoddy language, and consequently Peskotomuhkatiyik tend not to use that English term to designate their traditional chants, songs, and dances, but to use these more specific terms. "Music" is apparently too abstract to express Passamaquoddy concepts. My consultants repeatedly explained to me, "A song is not a thing. It's an experience." In other words, a "song" or "dance" carries specific connotations: it has efficacy, is associated with particular events or particular individuals.

The words "song" and "chant" correspond to the Passamaquoddy word *lintuwakon* (gerund of *-lint-* "to sing"), and the word "dance" corresponds to predicates formed from the verb stem *-(o)k(a)-* specifying dancing movements. Note that in Passamaquoddy there is no one word meaning "to dance" but rather words describing specific dance movements. The least specific term is *pomoka*, "s/he dances along." In conversation, songs are usually referenced by their specific function as well: *Qepiane*, "Greeting Chant."

Like many inanimate nouns in Passamaquoddy, *lintuwakon* is formed from a verb; fundamentally, it is conceived as the product of action. "Music," as an essentially abstract term for a class of objectifiable "things" in the Western conceptual system, cannot convey this understanding. The literal translation of *lintuwakon* is "sung tool" from the verb stem -lint- with the inanimate suffix -*akon* or -*ikon*. This lexical string is used with prefixes to designate specific genres of song as in *skawintuwakon*, "Welcome Song." The same suffix is used for other tools, such as *tomhikon*, "cutting tool" (from cognates of which came the English word "tomahawk"). The verb "to sing" follows the regular pattern for Passamaquoddy, distinguishing between one person singing *lintu*, two people singing *lintuwok*, and more than two *lintuhtuwok*.

In discussing the Passamaquoddy repertories, my teacher, Joseph A. Nicholas, used the English terms "song" and "dance" interchangeably to designate the pieces of music that are associated with dances. He was one of many singers who do not habitually distinguish linguistically between the song accompanying a dance and the dance itself, because they are bound together as a whole. As Bruno Nettl observed of the Blackfoot word for dancing, these terms cover several expressive domains (Nettl 1989:48). Contextual markers make clear which aspects of this whole are being referenced in conversation. The English word "song" on the other hand, is used by some of my Passamaquoddy consultants to refer to a text by itself, such as a poem that *could* be set to a melody whether it has been set or not (AMS 26Apr.95). Similar usage is found in Euro-American philological studies and even contemporary literary and cultural studies.

The distinction between the Passamaquoddy and musicological senses of the term "song" need not be belabored if readers will keep in mind that to a musicologist a song can be an abstract entity, whereas to a Passamaquoddy person a song is associated with its performance, immanent rather than abstract.[2] For the sake of clarity here I capitalize the term "song" to specify the meaning my consultants intended (e.g. Greeting Song), and lowercase the musicological object.

Concepts: What Songs Do

The Passamaquoddy concept of songs as tools suggests that they have more specific functions than in European cultural systems. Euro-Americans use the word "song" colloquially and often in a generalized sense to mean "music." They tend to think of songs and music as fulfilling a few broad and rather abstract roles: expressing and communicating emotions and entertainment are principal among them.[3] Hence, there is a great emphasis on the sensuous pleasure provided by music and songs. My consultants of all ages criticized this element of Euro-American culture, and younger people particularly pointed to the sexual content of pop music when claiming a higher status for Native music.

Wabanaki oral traditions collectively present evidence that songs, singing, drumming, shaking rattles, and flute playing are indeed tools that have specific efficacy. Sounds associated with instruments—drums, shakers, flutes, and so on—are discussed in the next chapter; the remainder of this chapter focuses on general concepts about songs, singing, and the dancing they inspire.

Passamaquoddy Song Style

Because this is an oral tradition, Passamaquoddy song style is revealed in performances. Performers have an idea of the song, a mental map, of which each performance is an instantiation. Transcriptions and recordings are rarely consulted, and by only a few singers; most do not read music. (Notable exceptions, involved in repatriation projects, are discussed in the concluding chapter.)

Although it is not part of traditional practice, by using recordings and transcriptions, we can examine Passamaquoddy songs as musicological objects. Doing so reveals the style features that distinguish them as a repertory. Within this repertory there are several genres, distinguished by function such as ceremonial association; but function also influences such features as form and rhythm, which can be analyzed musicologically. Style analysis can be valuable in reconstructing the context of historical recordings.

Even the most detailed transcriptions and recordings cannot show the full artistry of a singer or the power of a performance. One must experience the Wabanaki Confederacy songs in their ceremonial context to fully appreciate how they work, and the same is true of other genres. Hundreds of hours of observation over fifteen years, interviews with Elders and favored singers in the community, as well as study of the available recordings, transcriptions, and descriptions from the historical record inform my description of Passamaquoddy song style. All together, these sources reveal a core of aesthetic principles that govern performance and distinguish Passamaquoddy songs from other styles.

Musical sound has four basic parameters: pitch, duration, tone color, and volume. By combining these, style features such as melody and rhythm, form and texture are created. Form and texture in music are metaphorical, since music is not a material art. A transcription can give a map of the mental experience of the singer and her listener.

Passamaquoddy songs are sung solo or in unison, except for intertribal songs, which are antiphonal at the start of each verse. Antiphony (one group or singer answering another) is not evident in the historical record, nor was it recalled in practice before this style was adopted; however, Frank Speck observed that all dance songs except the Micmac Dance were sung antiphonally at Penawapskek in the early twentieth century (1997 [1940]:274). Polyphony was used within the memory of my consultants only to the extent of chanted monotone vocables as accompaniment. Mrs. Brown described this in her account of a *Sakomawkan* (Chief's Dance) in the late nineteenth century (Brown 1892). Exclamations are also added to the texture, and all songs end with singers and dancers calling out "*ta-ho!*"[4]

Melody

"Melody" is used here to mean the combination of pitches in certain durations to create the tune of a song. Melodies seem to move in time, which is reflected in the Western concept of mode.

The abstract concepts of scale and key are derived from the set of all pitches used in a song and how the melody flows, especially how its phrases end. Observation plus analysis of recordings and transcriptions reveals that Passamaquoddy singers use a variety of scales: some melodies are anhemitonic pentatonic; others are hexatonic or heptatonic with modal qualities that sound minor or major to the Western-tuned ear. Some singers have a habit of varying notes with half-step inflections.[5] The use of both major and minor thirds in performances of the *Tuhtuwas* Dance Song is a salient example of this technique (see example 12 in the Appendix), as is the use of a tone one half-step below the final of the Greeting Chant, *He, Qanute*, as performed by Wayne Newell and Blanche Sockabasin (example 4).

In performance, the scale of one song verse may not be that of the next: singers may change the tonic (resting pitch or orienting pitch) though keep the tune. Simply stated, scale and key are not operative concepts in Passamaquoddy musical practice. The Passamaquoddy singers I consulted never mentioned them, focusing instead on melodic phrases and phrase relationships.

Phrases are connected in a logical order that is signaled by cadences. A musical cadence is a formulaic combination of melody and rhythm that functions like intonation or punctuation in a sentence. Passamaquoddy singers use cadences to place phrases in clear antecedent and consequent relationships. The resulting forms are either arch shaped, with the first phrase ending on a higher pitch than the second; or constructed of parallel phrases.

Passamaquoddy song melodies combine phrases in antecedent-consequent and parallel structures to form verses or strophes. Melodies that have been adopted and set with Passamaquoddy words—for teaching language in the schools, for example—are similar in form, and perhaps chosen for this reason. Two examples are the melodies used in "Kumbayah" and in "Silent Night."

Recombination of these phrases is not uncommon, with singers repeating a consequent phrase or adding an extension. This can occur within one performance, so that variation and not purely strophic repetition is a feature.[6]

Melodic phrase relationships are the most important aspects of Passamaquoddy songs; this is how a song is conceptualized, as evidenced in performance practices of strophic repetition, variation, and antiphonal singing. When sung in a group, a leader may start any song verse on any pitch, but the following phrases must be kept in the correct intervallic relationship, even if they are sung antiphonally.[7] My notations are designed to make the phrase structures evident. Western key signatures are used only to show the interval set of the phrases within a verse.[8] The singers I have observed and recorded frequently change the tonic pitch from verse to verse, either when switching leaders or to increase excitement.[9] This flexible approach to pitch orientation is not unique to Passamaquoddy style and practice; it has been documented throughout eastern North America.

Several melodies are regularly employed as the basis for dancing and for extemporizing new texts. Since they are constantly reused, they can be referred to as "stock melodies" or "generic dance songs" rather than by proper titles. Other melodies are consistently used with the same text and for specific functions, such as the Greeting Chant (example 4). In performances of the wampum protocols, usually the proper chant or song will accompany the first part of the ceremonial action, which is then celebrated with a dance, accompanied at least in part by these stock melodies. This division is also found in Abenaki ceremonies, according to an Abenaki consultant.

Stock melodies will be strung together as long as needed for the occasion, a technique similar to southeastern Stomp Dances. This practice is found in many dance traditions from around the world: West African dance songs, Cape Breton *ceilidh* music, and others. A Passamaquoddy singer's skill is judged according to how long he can keep the people dancing, and transitions from song to song are crucial. One singer said of another: "He has the real old form that could keep a roomful of people dancing all night with a rattle[;]...it's in the transitions from one song to another, one section to another" (AMS 25Nov.94). Mrs. Brown found the social dances performed at the Passamaquoddy elections in 1892 to be "interminable, it is so difficult to see where one ends and the next begins" (1892:59)—a testimony to the skill of the singer.

Song Texts

In addition to melodic variation, song lyrics are extemporized to a greater or lesser degree. Many songs have refrains texted with *vocables*, nonlexical

58

syllables that keep the rhythm and place in the form.[10] These are often the most stable elements of the song. They may occur at the conclusion of a verse (in *Tuhtuwas*, example 12), as consequent phrases,[11] or as refrain verses (*Mahqan-kahtek ktolutanen*, example 22).

Other phrases are set with lexical text, forming sentences and phrases. Some song texts make cryptic allusions to historical events or to traditions that are kept within the community. An example is the dance song text *Itomuk Sipayik qayuwa...Itomuhk Motahkomikuk qayuwa* ("They were angry at Sipayik.... They were angry at Peter Dana's Point"). What they were angry about is never stated. Other texts make specific comments about the occasion for which they are sung: *Pemkiskahk wonakine sakomawka* ("Today we are dancing the Governor's Installation").

Although often extemporized, text is as important as melody in the structure of songs. Song texts create stress patterns, interacting with the rhythm of the melody; in performances when text is extemporized, this may alter the durations. Since pitch intonation in the Passamaquoddy language affects lexical meaning, text and melody must be carefully matched. Long vowels must be set to stressed pulses. It is impossible to rule text or melody superior in the construction and organization of phrases. Table 1 gives a key to Passamaquoddy pronunciation.

Many of my consultants showed an extreme concern for text in transcribed examples, being reluctant to sing songs if they could not with certainty pronounce the words as transcribed.[12] Another consultant spent hours with me going over a song transcribed by Natalie Curtis until he could determine the proper words. We tried beating the pulse several different ways, as the relationship of syllables to rhythm is crucial in determining vowel sounds.

The procedures that Passamaquoddy singers follow when extemporizing, and their emphasis on variation in performance, make the songs impossible to fit into European categories such as strophic and stichic.[13] The closest classification of their procedures is strophic variation, but this gives an incomplete idea of the extent to which verses are altered in performances.

As variation, recombination, and extemporization allow songs to be adapted to specific situations, they also accommodate changing sociocultural circumstances. New song texts may be fitted to melodies to reflect contemporary social needs, such as when David A. Francis and Joseph A. Nicholas wrote *Musa kotusomihkoc puktewick* ("Don't drink alcohol," example 28) to the melody of the dance song *Tuhtuwas*. Old songs have been fitted to the powwow drum rhythm, adapted to the Native American flute, and set with chordal guitar accompaniment.

Table 1. Passamaquoddy Pronunciation

A as A in English "father"	L as L in English "let"
AW as OW in English "how"	M as M in English "man"
AY as AY in English "aye"	N as N in English "not"
C unvoiced as CH in English "chip"	O as the schwa sound
C voiced as J in English "juice"	P unvoiced as P in English "pen"
E as E in English "bed"	P voiced as B in English "bed"
EH as A in English "apple"	Q unvoiced as KW in English
EW is a blend not found in English	Q voiced as GW in English
EY as EY in English "grey"	S unvoiced as S in English "sun"
H as H in English "hat"	S voiced as Z in English "zed"
I as EE in English "teenager"	T unvoiced as T in English "tin"
IW as EW in English "few"	T voiced as D in English "dog"
K unvoiced as K in English "King"	U as OO in English "boot"
K voiced as G in English "good"	W as W in English "wit"

Notes

An initial consonant is voiced unless preceded by an apostrophe. One consonant between vowels or preceded by the initial first-person marker N- will be voiced.

Otherwise, where two consonants come together, both will be unvoiced.

H after a vowel and before a consonant lengthens the vowel (except E, see above) and makes the consonant unvoiced. Y between two vowels represents a dipthong.

Vowels are semi-tonal, with AY being pitched lowest and I being pitched highest. O is the schwa sound and generally not stressed.

Performance Style: Traditional Singing

The tone color of older Passamaquoddy singers is significant, as it is quite different from the intertribal powwow style. Older generations of singers use a relaxed vocal tone with no strain or pulsation. They tend to pitch their voices low, and many women sing in chest voice rather than head voice. Many women are noted singers in this style today, although the historical recordings are dominated by men. Since men were the principal consultants for the fieldworkers, however, this may not be representative, as the historical record indicates that women did lead dances (Maillard 1758:14; Brown 1892).

The intertribal powwow style of songs and singing is based on historical Plains Indian styles. The vocal tone used is strained and incorporates pulsations of intensity. Singers pitch their voices high to get these qualities. Some contemporary singers, both male and female, have adapted this style of singing to Passamaquoddy songs; it appeals to them and accords with other singing at intertribal powwows.[14] Others eschew it, even when singing intertribal songs such as the ubiquitous "White Sky." "We sing like real men," insisted one consultant, with a grin. This Passamaquoddy adaptation of intertribal style can be heard on the recordings released commercially by Drum groups such as *Niwesqom eli*

Ckuwapok ("Spirit of the Dawn"). The tone color differences are very obvious, and rhythmic differences between the two styles are also felt keenly.

Most Passamaquoddy songs are accompanied by percussion, either beaten on a drum or an idiophone or by using a shaker.[15] The relationship between the vocal part and the percussive accompaniment is a crucial feature of performance style, marking the difference between older and more modern renditions of the same song. The hand drum is generally accepted as the "traditional" Wabanaki drum, although there is no true consensus on this point. Some older consultants believe that the shot-horn shaker (see chapter 4) is even more traditional; the accompaniment patterns that players could obtain with it are different still. The hand-held small frame drums are typically beaten in a light, quick duple stress pattern that subdivides the rhythmic motion of the vocal part of a song. Occasionally, a slow pulse is used to emphasize phrases. Over this beat the vocal line is set in flexible, often syncopated ("swinging") rhythmic patterns created by the lexical words. Vocables are usually set on the beat. The shot horn was shaken in subdivisions of the pulse and often beaten on a resonant surface as well, lending a complex layer of polyrhythm to songs.

On historical recordings, the vocal part is often heterometric, even when the text is composed of vocables. The same is true today when phrases are extemporized: one may have a triple feel, the following may be duple (see example 7, 1994 Election Dance Songs). This makes rhythmic sense because the subdivision is kept constant.

Transcription Style

The flexibility of the singers' voice part over the regular drum beats in the examples I recorded defies Western musical notation. Transcriptions showing all their rhythmic and melodic inflections and nuances are not easily apprehended. Notating the subdivisions of the beat, which is where the "feel" originates, makes them incomprehensible to all but musical specialists. I have chosen to follow historical precedent in notating only a kind of average of each song, regularizing and reducing performance style details. Since the songs are strophic to the extent that the melody is repeated for subsequent verses of text, I have also followed precedent in notating the melody for only one verse in most of the examples. This kind of representation has been standard in Native American musicology since studies began; it follows the same principles as a jazz lead sheet. The melodic system and formal features of songs are easily conveyed in this notation, and there is no pretense at having captured a song and removed it from the performance contexts that give each instantiation its meaning.

Various musicologists have approached the problem of notating Wabanaki rhythmic style with different solutions. My transcriptions do not use Western time signatures, because the song structures are phrase-based and the rhythm patterns text-based, rather than metrical. In *The Indians' Book*, Natalie Curtis changed meter signatures within songs as necessary. For example, she notated a Penobscot Greeting Song in shifting duple and triple meters ([1923] 1968:14).

Curtis did not notate any accompaniment for her Wabanaki examples, although there is ample historical evidence that drumming (with or without drums) and other rhythmic accompaniment was joined to these songs. Jacob Sapir did not transcribe accompaniments for any of Speck's song examples in *Penobscot Man* (Speck [1940] 1997), but this does not mean that there were none. Several of my consultants insisted that they could hear drumming and a shot-horn rattle on Speck's recordings, and such accompaniment is often unquestionably present. But when I suggested that in other cases this might be the noise of the recording equipment, one consultant advised me to listen to it anyway because "it sounds like they used to do it" (AMS 6Jun.95). The singers on these recordings have a flexible rhythmic feel, employing additive or syncopated groups of subdivisions. Speck described the relationship between singing and accompaniment thus: "It becomes apparent that the rattling, the singing, and the foot beats are not in the same rhythm; the effect not being discordant but so uniform to the ear that it is with difficulty that one is brought to realize that all three are moving in independent rhythms" ([1940] 1997:274).

Intertribal Adaptations

The intertribal powwow style uses a large stationary drum, beaten by a group in unison on the pulses in a straight rhythm unstressed except for Honor Beats.[16]

When singing intertribal style, Peskotomuhkatiyik sing on the drum beats, a difference from the swinging feel cultivated by Plains singers. When Passamaquoddy songs are sung in this style, the rhythmic feel is utterly changed. Within the wampum protocols, certain genres have been so adapted (Welcome Dance), while others have not (Greeting Dance between *Sakomak*), and I believe that the difference is based on the rhythm. Many of my consultants simply do not like the rhythm of the intertribal style—when pressed, one admitted he found it boring—and prefer the hand drum (AMS 23Feb.95). Many lament that the art of using the shot horn is lost.

Traditional Dancing Styles

Dancing is dependent on singing, for the most part (there are some instances where a drum beat alone might accompany part of the ceremonial action). Thus there is a mutually influential relationship between song and dance, and even as songs are adapted to fit dances (in length, occasion, etc.), dance styles are varied to suit song features. As with singing styles, the introduction of intertribal powwow dancing in the last half-century has resulted in changes in Passamaquoddy dancing.

There are parameters of dance motion just as there are parameters of musical sound. Dancing is structured movement, an expressive system within which significance is culturally attached to motions. Motifs—known colloquially as "steps," though they may be executed by the arms or head as well as feet—form the basic units of motion. Choreography is the ordering of motifs, the overall formation created by dance movements in time (Kaeppler 2007). The wampum ceremony dances are distinguished by their choreography, rather than by characteristic steps—though they all employ a kind of "stomp dance" step, which is traditional in the Eastern Woodlands area and historically documented. The term simply means that the leading foot is touched to the ground before it takes the dancer's weight. This preliminary touch can be very delicate.

The wampum ceremony dances are group dances, in each of which the formations of the dancers signify the function: to welcome a group of visitors, to join families in marriage, to show the alliance of warriors. The choreography is thus mimetic in the sense that the power of what is represented is accessed. I use line diagrams to show the formations, following the precedent of previous ethnographers in Waponahkik.

Within these dances, certain individuals are required to perform significant portions alone, as in the Greeting Dance between *Sakomak*. Further, several of the ceremonies require two segments of dancing: the first to perform the choreographed ceremonial action and a second, which participants dance in free style, to celebrate it.

Men's and Women's Styles

The movement styles of men and women traditionally have been clearly differentiated in Peskotomuhkatik. Men dance with more obvious energy, holding their arms and upper body slightly bent; women strive for grace and keep the upper body relatively still. In the past, consultants recalled even more differentiation than today. In the memory of one consultant, women barely moved their upper body, wearing shawls and allowing the fringe to swing in time to the drum.

Powwow Dance Style Adaptations

In the range of individual styles of dance encouraged in Peskotomuhkatik today, the influence of powwow dance styles is evident. Some men have adopted a kicking or jump step characteristic of the Fancy Dance. Women have taken on this element also; it was adapted in the 1970s for the women's Fancy

Shawl Dance. These steps encourage a more individualistic, freer style. Dancers employ them in intertribal dances or, rarely, for the celebratory second part of a ceremonial dance, but not for the dances or segments in which choreographed formations are the focus.

Contemporary performances of the wampum protocols are likely to include choreography and structural elements from the intertribal powwow as well. The 1995 meeting of the Wabanaki Confederacy opened with a Grand Entry, Veterans' Dance, and Flag Songs, all accompanied by intertribal songs. Sacred Runners arrived, who had started at Motahkomikuk, and then the Passamaquoddy Greeting Chant was performed. The dance, however, was an intertribal Round Dance.

An Exemplary Dancer: Steve Nicholas

One consultant pointed out Stephen Nicholas as a dancer who maintains an older style of dancing (AMS 14Jun.07). Steve is the son of Joseph A. Nicholas, who started the Sipayik youth dance group with Mary Moore in the 1960s. Steve is very light on his feet, steps high, and often dances solo at events. Some of his special dances are mimetic, such as the Canoe Dance (in which he mimes paddling and then dancing for joy) and "Flight of the Wounded Eagle." Steve sometimes engages in a friendly competitive dance with another man, where they dance facing each other for inspiration. At the Indian Day in 2002 he was joined by Mike Ranco of Indian Island. They danced with very high steps, a variation on the Stomp Dance but repeatedly touching the ground with one foot. It was individualistic yet controlled and artistic: they stepped very lightly and followed the drumming very well.

Style Differentiation between Wabanaki Nations

The older dancing styles may have varied more than they do today between Wabanaki communities. The same consultant who commented on Steve Nicholas noted that Mi'kmaq dancers used to step really heavily. I observed a Mi'kmaq man dancing this way at a powwow in 1994: each step was exaggerated and deliberate, while he held his whole body apparently suspended. Another consultant noted that "dancing like Mi'kmaqs" was a comical reference for some older Peskotomuhkatiyik. Frank Speck observed a Micmac [*sic*] Dance, performed by men, that was distinctive among all the Penobscot dances in the early twentieth century. Perhaps significantly, an alternative name for the genre was *Nawa'dawe*, translated as "Old Time, Ancient." It was danced by pairs of men who faced each other in a crouching position, arms outstretched and crooked. The step was to alternate stamping and shuffling, at times moving only on one foot, and was very energetic; Speck noted that heavy sweating by the dancers was a feature commented on by participants as a measure of success. This dance had distinctive songs as well and was the only dance he observed in which the song leader sang alone, without an antiphonal chorus, and did not dance. Speck also noted that for this dance the shaker, or a stick of wood, was beaten on the floor ([1940] 1997:285). He recorded four examples; one of them uses the melody associated with the Passamaquoddy women's dance *Tuhtuwas*.[17]

The heavy stepping I noted in 1994 called to mind the stories of shamans dancing. Throughout Waponahkik they are described as stepping into solid rock, and leaving footprints behind that can still be seen in the landscape.[18] Grand Manan Island at the outlet of Passamaquoddy Bay is said to be a place where shamans danced competitively. It lies between Etchemin (now Passamaquoddy) territory and Sourquois (now Mi'kmaq) territory in Nova Scotia. Clara Neptune told Fannie Hardy Eckstorm, "Old John Neptune [the Penobscot *Sakom*], used to go down Nova Scotia, fight Injuns there; always back in mornin'" (Eckstorm 1980:33).[19] It is possible that the heavy-stepping style was associated with powerful Mi'kmaq shamans who, in the early twentieth century, were ridiculed as a means of social control on their shamanic activities; but this is speculation.

The Power of Dancing

Dancing is viewed as healing, and getting everyone of all nations to dance together was often the stated goal of the master of ceremonies at public pow-wows I attended. When Native people gather together to dance, it is healing for their community especially in situations of social duress, such as where migrants have returned home, or federal recognition is being sought. Much is made of the occasion when someone first dances. To dance is to honor the drummers, honor your hosts, and honor your own people. Many consultants described it as a form of prayer.

Regalia that someone has worn to dance in are powerful partly because of the dances they have undergone. Sometimes regalia are passed on from one dancer to another, and it is a special honor to receive worn regalia.

On occasion, dancing can be a means of accessing spiritual power to affect events. At the 1995 meeting of the Wabanaki Confederacy at Sipayik, a group of dancers planning to "dance against" someone whom they suspected of bringing bad intentions to the dancing circle positioned themselves directly opposite that person in the circle of dancers (AMS 24Jun.95).

A dance may be given (performed) as a gift, for example at a Give-Away ceremony closing a powwow. Songs also may be given as gifts. When this happens, there is an ineffable quality to the performance; it is deeply moving to observe. On one occasion, an especially talented dancer gave up dancing for six months in memory of a close relative who had just died. Her last dance was for all those at the gathering (AMS 5Sep.94). On another, a young man still recovering from brain surgery, who had danced beautifully and bravely throughout the gathering, gave a final dance to his hosts (AMS 9Aug.93).

All these associations accrue to the power of dancing through individual and community experience. Experience and ideology influence each other and contribute to the many layers of meaning in the wampum protocol dances.

FOUR

Musical Instruments

The Passamaquoddy community today is affected by global musical influences, like the culture of the United States as a whole. A wide variety of musical styles is available over the airwaves, and instruments from around the world may be purchased a short distance from the reservations. The reservation communities themselves are magnets for multicultural artists.

As the previous chapter outlined, many musical genres coexist in Peskotomuhkatik, and have for some time. Even adhering to the limited definition of Passamaquoddy *music* as a style associated with the specific community of Passamaquoddy people, one could find a wide range of instruments used today in its performance, including those associated with popular, European classical, and traditional styles—guitar, piano, and shakers. Instruments used in music designated "traditional" by its performers would include recent imports (Native American flute) and some adopted within the span of recorded history (bass drum) alongside those used for centuries (shakers).

As the sounds of musical instruments make an essential contribution to the overall sound of a performance, they are the subject of a subfield of musicology called *organology*. The way sound is produced—manmade, intentionally, and so on—is also a feature expressed in the Passamaquoddy language. Further, instruments accumulate meanings from all the contexts in which they are used. Analysis of musical instruments thus illuminates the meaning of the wampum protocols.

Historically, Peskotomuhkatiyik did not have elaborate musical sound-producing instruments. A pragmatic reason was the damp climate of their territories, in which wood rots easily and other materials molder. Another was their migratory lifestyle, in which simplicity and ease of assembly of all material goods were highly valued.[1]

The oldest Passamaquoddy instruments are beaten idiophones and drums, shaken idiophones (rattles), and flutes. Drumming and flute playing are often mentioned in Passamaquoddy legends, and shakers of various kinds are described in seventeenth-century European accounts of the Etchemin, Souriquois, and Abenaki. Drums and hand-held shakers are the most ubiquitous instruments in contemporary performances. According to the historical record, these were used for all sorts of songs except Lonesome Songs, which were played on a flute if any instrument was used.

Various instruments of these types have been used over the last four centuries of recorded history, and their differences have significantly affected elements of musical style. For example, the large stationary drums beaten by multiple players in unison are a relatively new introduction from intertribal powwow culture, and the beat patterns obtainable on these drums are quite different from the patterns previous generations of singers obtained using a shot-horn rattle for accompaniment. Thus, along with the vocal style elements discussed in the previous chapter, instruments are principal features defining the different musical styles that Peskotomuhkatiyik perform today.

Instruments are not always used to accompany songs but also may be used alone, without singing. And a song sung while working or a lullaby might be accompanied primarily by the physical movement involved in the activity (paddling a canoe, rocking a child). Drumming is sometimes the only accompaniment to dancing or to ceremonial movements.

Within their respective genre contexts, musical instruments, and their material construction, have acquired symbolic meaning. But analysis of Passamaquoddy concepts about instruments reveals that their primary efficacy resides in the sound that they make. In this conceptual system, sound not only possesses aesthetic value but also may possess the power to heal, to charm, and to control nature. This chapter explores what has been recorded about musical instruments from historical and oral sources, how the different types of instruments are constructed, and the concepts about instruments that underlie their uses by Peskotomuhkatiyik.

Currently, the drum is highly valued in Passamaquoddy culture. The drum has become a general Native American symbol through the popularization of powwow drumming, and the political prominence of the American Indian Movement, which included "pan-Indian" drumming in its protests. These cultural movements have transmitted symbolic notions of the Dance Drum as a symbol for Mother Earth to Peskotomuhkatik.

The sound of drumming appeals to Worldbeat audiences, who are attracted to the distinctive rhythms of music fusing mainstream pop and traditional styles from around the world. Thus Native American drum traditions have become a focus of popular interest, raising the status of Native musicians. The growth of the New Age subculture has also increased mainstream interest in Native American ceremonial and shamanic drumming, and in the flute for its meditative qualities. As a result of the expanding popularity of Native traditions in global popular culture, Native American music and musicians have become part of larger distribution networks, and it is now easier to get access to Native music off or on a reservation. Several Passamaquoddy musicians have made commercially available recordings, ranging from traditional songs to powwow drum songs, folk songs with guitar accompaniment, and Native American flute.

Drums and flutes are the salient identifying features to the mass market of the Native American identity of a piece of music and of Native culture in general; for instance, Maine Public Radio often signals a story on local Native affairs with an introductory "sound byte" featuring the Native American flute, not a traditional instrument in the area. This strong association may have encouraged the adoption of powwow drums and the Native American flute in the Passamaquoddy community, as these instruments now are expected elements of Native culture and are immediately identifiable.

Changes such as these raise issues of misrepresentation of Wabanaki traditions, a problem at least since mainstream American culture began to take an interest in Native American culture in the nineteenth century as a means of defining its own identity. Penobscot vaudeville performer Lucy Nicola Poolaw sang popular "idealized" Indian songs by Thurlow Lieurance and Charles Wakefield Cadman in her stage act as Princess Watowaso (McBride 1995:45 and personal communication). These were versions of Native traditional songs given English words and made to fit European harmonies.[2] In the early twentieth century some Passamaquoddy singers adopted the tomtoms associated with Hollywood and vaudeville Indians, a change attributed to the influence of Bruce Poolaw, a Kiowa who had a career in vaudeville and married into the Penobscot Nicola family. Also around this time, men at Sipayik adopted Plains-style headdresses as regalia, and James Neptune of Sipayik became famous for making them (AMS 28Feb.95). Most men today wear the traditional Passamaquoddy headdress, into which feathers are arranged to stand vertically around the crown of the head.

My consultants did not believe that ephemeral trends in popular culture had affected Passamaquoddy traditions to a significant degree, however. Many emphasized its stable elements. Joseph A. Nicholas remarked: "It [the Passamaquoddy dance tradition] doesn't change; the foxtrot, square dance, those dances change." (AMS 28Feb.95).

But Passamaquoddy lifeways are part of a larger social system and it is a fact that at present it is more acceptable in mainstream contexts than previously for a young Native person to be interested in traditional songs. In reservation contexts, Drum groups have become central in youth organizations. They have taken on the function of representing the community abroad, fulfilled previously by community marching bands. Drum groups also have been significant components of counseling and rehabilitation programs.

Terminology

The key into Passamaquoddy conceptions of musical instruments is found in the language. The known terms for sound-producing instruments in all the Wabanaki languages are listed in table 2.

The distinction made between idiophones and drums is important. An idiophone is an instrument that produces sound by vibrating when struck, scraped, shaken, stamped, and so on. A drum, if it has a head, is a membranophone: the head vibrates when struck, but the sound also resonates inside the frame. Wabanaki oral traditions and the historical record often mention drumming but not always with a drum; technically, beating an idiophone is what is described. As explained below, the indigenous terms usually translated as "drum" do not correspond to the specific organological meaning of this term: a membranophone that is sounded by beating. Mi'kmaq terms given by Diamond, Cronk, and von Rosen (1994) are recent.

My consultants never referred to the drums, shakers, and flutes they use to accompany singing and dancing as "musical instruments" nor even as a general class of objects. To my knowledge, none of the Wabanaki languages have a term corresponding to "musical instruments"; however, this English-language term is used by Peskotomuhkatiyik to designate Western musical instruments (such as guitars and trumpets), which are well known in the community. Sipayik and Motahkomikuk each had a marching band from the late

Table 2.: Wabanaki Terms for Musical Instruments

English	Pas-Mal.	Penobscot	Mi'kmaq
drum or beaten idiophone	pokuhulakon	pekhola'gon	
shaker (shaken idiophone)	halonossis (specif., shot horn)	ah'lnahn	jitkasog' andkitc
flute	pipiqat	bibi'gwodi	bibigwa'an

References

Passamaquoddy-Maliseet: David A. Francis personal communication; Penobscot: Speck 1997:163–165; Mi'kmaq: Wallis and Wallis 1955:186,191.

nineteenth century on, and several generations of Peskotomuhkatiyik have played popular dance music. Joseph A. Nicholas recalls that formerly, people learned to play the piano and other instruments at the Carlisle Indian School in Pennsylvania (AMS 28Feb.95).

The word for "drum" in Passamaquoddy is *pokuhulakon*, parsed by David A. Francis as follows:

pok-	*uh-*	*ul-*	*akon*
beaten/(fill)/		hollow thing/	inanimate tool ("thing that does it")

An analogous word using the inanimate suffix *a-kon* or *i-kon* is *tomhikon*, "tool that cuts in two," from which the English derived "tomahawk." As noted previously, *lintuwakon*, "song," is a gerund literally meaning "sung tool," and the Wabanaki stories teach that songs also do things, especially with spiritual power.

The Passamaquoddy word for "drumming" is *'tolihtomon*:

't-	*ol-*	*ihtomon*
(person)/	hollow thing/	striking

These etymologies reveal that in Passamaquoddy there is no word that carries the typological specificity of the European term "drum," which is now used when speaking English; *-ol-* is any hollow thing, not just a membranophone with a resonant frame.

The distinction between drumming and drums is also crucial: the focus revealed in the language and oral histories is on the action of drumming, rather than on the instrument itself, which attains importance by virtue of its sounding capacity.[3] (This exactly parallels the situation with songs: the function or purpose of singing is what is valued, not the song as a thing.) Although the drum instrument was not always used, I continue to employ the English term "drumming" where musical beating of some idiophone is meant because this is the best equivalent of the Passamaquoddy word *'tolihtomon* .

Accompaniment

In the past, Peskotomuhkatiyik did not always employ drumming, even to accompany dance songs; sometimes rhythmic vocalizations were used. Joseph A. Nicholas and David A. Francis remembered that the tribal council (formerly all men) "used to go *huh-huh* in time" to accompany the *Sakomak* in the War Club Dance (AMS 28Feb.95). Mrs. Brown noted at the *Sakomawkan* in 1892, "A drum was beaten with short, sharp taps, very slowly at first; each beat of the drum was accompanied by a 'honk-honk-honk' from those in the circle" (Brown 1892:58). Frank Speck's informants described a dance done by men at the *Sakomawkan* feast which was accompanied only by the other men "who shouted 'he-he-he' in regular rhythm" ([1940] 1997:290). According to the Abbé Maillard, Mi'kmaq who were assembled for a ceremony uttered "a guttural loud aspiration of the word Heh! Heh! Heh!" in time with drumming (1758:13).

Historical accounts indicate that on occasion, idiophones were improvised by Wabanaki singers from rolled-up birchbark, or a fire log was beaten on the ground to accompany dancing. The missionary Maillard described a birchbark roll used by an elderly woman to accompany a women's dance (1758:13–15). William Mechling noted use of a birchbark roll in a Mi'kmaq ceremony he observed at Restigouche (1958–59:226). James Rosier described Bessabez's men drumming with sticks in 1605 (1605:[18]); Mechling observed Maliseet singers similarly drumming on boards (1917:297; 1958–59:227). When there is no other object available, contemporary singers often use their hands and feet to beat an accompaniment.[4]

The foregoing observations indicate how crucially important beating an accompaniment is in performing or even conceptualizing songs and dances. Accomplished Passamaquoddy singers whom I consult often cannot follow song melodies unless I try to beat an accompaniment while singing them. Drumming style is the principal means of distinguishing between songs used for different functions, as well as marking the intertribal and older styles of songs.

Drums and Drumming

There is some disagreement among Waponahkiyik over what sort of drum is traditional. I am not aware that any archaeological evidence of drums in Waponahkik has survived, but basing an argument on its absence would be unwise since the materials drums are made out of—skin, outer layers of wood, sinew, hair—decompose very easily.

Seventeenth- and eighteenth-century descriptions of Waponahkiyik dancing are conspicuously lacking descriptions of drums or shakers used as accompanying instruments. In their accounts of social and public ceremonial dances Marc Lescarbot ([1618] 1914:184), Pierre Biard ([1612] 1896(2):41), and Nicholas Denys ([1690] 1908) noted rhythmic vocalized accompaniment and responses. They do not mention drums or shakers in these contexts but do mention shakers as part of the equipment of *Aoutmoin* (shamans and healers). Jesuit missionaries Paul Le Jeune and Jerome Lalement used the word "tambour" in reports concerning the Abenaki from 1634 and 1647 but do not describe the instrument (Le Jeune 1896(7):99; Lalement 1896(31):192). John Gyles (1736) never mentions drums or shakers in his account of late seventeenth-century Maliseet life, though he describes dancing; however, the eighteenth-century missionary Maillard describes drummed accompaniment to dances among the Maliseet and Mi'kmaq (1758:14–15). By the nineteenth century, drum use is recorded, as the quotation from Mrs. Brown cited above exemplifies. Some secondary sources suggest that drums were not aboriginal but a later, introduced, feature of Wabanaki culture (Smith 1955:29; AMS 15May.95).

If the drum was a later introduction to the culture, it has certainly claimed an important position within it. Contemporary Peskotomuhkatiyik say in English that drums and drumming are "sacred."[5] For this reason, the word Drum is capitalized when it refers to the powwow style or Dance Drum. The Dance Drum is a ceremonial tradition originating in the western Great Lakes region in the mid-eighteenth century that influenced powwow teachings about drums and drumming (Vennum 1982:44–45).

Drumming is not done merely for recreation. For this reason, forms of the English term "to play [an instrument]," meaning "to cause to sound," make little sense when applied to drumming. One drummer told me repeatedly that to her, drumming is "a form of praying." Another drummer expressed her belief that it is possible to "drum too much," and that one must be careful not to abuse the power of the Drum (AMS 28Nov.94).

An idea often expressed is that the drumbeat is "the heartbeat of Mother Earth." Some think of the Drum itself as the Mother: one teacher admonishes young drummers to beat the Drum with care: "Remember that's your Mother you're hitting." This particular conception may derive from pan-Indian Drum teachings (AMS 22 and 24Apr.95). How far back the precedent for the contemporary role of the Drum may be set is conjecture, but drumming has been a symbolically powerful expression at least since the seventeenth century. Both the historical record and oral traditions attest to this: drumming is connected with shamanism.

Shamanism was one sphere of Wabanaki cultural activity that was often noted by outsiders, who either derided it or found it threatening.[6] Seventeenth-century descriptions of shamanic divining and healing involved singing, dancing, rattling shakers, and drumming. Missionaries in particular left good descriptions of the instruments used by healers and shamans throughout Waponahkik. Chrétien LeClercq ([1691] 1910:222) described a shaker made of moose dewclaws and Gabriel Druillettes reported drums were part of shamans' equipment (Lalement [1647] 1896(31):192). Pierre Biard, whose approach to traditional medicine was more confrontational ([1616] 1896(3):117), did not leave any descriptions of shamans' equipment, but given his attitude toward aboriginal culture, perhaps he was not shown any.

The Passamaquoddy-Maliseet word *motewolon*, corresponding to what anthropologists call a shaman, literally translates into English as "beaten hollow thing-sound person." *Mote-* designates a sound made by something unseen. Speck's survey of northeastern Algonquian languages showed that among them, words for shaman commonly reference the sound of drumming, and he argued on this basis that shamanic use of drumming was characteristic of their associated cultures (1919b:240–41).

Passamaquoddy evidence of shamanic drumming traditions is found in a song recorded in writing by Louis Mitchell and published by John Dynely Prince with commentary (1901:385–86). Prince never published any music for the text, nor did he allude to any melodic or rhythmic aspects of it. It is probable that the music was omitted to protect the song. All my consultants regard this song text as powerful, and concern was expressed by Mitchell's descendants that "The Song of the Drum" could be used improperly.[7] David A. Francis translated the words anew, and has kindly allowed me to use his translation (example 1). Wayne A. Newell, great-grandson of Mr. Mitchell, expressed belief that this song expresses a specifically Passamaquoddy philosophy of the Drum, as opposed to the more general Native American ideas noted above.

The aesthetic impact of this song text contributes to its power. It divides clearly into five verses constructed in parallel, each of which drives rhythmically to its point. The concluding verse gathers up all the preceding ideas with an insistent rhythm. Each verse *states* what the singer wills to happen, rather than asking for it; this mood is a linguistic feature noted by scholars in other Native American ceremonial texts (Vander 1997:332–34; Witherspoon 1977:34).

"The Song of the Drum" exemplifies the power of drumming to manipulate other entities. All those mentioned in the text cohabit *skitcomiq*—literally, "the surface realm," usually translated as "earth"—with human beings (*skicinuwok*). Each of the regular verses invokes entities from a different region: creatures of the air, water creatures, woodland creatures.

A most succinct demonstration of the power conveyed by drumming is James Rosier's account of a 1605 encounter between English Catholics and Native people in midcoast Maine.[8] A company of English under Captain George Weymouth had set out for the "North Part of Virginia" to ascertain whether they might establish colonies there. Coming into Muscongus Bay, they exchanged hostages with the local people. The English hostage, a Welsh boy by the name of Owen Griffin, reported to Rosier what he observed during his overnight stay:

> Owen Griffin which lay on the Shore, reported unto me their maner, and (as I may terme them) the ceremonies of their idolatry, which they performe thus. One among them (the eldest of the Company as he judged) riseth right up, the other sitting still, and looking about, suddenly cried with a loud voice, Baugh, Waugh; then the women fall downe, and lie upon the ground, and the men all together answering the same, fall a stamping round about the fire with both feet, as hard as they can, making the ground shake, with sundry out-cries, and change of voice and sound. Many take the fire sticks and thrust them into the earth, and then rest awhile: of a sudden beginning as before, they continue so stamping till the yonger sort fetch from the Shore many stones, of which every man tooke one, and first beate upon them with their fire sticks, then with the stones beat the earth with all their strength. And in this manner (as he reported) they continued above two houres. (Rosier 1605:[17–18])

Beating with sticks to accompany dances is described in several other sources, but the "ceremony" Griffin described seems to have been a display of several different kinds of power, perhaps for his benefit. The next night another man from the English ship stayed also to observe the "ceremonies." The pounding with stones (which is unique in all descriptions of Wabanaki ceremonies) may have functioned as signals to alert the companies of warriors who, at their leaders' summons, were gathering in the woods around the camp; for on the third day, when the English were led to shore ostensibly to trade, they were confronted with nearly three hundred Native men in war regalia (Rosier 1605:[21]).

This description was the source through which the word "powwow" entered the English language. The exclamation "Baugh Waugh" uttered by the Elder indicates that the "ceremony" was a show of spiritual power: even in Rosier's rendition it is recognizable as a form of the Mi'kmaq phoneme *buo*, from which derives *buoin* "shaman," equivalent to the Passamaquoddy *motewolon* (Erickson 1978:5). The contemporary Passamaquoddy term for a spirit helper, *puhikon*, is probably related to this root.

The English term "powwow man" was a common designation for a shaman or "medicine man" used by Native and non-Native persons alike in Waponahkik until relatively recently. "Powwow" is still used in the sense of spiritual power by some Native people. The annual gatherings hosted by several Wabanaki communities, including the Aroostook Mi'kmaqs and the Penobscot Indian Nation, are called powwows. The pronunciation recorded by Rosier is still used; someone had written "Bow Wow Van" in the dust on one of the vans used by a Drum group at the 1994 powwow at Big Cove, New Brunswick (AMS 3Sep.94).

On the basis of linguistic and historical descriptive evidence, one may say that drumming and (as the medium for producing drumming) drums are magical in the anthropological sense because they involve the supernatural manipulation of other entities. A *motewolon* uses magic but is not magic him- or herself. Drumming is a means of accessing supernatural force, *ktahant*, sometimes translated as "power."[9]

Contemporary Uses of Drums

Drums continue to be used for healing and in shamanic practice by Peskoto- muhkatiyik. These private uses are outside the analytical purview of this study but are relevant to the analysis of the wampum ceremonies of the Wabanaki Confederacy because of the associations that they contribute to the conception of drums when used in public.

At present, drumming is sometimes the only accompaniment to dancing or to ceremonial movements. During the Blessing of the Tribal Governor in the 1994 inauguration at Sipayik, the procession to the altar of the church was accompanied by a slow drumbeat (sounded by the Eucharistic minister) with- out singing (AMS 25Nov.95). Portions of the Peace Pipe Ceremony Dance and other dances performed for Indian Days are today accompanied only by drumming, and a videotape of the 1972 Indian Days in the collection of the Waponahki Museum shows that the dancers proceeded to their places accom- panied only by a drum.

Types of Drums

Contemporary Passamaquoddy singers and drummers use a variety of drums from different cultural traditions. The Drum groups use the large stationary Drum characteristic of the powwow; singers in the older style use hand drums. In the 1960s, stationary drums that could be supported and played by one per- son were popular. According to a Penobscot Elder, former vaudeville star Bruce Poolaw brought the tomtom to the Penobscot about 1930 (AMS 15May95).

Large drums, beaten by one person while balanced against the body, were used by some singers within the memory of my consultants to lead dances before the group drum became popular. The historical record before the twentieth century contains scanty references to drums and does not specify whether they were single- or double-headed. Most of those described since the nineteenth century had heads made of hide. Joseph A. Nicholas used a large double-headed drum to lead the Indian Day ceremonies in the 1960s and

1970s, and there are many pictures of him with it. This type of large drum for one person is still made and used, notably by Peter Neptune of Sipayik. In the last twenty years, Nicholas most frequently used a hand-held frame drum for solo singing. All these drum types have been used to accompany dancing. Since microphones are now often used for outdoor occasions, any size drum can be made audible.

The different drums used by contemporary Waponahkiyik are supported (or held) and beaten differently according to their construction. The difference in the quality and pattern of the beat is quite clear between different types of drums, and this was the aspect of drumming style most commonly commented on by my consultants. The different sounds these instruments produce have influenced performance style as well. The different beat patterns characteristic of various drums and shakers are detailed below in the discussion of old and new song styles. The following survey clarifies differences in drum construction.

HAND-HELD DRUMS

The hand drum is generally accepted as the "traditional" Wabanaki drum, although there is no true consensus on this point. Neither oral tradition nor the historical record specifies that this is the oldest type.

Several kinds of hand drum are currently used. The most common is single-headed, made of hide laced over a circular, hexagonal, or octagonal wood frame. The laces are woven together in the center of the open side, and to hold the drum the drummer grasps the center where they are tied together. This sort of drum, beaten by one person with a stick or small beater, is used to accompany solo singing or singing by a small group of two or three. It is typically beaten in a light, quick duple stress pattern that subdivides the rhythmic motion of the vocal part of a song; the vocal part may be syncopated against it. Some Waponahkiyik believe that this is the traditional performance style of their culture. It is close to the style recorded in the early twentieth century, with singers using shot-horn rattles for accompaniment.

Many women use hand drums exclusively to avoid proscriptions against women participating in Drum groups, proscriptions that adhere to the powwow-style Drum. During my fieldwork one Mi'kmaq medicine man was teaching that women should not use such Drums because to do so would bring evil on the men of their community (AMS 29Nov.95). Other Elders agreed, asking that women not drum at all until they were "grandmothers." These teachings enforce the aesthetic choice of many older people with supernatural sanctions.

Although Frank Speck reported that "the drum has never been used in dance performances within memory" ([1940] 1997:271), he had one of his Penobscot assistants make a drum for him. He accepted the example as aboriginal in type although the source for the style of construction was not identified. This was a double-headed hand drum, made of a hoop of cedar 3.5 inches deep and 11 in diameter. The heads were made of green deerskin, stretched across the hoop and laced on the side "somewhat irregularly" with babiche. It had a wrapped rawhide handle fastened on one side. Across one side were two snares made of babiche while the other side had babiche fringe. The drumstick was carved of cedar, 10.5 inches long, with a 1.5 inch wide carved head (Speck [1940] 1997:164–65). Speck noted that this type of drum is similar to those used by Naskapi people, northern neighbors of Waponahkiyik.[10]

In the early twentieth century William Mechling reported that Wolastoqewiyik made both single- and double-headed drums, with the heads stretched over a hoop of cedar (1917:227). He obtained a single-headed drum made by one of his Maliseet assistants for the Canadian Museum of Civilization.

During his fieldwork in the mid-twentieth century, Nicholas Smith was told of three types of Wabanaki drums: one, a hand drum with a snare across one of the heads (it probably had two hide heads); the other two, stationary drums made from hollowed cedar logs covered with hide heads, one of which was partly filled with water. Smith, however, stated that he himself had never seen any of these drums used (1955:29).

STATIONARY DRUMS

Stationary drums can stand alone, sometimes in a special support structure called a cradle. The powwow-style Drum is a large instrument of this type. It typically has two heads made of hide, stretched over a straight-sided circular wooden frame. The heads and other parts of the Drum may be decorated. It is similar to the Ojibwa Dance Drum but is not associated with the same ceremonies.[11] This kind of drum is beaten by a group of people in unison. Peskotomuhkatiyik sing on the beat, a stylistic difference from other cultures and from powwow style in general.

Neither historical nor oral records of the past mention this specific type of drum or the group performance style; they seem to have been introduced into the Passamaquoddy communities in the 1970s (AMS 28Feb.95; AMS 7Mar.95). Drumming on a hollowed-out log cannot be ruled out as aboriginal, however, and given the close cultural connections between Waponahkiyik and Anishena'abeg, there could have been contact with Ojibwa drum styles.

Robert Ritzenthaler recorded a tradition from Ojibwa John Bisonette that Dance Drums must not be kept too long and therefore are given away, passing from community to community (Vennum 1982:263).[12] Wabanaki communities are not represented in the "Path of the Drum" given by Bisonette, but the presentation of Drums to other communities is an established part of midwestern Algonquian teachings. Since Waponahkiyik feel strong connections to the other Algonquian nations, they are a natural extension of this tradition.

In 1993 the Red Dawn Drum group at Pleasant Point was using a powwow-style Drum which, according to several of the drummers, they had received from a Native community "out west" as a gift to the youth of Sipayik (AMS 25Jul.93). As of 1995, the group had retired three such Drums, all made outside the community.

WATER DRUM

Another type of stationary drum used by Peskotomuhkatiyik is the water drum, which may be small (as in the Navajo tradition) or large. Water drums are so called because their frame can be filled with varying amounts of water, making them tunable. Nicholas Smith was told of such a drum, its body carved out of a stump, but he did not see any in Wabanaki contexts (1955:29).

It is not clear how long this type has been in use. A large water drum suitable for group drumming was used by the "All Nation" Mohawk Drum group from Ontario at the Big Cove Powwow in August 1994 (AMS 3Sep.94). After a council of Elders decided that women should not use the powwow or Dance Drums, all of the women present used this water drum; one of the Passamaquoddy women declared that she believed "this was our Drum." The Mohawk of Kahnawá:ke were part of the Wabanaki Confederacy, and there has been much cultural exchange between the two peoples during centuries of conflict and alliance, so the water drum's historical use in Waponahkik is probable.

Drum Making

The following observations about contemporary Wabanaki drum making are drawn primarily from my experience in drum-making sessions led by Rob Coyne at Sipayik's Annual Native Gatherings.[13] During these, Rob and the primarily Wabanaki participants exchanged a great deal of information about different kinds of drums. Rob emphasized that there are different traditions of hand-drum making, and he was careful to note that what he was doing was not necessarily Wabanaki by making references to "your tradition." He explained to me later that he knew mainly Iroquois traditions but had been learning how to make different styles of drums from various North American Native cultures (AMS 14Aug.94). In addition, several other men discussed making drums with me, either during Rob's workshops or privately during other parts of the Gatherings. These conversations were not formal interviews but incorporated into my fieldnotes for the occasion, and the men whose stories are related here remain anonymous.

The materials out of which hand drums are made are considered carefully, with two principles in mind. The first concerns practical matters: how to procure the materials and what is available. The second concerns the relationship between those materials. Table 3 at the end of this chapter summarizes all known descriptions of the material construction of Wabanaki drums, beaten idiophones, shaken idiophones, and flutes.

Different kinds of wood may be used for frames, but Rob recommended that each frame be made entirely out of one wood. If the frame is pieced, the pieces need to be chosen for consistent texture. These procedures help control warping and splitting as the drum ages and weathers. Horsehide and deerskin are often used for heads, but moosehide is prized for some drums. Synthetic materials are sometimes used for laces, and a plastic disk might form the center around which the ends of the laces are tied in the back. When I observed drums being made by beginners, they all accepted the use of synthetics as part of the learning process. When more accomplished, they expected to use sinew laces and bone centers, and some participating in the group lessons did so. In addition, materials may be reused from one drum to make a new drum. A sense of continuity seems to be achieved by doing this. The notion that properties of an old instrument will be transferred to a new one made from its materials does not seem to be exotic; it was expressed by a Penobscot consultant in relation to making a canoe (AMS 15May.95). The idea is similar to passing down regalia.

The relationship between the materials used in constructing a drum has symbolic importance. Rob spoke of the hand drum as "balanced" because to make it one uses materials from both plants and animals: the frame is wood from a tree trunk; the beater is a branch; the center of the laces is bone; the laces themselves are sinew; and the drum head is hide from an animal. When, in making their hand drum at the session, a young man and woman accidentally tied a leaf into their lacing, Rob was delighted because now the drum had three parts of the tree—leaf, branch, and trunk—as it had three parts of the animal: hide, sinew, bone. When the couple pointed this feature out to newcomers, the symbolic symmetry was immediately appreciated.

The relationship between the materials used in the drum and in the beater is another factor to be considered in making the drum. Rob recommended using the ball-head type of beater, a straight stick about a foot long with a ball of deer hair covered with hide tied on one end. He said that he saved the hair from scraping the deer hide of which the heads were made but also collected it from other hides.

The materials used for the large drums likewise are of deep spiritual and symbolic importance. Because the frame for large drums is carved out of the trunk of a tree, the relationship with the tree itself is very powerful. One man told me that he had not planned to make a drum but that one day while hunting he had come upon a huge old cedar tree in the woods, out of whose trunk an entire drum frame could be carved. Right then and there he made up his mind to make his son a drum. So he offered tobacco and then cut down the tree. (In addition to being a favorite material for drums, cedar is a medicinal and sacred tree in Wabanaki culture.) Getting it out of the woods was hard, because he had not come prepared, but he managed without accident and at the time of our conversation was well along on the project, which he obviously considered he had been guided into (AMS 14Aug.94).

The look of a drum is important as well as its sound, making its materials aesthetically crucial. The color of the frame wood and the presence of knots and striations in it are carefully studied when making a big drum. Likewise, the hide is examined for discolorations and texture differences that might make it stretch unevenly. Natural coloration may be turned to advantage. One man at Rob's 1994 session carefully and silently stretched the precut head across his frame, while onlookers worried about a discoloration in the hide: was it from the end of the backbone, and would it therefore split? When finished, the man proudly displayed the head: the discoloration had formed into the figure of an eagle. A couple of weeks later the head had mellowed, and the drum had an excellent tone. Drums may be painted on the head or sides and decorated, but ornamentation is usually minimal so as not to affect the sound. On the whole, decoration is applied only to larger drums.

The process of making a drum seems to be a significant life event for contemporary Waponahkiyik. Several men discussed making drums for their sons, carving the frame out of a cedar or ash stump and making the heads of hide. One man constructed his like a smaller version of the Dance Drum, complete with supporting cradle. Rob's description, paraphrased above, is typical of many that were offered in normal conversation but is more detailed.

Drums are given as gifts, and those presented at Give-Away ceremonies were handled with reverence. A hand drum made at the first gathering of the modern Wabanaki Confederacy at Restigouche was presented to the Sipayik governor, Cliv Dore, at the opening of the third gathering in 1995, to symbolize his duty to honor the spirit of the Confederacy (AMS 20Jun.95). In this case, the Drum could be understood as symbolizing the reunification of Waponahkiyik in the ceremonies of the Confederacy, where drum beats set the pulse as they join in song and dance. Thus, in contemporary culture the drum object may take on the significance of a *rite de passage* when given from father to son, or constitute an honor, when presented at a Give-Away, or symbolize unity. As linguistic analysis suggests and historical comparison confirms, however, a drum's value derives from its ability to sound, and the efficacy of that sound.

Shakers

Shakers were being used by Wabanaki shamans at the time European colonization began. The Recollect missionary LeClercq described one found among the equipment in the medicine bundle belonging to a former shaman in Gaspesia who had converted to Catholicism: "I found there a stick, a good foot in length, adorned with white and red porcupine quills; at its end were attached several straps of a half-foot in length, and two dozen dew-claws of moose. It is with this stick that he makes a devilish noise, using these dew-claws as sounders" (LeClercq [1691] 1910:222). Shamanic use of shakers contributes to the conception of their efficacy when used in public ceremonies. The words for shakers in Mi'kmaq and Passamaquoddy, given in table 2, emphasize that their sounds are not natural sounds, such as leaves rustling, but are created with intent. In Passamaquoddy, the sound of rattling is *metiyamkihputek*.

Fewkes (1890a) and Hagar (1895) referred to the tradition that rattlesnakes are the origin of shakers in the Passamaquoddy and Mi'kmaq communities. Both noted the importance of the rattling sound in medicine. A shaker held by the dance leader was formerly the only accompaniment to the Passamaquoddy and Mi'kmaq Snake Dance, a dance that has connections to traditional medicine. These ideas are discussed further in chapter 7.

The historical record describes several types of shakers used by Waponah-kiyik as accompaniment to dancing. The shot-horn shaker seems to have taken precedence by the late nineteenth century, and the Passamaquoddy word *ahal-nossis*, now commonly used for shaker, most likely derives from the English word "horn." By the time Fewkes wrote his account of Passamaquoddy songs and dances, shot horn shakers were commonly mentioned as used by dance leaders (Fewkes 1890a:262; see illustration 3).

Shot horns—cattle horns filled with metal shot—were acquired through European trade. Turning equipment essential to warfare into a musical instrument essential to dancing is not merely a poetic irony; it is entirely in line with the connections between the protocols of warfare and peace in Wabanaki culture (as discussed in subsequent chapters). Sabatus Tomer and other favored song leaders used shot-horn shakers, drumming them on the floor, within the memory of many of my consultants. This technique resulted in a complex rhythmic sound that many associate with the older style of song and dance performance and prefer to modern styles.

Frank Speck noted that during his fieldwork in the first decade of the twentieth century, the shot horn had "entirely replaced" gourd and birchbark shakers as a Penobscot dance instrument ([1940] 1997:163). By the time Speck's work was published, the tomtom had been adopted by many singers, according to a Penobscot Elder I consulted; before this, he said, "They all used the shot horn," which he classified as a different instrument from the hand-held shakers made of dried gourd, turtle shell, birchbark, or carved wood. Contradicting Speck, he asserted, "They had those too" (AMS 15May.95).

Mechling found that Wolastoqewiyik were using shot-horn shakers exclusively in the early twentieth century but that birchbark shakers had been used within memory. They were described to him as "cylindrical, about 6 inches long and three in diameter... attached to a wooden handle." He noted the similarity of this type to those used by the Menominee and Ojibwa (Mechling 1958–59:228).

Smith tried to ascertain what types of shakers were aboriginally Wabanaki. In addition to birchbark he mentions a turtle-shell shaker of local provenance in the collection of the Peabody Museum in Salem, Massachusetts (Smith 1955:29); anthropologists consider the Cape Ann area the southern boundary of Wabanaki cultural influence. Turtle-shell shakers are used by contemporary Passamaquoddy singers, especially women. Although no historical source describes their use, Alma Brooks stated that in the past, turtle-shell shakers constructed of the shell affixed to a wooden handle were used in sweat lodges by Wolastoqewiyik. If so, they may have been reserved for that purpose and not used publicly in Peskotomuhkatik. Turtle is a prominent helper animal in the Koluskap stories, and turtle-shell shakers had important significance in Mi'kmaq traditions. The thirteen plates of the turtle's shell represent the thirteen moons of the lunar year. (Diamond, Cronk, and von Rosen 1994:135).

I have observed Wabanaki singers using shakers of various types drawn from several different American cultures. A singer is likely to own more than one, and they are often shared. In addition to birchbark and turtle-shell shakers, a common type is made of a wide section of horn, sometimes trimmed with fur and mounted on a stick handle. One of the women drum teachers at Sipayik used this type. Shakers are also made of dried gourds, with the seeds functioning as the noisemakers. This type was historically typical of more southern, semihorticultural North American cultures.

Many styles of shakers are usually for sale at gatherings and powwows in Maine and New Brunswick, though turtle shells are uncommon. Others of northeastern cultural origin include birchbark cylinders and shakers made of hollowed-out logs or sticks, filled with beads. Richard Keezer of Sipayik specializes in these, which he ornaments by burning designs on the wood. One design (illustration 4) has "instruments of war" (*tomhikan*, knife, and a spear ornamented like a Calumet) on one side, and "instruments of peace" (drum, beaters, and shakers) on the other; hence the way the instrument is held when in use is significant (Richard Keezer, personal communication).[14]

At the 1995 Confederacy meeting at Sipayik I noted shakers made of hide, stretched while wet around baseballs and allowed to dry to form a sphere bearing the clear imprints of the baseball stitching. After the baseball was removed, the hollow was filled with seeds and a stick handle attached. Baseball is a highly important part of contemporary life, and the Sipayik team is a source of local pride; its travels for league games have always been accompanied by fans and formerly by the Sipayik marching band. When the game is in another Native community, traditional and powwow-style social dancing sometimes follows.

I have observed shakers used mostly by women when men are drumming, but I have also seen men use them if they are not drumming: for example, when there are not enough drum beaters and a man wants to sing with a Drum group. There does not seem to be a notion that men should not use shakers, as there is that women should not drum. People still remember Sabattus Tomer and other men leading dances with the shot-horn shaker. When a man of political prominence in the Passamaquoddy Tribe was handed a horn shaker to use with a Drum group at a public occasion, he did not hesitate to use it, and there was no discussion about it (AMS 22Apr.95). With the recent concern among Wabanaki communities over women drumming, however, their use of shakers may take on new significance.

The making of a shaker was not mentioned to me in normal conversation as a significant event in the way that men in particular publicly discussed making drums. Factors such as the social and symbolic significance of the Drum may be obscuring the importance of the formerly ubiquitous shaker.

Flutes

According to published stories and to oral tradition, flutes were used by *mote-wolinuwok* (shamans), supernatural creatures (especially the woodland *mihko-muwehsisok*),[15] and even ordinary humans to charm other people. In these sources, power is attributed to the sweet sound of the flute.

"Lonesome Songs," one of the few genres not accompanied by drumming, were played on flutes to attract the player's beloved. One story teaches that the *mihkomuwehsisok* gave the flute to men so that they could attract women and game (Leland 1884:82–83). In the oral traditions, when women wish to attract a lover they always sing Lonesome Songs, and some men play them on

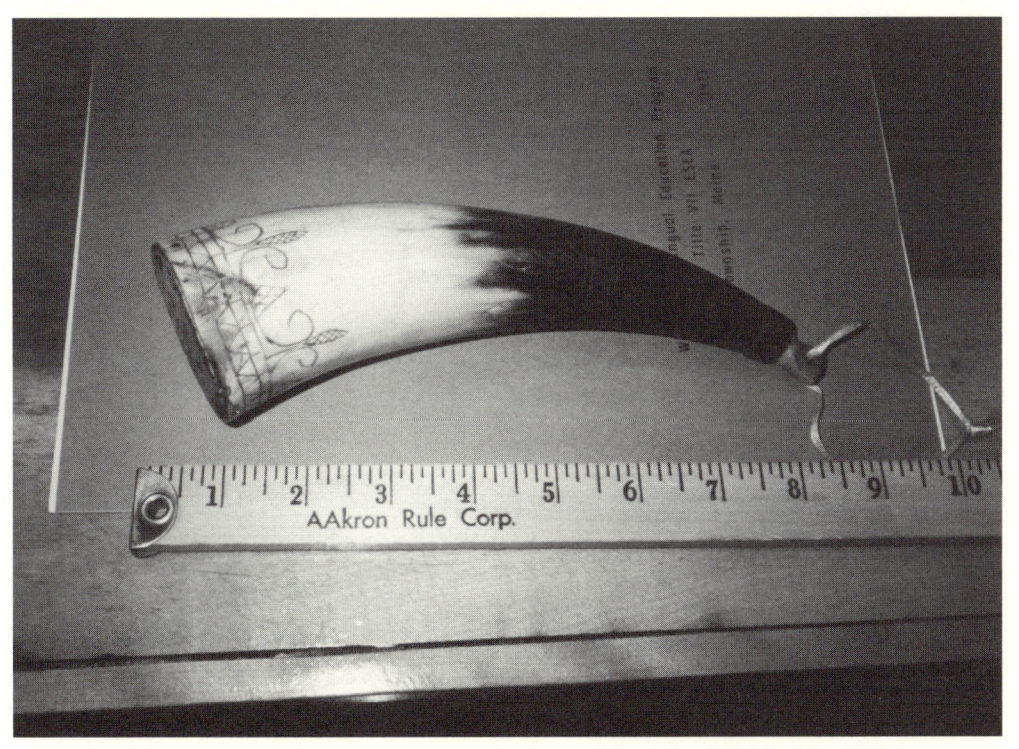

3. Shot Horn Shaker, Waponahki Museum, Photograph by Ann Morrison Spinney.

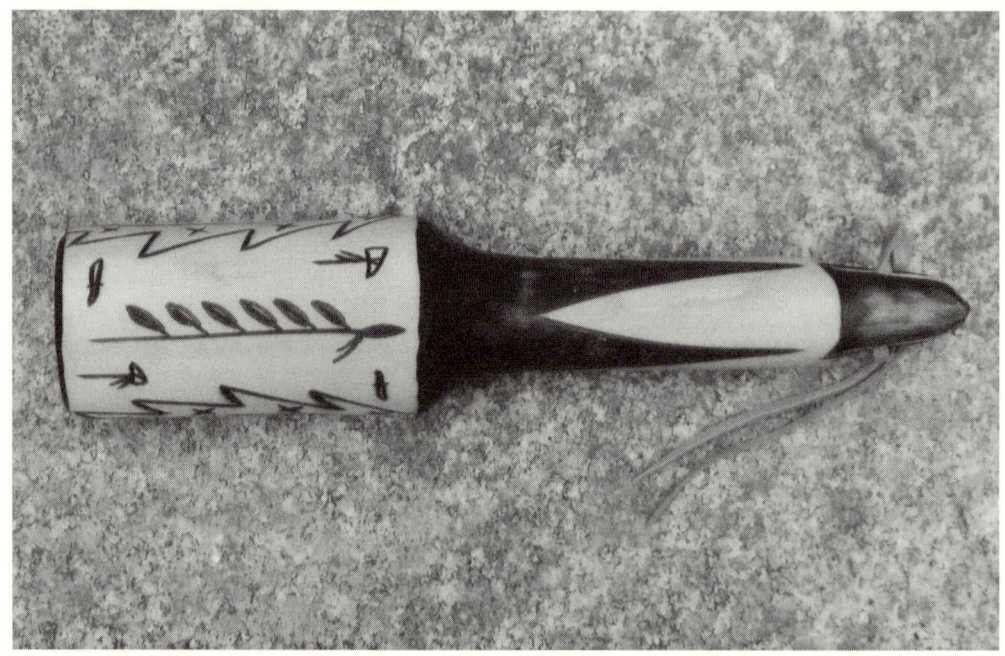

4. Shaker by Richard Keezer (Passamaquoddy), ca. 1999. Photograph by Ann Morrison Spinney.

the flute. The transcriptions of Lonesome Song texts that survive are all from a man's point of view, perhaps because they were transmitted by a male singer (Curtis [1923] 1968:27; Prince 1898:375; Speck 1926:197; Wallis and Wallis 1955:194).

Among Peskotomuhkatiyik at present, I did not find any sanctions against women playing flutes. I occasionally used a German *blockfloete* to demonstrate melodies from historical transcriptions to my consultants and was encouraged by some to record my playing of Passamaquoddy song melodies on this instrument. Because prohibitions against women even touching a flute do exist in other Native American traditions, I inquired whether there were any such restrictions in Wabanaki culture and was assured that there were not. In the Passamaquoddy stories, however, flutes are played or carried only by men.

It seems to be common knowledge among Peskotomuhkatiyik that flageolets—small end-blown flutes—can be made out of poplar saplings. Many middle-aged and older individuals can remember making and playing them. David A. Francis explained the process to me. They are best made in the spring. A segment free of nodes is chosen and cut from a branch, then tapped all around "like you're pounding ash" until the outer bark core separates from the pith, allowing the center to be pushed out. An aperture is cut near one end of the bark tube, and a trimmed plug of the pith inserted in that end of the tube to make a whistle. After testing the whistle, finger holes may be cut down the length of the tube to suit the player. Another man who went with me to cut poplar remembered his father making these fifes; he himself had not. He carefully selected a good branch but did not know how to proceed beyond that point. In his forties at the time, my friend wondered out loud why his father had not taught him more cultural knowledge of this sort. None of my contacts attributed much value to these fifes. David Francis indicated they were a sort of toy, and he used to make them for Native and non-Native children.

Mechling reported that the Maliseet and Mi'kmaq both had a type of flageolet, but he apparently did not see any used, nor was he able to obtain a full description of how they were made. The directions he did obtain are highly unsatisfactory, beginning with the choice of wood. He was told that they were made out of alder, wild cherry, or sweet elder, the last preferred because of its pithy center. My Passamaquoddy consultants regarded this as misinformation.

Speck was told about flutes and informed by his Penobscot assistants that they were associated with shamans, but he did not see any of these instruments (Speck [1940] 1997:165). He was also told that flutes were used to accompany dancing, but no other source corroborates this, and Smith has questioned it. Smith asserted, "We know that the Indians made flutes of bone" (1955:29), but it is not clear whether he was referring to the presence of bone flutes in

North America generally. I have found no reference to Wabanaki bone flutes in any of the sources, oral or written. One contemporary Elder uses a bird-bone flute for certain ceremonies, but I was told that his flute came from "out west," where such flutes were traditionally used in the Sun Dance.

Most of my contacts were very familiar with other Native American flute traditions, and the popularized flute playing of Kevin Locke and R. Carlos Nakai.[16] Kevin Locke has visited the Passamaquoddy reservations and is much admired in the community, as is the Nipmuc flute player and maker Hawk Henries (AMS 21Jun.08). Flute music was sometimes played over the PA system after social dancing had ended at powwows, while crews cleaned up and closed down (AMS 3Sep.94). Rolfe Richter from Sipayik took up the instrument and is now an acclaimed player; his debut recording was released commercially in 2005.[17] It contains some traditional Passamaquoddy melodies as well as newly composed pieces.

Analysis: Musical Instruments in Cultural Context
Gender Restrictions

I have noted gender associations and restrictions for all three classes of musical instrument. Whereas flute playing seems to have been restricted to men in the past, no proscription against women using flutes was acknowledged by my consultants. Women's use of shakers is being encouraged, whereas in the past there seems to have been no gender association. The use of drums is now restricted to men in some contexts, but there is no clear record that it was in the past. Gender issues surrounding drumming are most vexing in public contexts such as powwows and ceremonies of the Wabanaki Confederacy. Different communities have different standards, with Mi'kmaq being more restrictive.

Some of the ideas about gender and instruments have been imported into Passamaquoddy contexts along with musical practices adopted from other cultures. They correspond, however, to an indigenous Wabanaki conception of women as powerful enough to conflict with the efficacy of the sound of drums, shakers, and flutes.

The idea of women as essentially powerful stems from menstruation. I have been told repeatedly, by male and female consultants, that women are powerful because they cleanse themselves once a month; men have to do sweats because they cannot cleanse themselves (see Augustine et al. 1994). One consultant suggested that men are alcoholics at a higher rate than women because they lack this power to cleanse themselves. I was taught that menstruating women should not dance in a circle, stand in the circle around a drum, or enter any ceremonial circle or area where there is smudging, a religious ceremony akin to sanctifying in Christian tradition. Once the smudging is over, a menstruant may reenter the area as long as she does not come into a circle.

These contemporary practices are corroborated in records of the past. According to European accounts, menstruating women were excluded from group activities and prohibited from cooking or handling any implement, particularly those connected with hunting (Biard [1616] 1896(3):105); Denys [1672] 1908:409–10; LeClercq [1691] 1910:227; Maillard 1758:51). Recalling that the Passamaquoddy terms for "drum" and "song" use a generic suffix indicating they are tools, these sanctions can be understood as extending to drumming and singing in public, though specific information about these activities is not mentioned.

Bernard Hoffman, relying solely on historical accounts, believed that these restrictions were because "supernatural power was incompatible with anything so secular and profane as menstruants" (1955:278), but the information I was given suggests the opposite: that menstruating women are so powerful they would interfere with the power invested in these instruments. This is an equally viable explanation of what is recorded about past practices, and it is in accordance with the present sanctions. The danger perceived by Waponah-kiyik in a menstruating woman seems to come not from her being unclean but from her exercising this natural and unconsciously present womanly power. Since in Wabanaki thought the premier concern with power appears to be controlling it for the common good, doing so could logically be the target of restrictions.[18]

Proscriptions against drumming by premenopausal women may be reflections of the social order, as Mary Douglas (1966) suggests are most cultural rules governing contact with bodily fluids. Charlotte Frisbie noted that among Navajo communities the restriction of women from ceremonies was not based on "fear of menstruation, which is actually welcomed and publicly celebrated...but [came] from fear of menstrual fluid" (1989:27). Douglas associates uncleanliness with transgression of cultural categories, but also with the need to control supernatural power, which could destroy culturally defined categories such as social roles (1966:35, 99). Oral traditions and the historical record evince clear divisions by gender in Wabanaki society. These are reflected in the dance styles (see chapter 7). Women's role as bearers of children is strongly emphasized throughout Wabanaki culture. When a woman is menstruating, she cannot be gestating or giving birth but is preparing herself to do so.

Menstrual restrictions are still observed with regard to ceremonial regalia and materials such as smudges. They are even observed in commercial situations such as Penobscot Elder Anne Pardilla's store in Old Town, Maine, and at powwow vendors, where posted notices request that "Women on their time" not handle the tobacco (AMS 29Oct.95)

These restrictions on ceremonial participation are extended by some in the Passamaquoddy community to Catholic practice. At a social gathering of women, one mentioned the idea upheld by a friend of hers that women should not be Eucharistic ministers at Mass "because they bleed once a month." Another friend, a postmenopausal Eucharistic minister, guffawed and said there was nothing to fear from "an old woman like me" except hot flashes. But in the immediately ensuing conversation hot flashes were linked by both women to revelation experiences (AMS 24Apr.95). Thus, the question of whether women's power is harmless at any age was left unresolved. [19]

The question of whether women should drum was under debate within the Passamaquoddy and larger Wabanaki communities during the 1990s. Several prominent Passamaquoddy singers and drummers at that time were women, as is the case at present. The situation is complicated by the different types of drums and traditions of drumming currently in use. It is also influenced by the intertribal nature of most ceremonial occasions, such as powwows and meetings of the Wabanaki Confederacy. Both historical records and oral tradition were consulted, but lack of clarity on which types of drums were the oldest left open questions.

A disagreement over whether women should be allowed to drum created a disturbance at the thirteenth Annual powwow held at a Mi'kmaq reserve in New Brunswick in August 1994. The problem arose because two Drum groups that included women drummers—one Passamaquoddy, one Mohawk—and one all-female Mi'kmaq group had been offered tobacco to come and participate in the powwow. Their obligation to the tobacco offering had to be honored, but some of the assembled Mi'kmaq Elders were gravely disturbed by the notion of women drumming. The female groups had been invited by the powwow committee of the sponsoring community. On Saturday, the first full day of the event, afternoon and evening meetings were held in a special tipi to discuss the issue. Drummers and Elders were all asked to contribute their thoughts to the discussion, which continued up to the end of the last night of singing and dancing.[20] During the discussion, women began to gravitate toward using the large water drum brought by the Mohawk group. Only two Drums, the host and another all-male group, participated in the final Give-Away and closing ceremonies.

Some male Mi'kmaq leaders have upheld the proscription against women using the large group Drum. Some believed women should be restricted to using hand drums, and then only after they have become grandmothers—though not necessarily postmenopausal (AMS 28Feb.94). Most of my women contacts dismissed these ideas as men trying to put women down: as one pointed out, it's the men that are making these rules, not the women Elders (AMS 3Mar.95).

Others have taken them seriously. A Passamaquoddy woman who teaches singing, drumming, and dancing to children in her community and who has been active in an adult Drum group ceased to drum in public after hearing of these proscriptions from a visiting Mi'kmaq shaman. He told her that the men in the community would be sick if the women drummed. This profoundly affected her, because she felt that the men and boys were indeed sick. Although she still led the singing, she stood outside the seated circle of male drummers and used a shaker for all the public occasions I witnessed during 1994–95, until she became a grandmother. She has since continued to lead the children's Drum group, earning praise from many in the community for her dedication.

A resolution has been reached by following the proscriptions proper to each style: premenopausal women use hand drums but do not participate publicly in powwow-style drumming.[21] Women stand outside the circle of drummers and sing on the chorus parts; and they add shakers.

The notion that women should neither drum nor have physical contact with a drum is often encountered among powwow drummers and participants at intertribal powwows and gatherings. The Anishena'abe Dance Drum tradition excludes women from drumming or singing (Vennum 1982). The Grass Dance and Sun Dance traditions of the Sioux nations also restrict women's participation. As these were important sources of the contemporary intertribal powwow, the restrictions on women have been incorporated. The powwow amalgamates and reinterprets elements from these and other traditions. In the powwow there is a concern with balance: the Drum is conceived of as female, and the beaters male. Teachings from the Ojibwa and other Algonquian groups carry more weight with Waponahkiyik than teachings from other cultures, but all have been given careful consideration when a conflict of ideas has arisen.

The question in part revolves around the use of drums from outside the Wabanaki cultural tradition. I asked several female drummers whether they thought there was a connection between the introduction of Dance Drums and the Teachings prohibiting women from drumming. Several were struck by my coupling of the borrowing of drums and the responsibility of accepting the Teachings they carry in their indigenous culture. This is not necessarily how borrowed ideas are treated. One woman pointed out that anything that Passamaquoddy people do becomes part of their tradition, regardless of where it came from. She indicated that the use of the Dance Drum is now part of their culture and can be treated as such, both internally—by applying Wabanaki concepts to it—and externally, by outside observers (AMS 3Mar.95).

Historically, there is evidence supporting the inference that Mi'kmaq people maintained some restrictions on women drumming. Only older women are recorded as drumming in the historical accounts (LeClercq [1691] 1910:14; Maillard 1758). To my knowledge, there are no examples of young women drumming in the oral tradtions. Thus, the current Mi'kmaq teachings may have a historical basis at least in Mi'kmaq culture rather than being a borrowed or invented tradition, as some women suspect.

Drumming and Healing

Concepts linking drumming to healing are an important factor in the debates surrounding women drumming. Drum groups have provided many significant benefits in the Sipayik community that many of my contacts believe would be unfair and even shameful to withhold from young women.

Drum groups provide therapeutic group activity for young people, from preschoolers to teenagers. Talking Circles connected with the Drum groups address constructive problem solving and sharing experiences.[22] Drumming and talking nurture deeper connections between individuals in the Native community, furthering the paramount goal of tribal unity. In the past, individuals were isolated by poverty, alcoholism, and off-reservation prejudice. Drum groups provide a support network for those in trouble, helping young people especially to achieve self-esteem through pride in Native heritage, self-expression, and spiritual growth, according to participants and staff at the Sipayik youth center and *Kilun Kikun* (our house) Transition House.[23]

Drum groups are understood to be central to the healing process that the Wabanaki nations are now undertaking. Drumming encourages a drugfree lifestyle: many of the drummers I encountered in Waponahkik observed the protocol of avoiding all drugs—even cold medications—for twenty-four hours before drumming (AMS 26Nov.94). Therapy combatting physical and mental problems as well as emotional disorders has been conducted in children's Drum groups. One drum teacher reports that drumming has helped train children with attention-deficit disorders to focus (AMS 3Mar.95).

Summary Conclusions

Drums, beaten idiophones, shakers, and flutes are all considered to be traditional Wabanaki instruments. Several construction styles of drum and shaker currently coexist, and their relative preeminence is arguable. There is no consensus within the community on what type of drum is most traditional, and the historical record is not clear. There is ample historical evidence that beaten idiophones were used as well as drums in performance and not differentiated

Table 3. Materials Used by Waponahkiyik for Musical Instruments

Instrument	Material	Purpose	Source
SHAKERS			
	moose dew claws on straps	shaman	LeClercq 1691
	birchbark on stick	dancing	Speck 1940; Smith 1955; Mechling 1958
	gourd	dancing	Speck 1940; Smith 1955; in use
	turtle shell	dancing	Smith 1955; in use
	shot horn	dancing	Fewkes 1890; Mechling 1958; Speck 1940; Smith 1955; remembered 2000s
	horn on stick	dancing	in use
DRUMS			
hand drum	white cedar frame	multipurpose	Mechling 1958; Speck 1940
	maple frame	multipurpose	in use
	pine frame	multipurpose	in use
stationary	yellow birch stump	multipurpose	Mechling 1958
	ash stump	multipurpose	Mechling 1958
	cedar stump	multipurpose	Mechling 1958; Smith 1955; in use
heads	caribou skin		Mechling 1958
	"green" deerskin		Speck 1940
	deerskin		in use 1990s
	moose hide		in use 1990s
laces	babiche		Speck 1940
	sinew		in use 1990s
	plastic		in use 1990s
snares	babiche		Speck 1940
beaters	cedar stick		Speck 1940
	caribou skin head		Mechling 1958; in use
	deer hair ball head		in use
	deerskin ball head cover		in use
BEATEN IDIOPHONES			
birchbark roll		dancing	Maillard 1758; Mechling 1958
board		dancing	Mechling 1958; Speck 1940
logs		dancing	Rosier 1605; Speck 1940
FLUTES			
end-blown	poplar	children's toy	remembered in 1990s
	sweet elder	?	Mechling 1958
	wild cherry	?	Mechling 1958
	alder	?	Mechling 1958
end-blown?	bone	ceremonial	Smith 1955; described in 1990s; *Waponahkik* provenance doubtful

linguistically in either Passamaquoddy or English. Only a musicologist would use the term idiophone.

The importance of all these instruments resides in their capacity to produce sound, although the materials of construction are also philosophically and aesthetically significant in the case of drums and shakers. The uses instruments are put to accrete symbolic value to them. The percussion instruments have been retained in their traditional functions as dance instruments, for healing, and for other kinds of supernatural manipulation in private contexts. Flutes, which the oral tradition suggests were primarily used for love charms and other supernatural manipulation, have not been so consistently utilized. The principal public genre associated with them, Lonesome Songs, has largely been supplanted by Euro-American popular music genres. But recently Peskotomuhkatiyik have adopted the Native American flute for performing traditional Passamaquoddy songs as well as popular meditative genres.

Genre associations of traditional instruments seem to have been largely maintained in the practice of Peskotomuhkatiyik: drumming for dancing, flutes for charming. In addition, gender restrictions, though under debate, are still factors to be considered. In general, both the Passamaquoddy and larger Wabanaki cultural systems are less rigid regarding gender discrimination in the use of musical instruments than other Algonquian cultures. An exception is the unresolved question of women drumming, which is complicated by diverse cultural influences.

The primacy of percussion instruments invites comparison with other uses of percussive sound in Wabanaki culture and the significance attached to them. Salutes using guns became part of ceremonial welcomes (see chapter 5) among Waponahkiyik—as noted by Eckstorm ([1945] 1980:172–73); Speck ([1940] 1997:289–90) and Wallis and Wallis (1955)—perhaps beginning in the seventeenth century, for Lescarbot noted that the Souriquois leader Membertou requested this show of respect from the French. Williamson's description of the 1816 inauguration of the Penobscot governor Aitteon included firing a cannon as the leader was installed in office (Williamson 1832(1):495–98). As late as the twentieth century a cannon kept at Sipayik was fired when the bishop visited and, on the feast of Corpus Christi during certain points in the procession with the Host around the reservation.[24] In addition, it used to be the custom that when a person died at Sipayik, one of those attending the deathbed went outside the house and shot off a gun. Rodney Needham (1967) noted that percussion is almost universally associated with moments of transition between states of being, and his hypothesis seems to apply to these instances.

FIVE

Welcoming Ceremonies

Every school child in the United States has heard a story of how the Pilgrims were welcomed by Native Americans when they landed at Plymouth Rock: meetings were held between their leaders; treaties were signed; the Pilgrims were taught to plant corn; and it all culminated in feasting at the first Thanksgiving. These stories have achieved the status of foundational myths (Ceci 1990:83 n15).

In fact, welcoming ceremonies involving both formal greetings between leaders and feasting were historically, and remain, an important part of the ceremonial life of all the Wabanaki communities. In these ceremonies songs, dances, speeches, and other formal actions are combined into a complex social interaction. The songs that signify welcoming in these ceremonies are also performed independently as part of many civic and spiritual events. The ceremonial actions of the welcoming ceremonies encode layers of meaning: histories of warfare and alliance, social structure, spiritual beliefs, and cultural pride. Analysis of the songs and dances involved can illuminate the resonances that have accrued to their continuing practice in Passamaquoddy communities.

Welcoming ceremonies are well described in the historical literature, including some of the earliest descriptions written by European visitors. The accounts reveal historical continuity up to the present time, as well as common features of these ceremonies shared among all the Wabanaki communities. Peskotomuhkatiyik have extended welcoming ceremonies to groups of visitors who come to trade, confer, or simply socialize. Today, the songs associated with welcoming are sung wherever and whenever the community wishes to express welcome. The dances associated with the songs are not so often performed today, because they require the organization of groups of dancers; but they are features of intertribal gatherings hosted by the Passamaquoddy communities at Sipayik and Motahkomikuk.[1]

Visiting and hosting guests are important activities in modern Wabanaki culture and seem to have been so traditionally. Indian agents in Maine complained that Peskotomuhkatiyik were profligate hosts during summer gatherings (Erickson 1982:171 n6). During my fieldwork I found that visitors are fed, entertained, and given gifts to the best of the hosts' abilities. Engaging in a formal welcome ceremony is a way of showing alliance and signaling the absence of aggressive intentions.

Reciprocal visiting is a form of exchange, and the welcoming ceremonies of the Wabanaki Confederacy may be related to gift-giving ceremonials of other Native North American peoples. Ceremonial exchange of gifts is typically involved in alliance-building events such as trade, marriage, and treaties conducted between First Nations. Give-Away ceremonies at contemporary events in Waponahkik are similar to those held in other Native communities at the closing of a powwow. The most illuminating comparisons of Passamaquoddy exchange protocols past and present, however, are to cultural practices of neighboring groups with whom they have had extended contact: Iroquoian peoples and others in the eastern coastal and Great Lakes regions. As shown in the analysis of songs and dances, there seem to have been influences between these groups in the development of intertribal ceremonies.

The elaborate extent of the welcoming ceremonies and their persistence into the present day speak for the centrality of generosity as a core value in Wabanaki culture. In historical perspective, this appears to be a crucial factor in developing mistrust of Europeans, whose colonial cultures were and are still based on competition and driving hard bargains.

A Ceremonial Complex

The complete welcoming ceremonies comprise several dances interspersed with speeches and prayers. My teacher Joseph A. Nicholas spoke of these as separate dances but also indicated they were related. I find it helpful to think of the dances as forming a ceremonial complex. The historical literature—based on the testimony of insiders as well as outside observers—invariably presents the different stages of welcoming (welcoming the visiting party, formally greeting their leader, smoking the Peace Pipe) as one event, and this is also how I have experienced them.

The welcoming ceremonies are linked to three of the other dances associated with the Wabanaki Confederacy and defined by Joe Nicholas as "the core of the Passamaquoddy repertory." On some occasions the Welcome Dance between communities and the Greeting Dance between their leaders (*Sakomak*) are followed immediately by the Peace Pipe Ceremony between tribal council members and the War Club Dance between esteemed men. Depending on the context, the Welcome Dance might be shortened and move immediately to a War Club Dance (AMS 25Nov.94). On other occasions, these dances are interspersed with modern intertribal style dances.

There is an entire repertory of songs that are proper to the Welcome and Greeting Dances, marked by the archaic lyric *qanute*. These songs were generally singled out as a group by my Passamaquoddy consultants with the term "*Qanute* Songs," and "Welcome Songs" is a common translation.[2] At least one of these songs was always sung during the welcoming ceremonies that I have observed or have been told about. There are various stages in the ceremony requiring that other types of songs be used as well. The *Qanute* Songs are also used alone for occasions when it is appropriate to express formally the sentiment of welcome, often without performing a formal Welcome or Greeting Dance. Detailed analysis of the style features of these songs is undertaken below, after consideration of the ceremonial contexts in which they function.

Previous researchers have labeled all the songs of the various dances in the welcoming ceremonies "Greeting Songs." I prefer to distinguish the songs used for different parts of these ceremonies. There is a specific Welcome Dance done between host and visiting parties as well as a specific Greeting Dance performed by their leaders, and both are parts of the protocols of welcoming. Historical accounts suggest that these distinctions are quite old.

Historical Accounts

Jacques Cartier's account of his 1534 voyage indicates that he was welcomed on the Gaspé peninsula with ceremonies from which trading ensued. His description of an encounter with people who were probably Mi'kmaq at the mouth of the Restigouche River includes actions similar to the welcoming ceremonies described by nineteenth-century sources: "Some of their women, who did not come over [to trade], danced and sang, standing in the water up to their knees. The other women, who had come over to the side where we were, advanced freely towards us and rubbed our arms with their hands. Then they joined their hands together and raised them to heaven, exhibiting many signs of joy" (Cartier 1924:56).

Samuel de Champlain observed an event similar to welcoming ceremonies between allied parties of Etechemins (ancestors of the Passamaquoddy), Montagnais, and Algonquins near Tadoussac, Quebec (Champlain [1603] 1922:102,

109). War parties from these three communities had allied against the Iroquois, and a ceremonial celebration was held on their successful return there. At the feast held in honor of the occasion one league from Tadoussac, men danced between the cooking pots of stew: "The men sat on both sides.... Before their meat was cooked, one of them rose up, and took a dog, and went leaping about the said kettles from one end of the lodge to the other. When he came in front of the grand Sagamo (leader), he threw his dog violently upon the ground, and then all with one voice cried Ho, ho, ho. Immediately another rose up and did the like, and so they continued until the meat was cooked" (Champlain [1603] 1922:101–2).

When the successful war party arrived at Tadoussac, the Algonquin men lined up with their women kinfolk and sang and danced, facing the others (Champlain [1603] 1922:107–8). The Jesuit Father Pierre Biard reported that the Mi'kmaq and Etechemin insisted on ceremonies before they would trade: "Gifts must be presented and speeches made to them, before they condescend to trade; this done, they must have the Tabagie, i.e. the banquet. Then they will dance, make speeches and sing 'Adesquidex, Adesquidex,' That is, that they are good friends, allies, associates, confederates, and comrades of the King and of the French" (Biard [1616] 1896(3):80–81).

In several of these accounts, welcoming is linked to trading activity, and both imply an alliance, even if only temporary. Alliance seems to be the rubric under which these complicated interactions best may be understood.[3] Gilles Havard (2001:16–18) argues that "the Native understanding of trade" was much more than economic activity; trade was symbolic of alliance.[4] In the alliances that Native peoples and Europeans constructed, gift-giving was also important, as was the quality of gifts. Trading and gift-giving are different forms of exchange: where trading may have limited significance, gift-giving is generally understood to be part of a symbolic economy or a system of ethics.[5] Other aspects of traditional Wabanaki political life were also conducted on a symbolic level (see the discussion of warfare in the following chapter), and keeping in mind the symbolic elements of trade illuminates the role of singing and dancing in these interactions.

In contemporary practice as well as the historical record, welcoming ceremonies are most closely associated with any activity that implies alliance, and they are an important event independent of any trading activity. When interpreted under the rubric of alliance, continuity in practice is revealed from earliest European contact records to protocols of the present day. Details of the historical observations correspond with several aspects of the modern welcoming ceremonial complex.

The Passamaquoddy Wampum Records on Welcoming

Descriptions of various specialized versions of the welcoming ceremonies can be found in the Passamaquoddy Wampum Records. As explained in chapters 1 and 2, these specify the laws by which the historical Wabanaki Confederacy was established in the early eighteenth century and the protocols with which it functioned. An oral record, the Passamaquoddy version was preserved by Louis Mitchell, who shared it with philologist John Dyneley Prince at the turn of the last century. Several printed versions are now available (Prince 1898; Leland and Prince 1902; Prince 1921; Leavitt and Francis 1990). The commentary devised by Joseph A. Nicholas for the program of dances presented at the Indian Day is a contemporary adaptation of the Wampum Records, and these texts continue to be reproduced through practice by other ceremonial leaders in the Passamaquoddy community.

In the Wampum Records, welcoming ceremonies are described as part of the protocols for installing new leaders among the member tribes, a task done by delegates from the entire Wabanaki Confederacy. The function of these ceremonies was to signify the gathering in peace of tribes that had formerly been at war; thus continuance of the ceremonies served a symbolic function, reminding those present of the original coming together of the tribes to end the warfare between them. The support offered to a community that had lost its leader or was choosing a new one could be powerfully evident in such ceremonies.

Bernard G. Hoffman (1955:608–58) has argued that warfare among the Mi'kmaq was waged in part symbolically through ritual events (discussed below).[6] The evidence for symbolic struggle suggests that efforts to maintain peace might also have symbolic components. The welcoming ceremonies are particularly emphatic in signaling peaceful intentions.

A summary of the welcoming ceremonies of the Wabanaki Confederacy, extracted from their context in the various Passamaquoddy versions of the Wampum Records, goes as follows. Messengers bring news of the council to be held at their settlement to the settlements of the other tribes. They travel by canoe, carrying a flag. One of the messengers steps ashore singing a Greeting Song, *noskawewintuwewan*, and walks back and forth between the men arrayed onshore greeting them. His greeting is returned by one of the hosts (*noskawan*). The visiting messengers go with their hosts to pray at the church. Then they are taken to their lodging, and the whole community greets them informally (*wolasihkuwawa*, or '*sokiptinenawa*). At night they dance, and then they meet in council to set the date for the *Oliyut Sakom* (chief-making). The departure of the messengers is delayed with the ceremony called *Okelhutin*, and there is more feasting (*Okelhutuwi Wiqhopaltin*), at which more greetings are ceremonially exchanged (*nskawhotin*). Finally, the messengers are allowed to depart. The *Oliyut Sakom* opens with welcoming ceremonies as well: when the visitors arrive, "they go to shake hands, dance and make their greetings" (Leavitt and Francis 1990:41–45).

No published version of the Wampum Records describes details of the actual songs and dances, but different genres are named and placed in context of the ceremonies. This allows comparison with ethnographic and historical records.

The origin of the welcoming practices detailed in the Wampum Records is intriguing. We know that the historical Wabanaki Confederacy was based on older, preexisting alliances (A. H. Morrison 1975). It is possible that the protocols described in the Wampum Records were also existing practices that these First Nations already shared; it is also conceivable that significant new protocols were devised to mark the occasion of this alliance, which profoundly changed the political power structure of the area.[7] Some obviously new elements in the protocols were drawn from Catholic practice, which by the 1701 Treaty of Montreal had become indigenized.[8] The Wampum Records include prayers in church and blessings by the resident priest as part of elections.

Welcoming ceremonies are mentioned in the context of elections in both the Wampum Records and the ethnographic accounts of Penobscot culture collected by Frank G. Speck ([1940] 1997). But there is evidence, including modern practice, that welcoming ceremonies were held on other occasions when the Wabanaki nations gathered together, such as St. Anne's Day (Wallis and Wallis 1955:184, 188). The installation of a new governor in a constituent community may have required the most elaborate greetings, and on such an occasion, the welcoming ceremonies would have fallen under the protocol of the Wabanaki Confederacy.

Observations of Welcoming Ceremonies in Other Wabanaki Communities

In the early twentieth century, accounts of welcoming ceremonies in Mi'kmaq, Maliseet, and Penobscot communities were gathered by anthropologists. Louis Mitchell's rendering of the Wampum Records was passed down across generations; similarly, the ethnographies presented the recollections of elderly consultants. Taken together, they allow for comparison among the versions of each First Nation and across time.

Speck's consultants in the first decades of the twentieth century indicated that the Penobscot welcoming ceremonies had formerly been very complex. They also remembered the welcoming ceremonies as part of the election ceremonies, so that Speck presented them together as "Greeting or Election Dance" (Speck [1940] 1997:292, 288). This corresponds to the presentation of the ceremonies in the Wampum Records. Note that Speck refers to the whole ceremonial context as a "dance," following the Native terminology. His use of the term "greeting" instead of "welcoming" is idiosyncratic but may also reflect his informants' terminology.

The Greeting Dance (i.e., welcoming ceremony) as Speck described it was a "solemn...ceremony" of which there were two aspects "according to whether the Penobscot were visiting others or whether they were hosts receiving visitors" ([1940] 1997:288–89). It was called *skawohe*, or *skawintowakan*, the latter meaning "Greeting Song." The other Wabanaki languages have similar terms, perhaps reflecting a common origin in this ceremony, the purpose of which was to cultivate an alliance between tribes. Mechling (1917:241) gives *skauwe* as the Maliseet term for the councilmen's "personal songs" sung during election procedures. Leland and Prince (1902:347) give *n'skawewintuagun* as the Passamaquoddy term for "Salutation" or Greeting Song. W. D. and R. S. Wallis give *ne'skawe't* as the Mi'kmaq term for a Greeting Song (1955:119). The last two forms indicate with the particle *n-* that the greeting is *from* an exclusive "us" party and presumably to a "you" party.

Speck's consultants described how the visiting party would approach their village (Indian Island Reservation) by water in canoes. They would assemble in a line off shore and paddle in slowly, singing their Greeting Song. Meanwhile, the Penobscot men had assembled on the shore in two lines with loaded guns. These they fired into the air, "symbolizing the reception of an enemy as well as being a salute." As the leader of the visitors (remembered as a man) walked the length between their lines, singing along with his party, the hosts fired again. Speck understood this action as symbolically "'running the gauntlet'...a dramatic gesture of hostility and peace summarizing the periods of Wabanaki [intertribal] contact before and after the foundation of the Confederacy." The ceremonies continued later in a feast, at which the (male) visitors danced around the hall shaking hands with the (male) hosts before eating (Speck [1940] 1997:289–90).

An alternative interpretation based on the choreography is that the lines of dancers symbolically form a longhouse. This accords with the Iroquois metaphor of confederation and also matches one translation of the archaic word *qanute* used in Welcome Dance Song lyrics (discussed below). As previously explained, the Wabanaki Confederacy was influenced by the Iroquois Confederacy, through the participation of the Mohawk community at Kahnawá:ke.

Speck's information came from elders who were remembering the songs and the ceremony. Whether Speck personally observed the Penobscot or Passamaquoddy welcoming ceremony during his fieldwork—undertaken between 1907 and 1918—is not clear from his account of it. It was most likely in use occasionally at least, since my archival research corroborated that the ceremonies were performed during the 1940s and 1950s, even if only for public exhibitions. These were still occasions for the different tribes to gather together, and the *Sakomak* often attended in their regalia.[9] Nicholas N. Smith also documented and recorded a Greeting Song used in the ceremony inaugurating William Neptune as governor of Motahkomikuk in 1953 (Smith 1955:32).

Speck noted that "there were originally ten songs or parts to the whole [welcoming] procedure" ([1940] 1997:292). At the time of Speck's fieldwork, the Penobscot recognized two forms of songs associated with welcoming ceremonies: an older, slower and more impressive version originally used for the opening greeting upon the guest's arrival; and a style the singer identified as "new," more rapid and less stately, originally used for dancing at the welcoming feast. He reported that the fast type seemed to have replaced the slow type some time before; however, he recorded examples of both slow and fast songs and included transcriptions of them in his book *Penobscot Man* (labeled PR 66b, PR 72, and PR 18; these examples are discussed below). No other source mentions a ten-part procedure, although it is probable that in the past there were different types of songs for the different dances in this ceremonial complex, as there are now.

An onshore greeting ceremony and feast consistent with the details presented by Speck were described by W. D. and R. S. Wallis, based on information from Mi'kmaq consultants in 1911 (1955:184–89). The *neskawet* was sung only by the two chiefs, while the host placed a gun on the shoulder of the visitor and discharged it. There was no gauntlet formation. The feast was called *tiwig'oba'ktim* (compare Passamaquoddy *wiqhopaltin*, above), and the description of dancing beforehand by the men is remarkably similar to what Champlain observed in 1603 (quoted above). The dancing afterward included women, all accompanied by a man drumming on birchbark.

The Abenaki Friendly Dance observed by Nicholas Smith at the 300th Anniversary of the St. Francis community at Ôdanak, Quebec, was similar to the Welcoming Dance of the other Wabanaki (Smith 1962:15–16). The form of this line dance was like a gauntlet formation, but as Smith suggests, it is perhaps closer in form and even in function to a Virginia Reel. It is possible that an older Abenaki dance, in form like those described by Champlain and Speck (Champlain [1603] 1922:102, 107; Speck [1940] 1997:289) was influenced by Euro-American country dancing. It is not clear from Smith's description whether the Friendly Dance was used to open the ceremonies on this occasion; it is the second genre he discusses, after the Snake Dance. The Snake Dance was sometimes used to gather dancers together (see chapter 7).

Maintaining the Ceremonies

Speck and Smith both felt that the ceremonies they observed had degenerated from the practices described by their older consultants in the Penobscot community. Occasions on which welcoming ceremonies were employed such as electing a *Sakom* were altered over the years to conform to state election laws. Although documentation does not exist for every occasion, ethnographic sources reveal that traditional practices were maintained.

In 1995 I interviewed a Penobscot Elder who reported that the last time he saw a Greeting Dance done "properly" was when the Sipayik governor, Hartley Nicholas, and his tribal council came to Indian Island. Hartley Nicholas was governor from 1980 to 1984. The two tribal councils were seated on the ground in two facing lines. Hartley danced in from one end. He sang "an introduction" first. Then he sang and danced toward the Penobscot governor "with a measured step." Then the Penobscot governor greeted him. They smoked the Pipe in the Four Directions, then Hartley danced back and took his seat at the end of his Council (AMS 15May.95).

This Elder's judgmental description indicates that the division of the welcoming ceremonies into parts, with a Greeting Dance reserved for the leaders and a different type of song for each segment, never disappeared from Waponahkik—contrary to ethnographic reports of the demise of the traditions, such as the assertions throughout Speck's *Penobscot Man*. The protocols had been kept alive in Hartley Nicholas's family, at least. His mother was active in promoting traditional culture through traditional ways. She used to teach young people by example, including chaperoning groups from Sipayik to Indian Island for traditional dances (AMS 27Apr.95). Because cultural knowledge is passed down through practice, as long as one person knows older procedures and carries them out, the tradition cannot be said to have disappeared. There is the possibility that it will be returned to general knowledge, as the multipart welcoming ceremony has been in the contemporary meetings of the Wabanaki Confederacy.

Contemporary Ceremonies

Whatever the case in other communities, multipart welcoming ceremonies were continued in Peskotomuhkatik. They are used on formal civic occasions, such as the inauguration of the tribal governor and council. They are also demonstrated at the Sipayik and Motahkomikuk Indian Days, where they serve both to welcome visitors and to educate the public about Passamaquoddy traditions.

At the Indian Day ceremonies I have observed, the Welcome Dance usually follows the Grand Entry of the dancers, elements of which correspond to the Grand Entry of powwows. In 1993, at the Sipayik Indian Day, the Welcome Dance was the first dance, opening the celebration; in 1995 the traditional dancers were "smudged"[10] in the new Ceremonial Grounds before proceeding across the state highway into the old Ceremonial Grounds in a Grand Entry accompanied by the Eastern Fire Drum. A verbal welcome was offered by the master of ceremonies (MC) and the tribal governor, and a Flag Song and Veterans' Honor Song preceded the Welcome Dance. Subsequent Indian Days have followed this procedure, blending traditional Passamaquoddy protocols with those of an intertribal powwow.

Choreography

The movements of the modern Passamaquoddy Welcome Dance are as follows. Traditional dancers (those dressed in regalia) form into two long lines, facing each other (illustration 5). According to former dance leader Joseph A. Nicholas, the lines are supposed to be separated by sex, but where there is a problem of matching length, they are mixed. The host and visiting *Sakomak* are positioned one at each end. To the accompaniment of a fast paced *Qanute* Song and a drum (examples 2 and 3), the dancers step toward each other. The step common to many Native American dances is used: with weight on the left foot, dancers move their right foot forward, touch the ground and lift once, then step forward onto it. With weight on right foot, the touch-and-step is repeated with the left foot and so on.[11] When the lines are face to face, generally not more than four to six steps, the dancers turn around and step away with their backs toward each other. The song is repeated as many times as is necessary for the dancers to move toward and away from each other. Sometimes directions are called out to the dancers as part of the song, and the exclamation *Taho*! signals the end. The *Sakomak* do not change position during this dance but step in place.

The Greeting Dance often is done immediately after the Welcome Dance, since the end of the Welcome Dance leaves everyone in position. Joseph A.

5. Welcome Dance, Sipayik Indian Day 1995. Photograph courtesy of the *Quoddy Tides*.

6. Greeting Dance, Sipayik Indian Day 2005. Photograph by Roger Spinney.

Nicholas described the Welcome Dance and its relation to the Greeting Dance as "page one and page two." These two dances are very different in style and have specific functions within the welcoming ceremony, similar to the old multipart ceremony described by Speck's Penobscot consultants.

The Greeting Dance itself is in parts: first the two *Sakomak*, sometimes accompanied by their lieutenant governors, step toward each other from their positions at the ends of the lines of people and offer each other a greeting (illustration 6). Sometimes they meet in the middle; sometimes each comes to the other's place. On every occasion I have observed, this motion was done to the slow chant *He, Qanute* (example 4). The step used is the same step used by the lines of dancers in the Welcome Dance, but the *Sakomak* may slow the motion down markedly by touching each foot twice before shifting onto it. As shown in the analysis of songs (below) the slow pace of the Greeting Dance is a marker of the prestige of the *Sakom*.

After this ceremonial exchange of greetings, there are several ways of concluding the Greeting Dance. The two *Sakomak* may perform a fast freestyle dance in celebration, for which a variety of fast dance songs may be sung. Alternatively, after returning to their places at the head of the lines of participants remaining after the Welcome Dance, the host may summon the Pipe Bearer and offer the visitors the Peace Pipe. At an election ceremony I observed in 1994, the *Sakomak* moved directly from exchanging greetings into a War Club Dance with men representing each of the tribal councils, after which a fast dance was done to conclude. The Election Ceremony Dance, Peace Pipe Ceremony Dance, and War Club Dance each require detailed analysis and interpretation (see chapter 6).

Analysis and Interpretation of Welcome and Greeting Ceremony Dances

The line formation of the Welcome Ceremony Dance and Greeting Dance as performed today recall the historical descriptions given above. The lines moving together and apart seem to mimic confrontation between the communities, but the significance of the motion is that confrontation does not occur. Speck's suggestion that the lines in the Penobscot dance were similar to the "gauntlet" that prisoners of war were forced to run is based on a similar interpretation of the dance as symbolic action (Speck 1997 [1940]:290). The motion of turning around so that the parties have their backs to each other indicates trust. The overall formation is like a longhouse in which the people are assembled on two sides. The dance thus represents what the meeting should accomplish through the metaphor of confederation as a longhouse. William Fenton's summary of the Condolence Council ceremony at the heart of the Iroquois Confederacy protocols indicates a similar formation when representatives of the allied nations met in the segment, "At The Woods' Edge" (Fenton 1998:727, 731).

The Welcome and Greeting Dances do not allow freestyle expression except to the *Sakomak* in concluding the Greeting Dance. Solidarity within the community is expressed by the long lines of dancers moving together. The use of fast dances to conclude the ceremony seems celebratory, to complement the careful symbolism of the leaders' exchange. The words I have observed extemporized for the songs sung in accompaniment to this segment are often praises for the leaders, the dancers, and the community (see examples 4 and 7).

Analysis and Interpretation of Welcome and Greeting Ceremony Songs

In current practice, there are two types of song associated with the welcoming ceremonies: a very formal type, with long note values performed in slow tempo, always sung on occasions of state when governors of different tribes come together; and a fast type, employing shorter, more patterned note values in a faster tempo. Examples of the slow and fast *Qanute* Song types sung today by Wabanaki singers may be found in examples 2, 3, 4, and 7.

Peskotomuhkatiyik reserve the slow songs for the more stately parts of their welcoming ceremonies: the first Welcome Dance, and the first part of the Greeting Dance, War Club Dance, and Peace Pipe ceremonies performed by the tribal leaders.

One singer believes that the fast songs (specifically example 3) may have come from the Penobscots. She agreed with other consultants that the slow song *He, Qanute* is originally Passamaquoddy. In any case, as this singer noted, all Wabanaki singers know these songs because their function is intertribal. Different individuals, and different Drum groups give them slightly different renditions; they are sung both by individuals with hand drums and by Drum groups, with corresponding changes in the pulse and organization.

As described in chapter 3, Peskotomuhkatiyik generally sing with percussive accompaniment, usually a drum or shaker played by the lead singer; rhythmic chanting by other participants is also mentioned. Portions of the welcoming ceremonies when performed today may be accompanied only by a drum beat. I maintain the conventions followed by other sources in transcribing songs, as explained in chapter 3. Because transcriptions showing all the rhythmic and melodic nuances of each performance are not easily apprehended, the transcriptions provide only a basic map of the form, melodic system, and rhythmic flow of the songs. Features of performance style such as the relationship between the singer's line and the drum or shaker must be kept in mind when reading them.

Melodic phrase relationships are the most important aspects of Passamaquoddy songs; this is how a song is conceptualized, as evidenced in performance practices of strophic repetition, variation, and antiphonal singing. Comparative analysis of melodic phrase structures yields important information about the stability of Passamaquoddy song repertories. The *Qanute* Songs proper to welcoming ceremonies have parallel phrases, and their melodic motives are found in recordings that span the twentieth century.

All the contemporary songs are constructed of three and five phrases, parallel phrase structures being elaborated with extensions. This is easiest to spot in the fast songs: example 3 soars into a higher range "interrupting" the second of two otherwise similar sections. The second phrase of the slow song *He Qanute* (example 4) begins like the first but turns down and is extended with a cadential formula; the third is set in a lower range but repeats the cadence.

Text is as important in the structure of these songs as melody is; lexical and ceremonial words are interspersed with vocables used to keep rhythm. Since pitch intonation in the Passamaquoddy language affects lexical meaning, text and melody must be carefully matched. It is impossible to rule one superior over the other as regards phrase organization. In performance, extemporized texts often change the durational pattern of melodies. Many of my consultants showed an extreme concern for text in recorded examples, being reluctant to sing the songs from Curtis's *The Indians' Book* ([1923] 1968) because they could not with certainty pronounce the words as she idiosyncratically transcribed them.[12] Another consultant spent hours with me going over a song transcribed by Curtis until he could determine the proper words; the relationship of syllables to rhythm is crucial in determining vowel sounds.

All the songs associated with welcoming ceremonies employ various forms of the archaic word *qanute*. One Elder who is considered an authority on Passamaquoddy songs insisted that *qanute* is "not a regular word," although another Elder who is a resource person for the language gave *aqane* as the Passamaquoddy for "you [singular] are welcome." The ending *-ute* is the first person plural suggestive of animate intransitive verbs, so that *aqanute* might be translated as "Let's welcome [each other]" or "Let's do the Welcome Dance." Probably the best explanation given to me is that it is "an expression of welcome" (AMS 18Oct.96). The word is found in Abenaki, Penobscot, Maliseet, and Passamaquoddy songs from the past, as well as those used at present. As in the Passamaquoddy repertory, songs using this word are associated with welcoming. The word *qanute* is also found in Iroquois longhouse ceremony songs, where it is given different translations, including "the long house" and "a voice is rising."[13]

Comparison with the Historical Record

Natalie Curtis included three Wabanaki Songs of Greeting [*sic*] in *The Indians' Book*: one Passamaquoddy example as sung by John Salis in Eastport and two Penobscot songs, one sung by Salis and one by Francis Joseph Dana in Lincoln, Maine.[14] The description of the welcoming ceremonies that she received (Curtis [1923] 1968:7) conforms to the one that Speck was given ([1940] 1997:288–95). Her consultant indicated that the people responded to the visitors' first song by singing *Hega, hega*. The second and third songs have these vocables as their text (Curtis [1923] 1968:15, 16) This kind of rhythmic exclamation was traditionally sung by men to accompany dancing and melodic singing, according to my Passamaquoddy consultants. Readers can infer that the first song was the greeting of the visiting *Sakom* and the other two were the hosts' Welcome Dance Songs. This fits with some of their style features, but Curtis's materials and methods raise questions. Melodically, the "Greeting Songs" she transcribed bear little resemblance to those sung today, nor do they correspond with songs recorded by Speck or Mechling. Whether this lack of correspondence is significant is debatable. Curtis did not do extensive fieldwork but rather paid a quick visit to each Native community represented in the book. Once her transcriptions were made, by having the song repeatedly sung to her, she did not return to check them. The repertoire she was entrusted with was meant to be only a sample of the community's song style, and what she ended up with may not be representative.

Structurally, the songs Curtis gives are very regular: each has four phrases. The second and third songs are periodic, whereas the first song contains an echo between the two interior phrases. These forms contrast with the rounded three- and five-phrase song forms used today. The range of the first song is over an octave; the modern slow song *He, Qanute* (example 3) spans a sixth. The second and third Greeting Songs given by Curtis are more limited in range, more like the modern songs. The tempo she gives is the same for all three: a good walking pace, the quarter note at 116 beats per minute. But the beat of the accompaniment—whether footsteps, rattle, or drum—is not indicated, and this is the real determinant of slow or fast genre today. Curtis barred the first song in mixed meter, changing between triple and duple, and the penultimate measure contains only three eighth notes. If sung freely, with drum beats marking where Curtis has bars, this nearly conforms to the style parameters of a slow Greeting Song. Its lyrics are:

> Ye Kwa no da Kwa no da no Kwa ye
> Kwa no da Kwa no da no Kwa ye etc. (Curtis [1923] 1968:14)

The relation to the Passamaquoddy text *qanute* is obvious (see example 4).

The following two songs, another "Penobscot Song of Greeting" and a "Passamaquoddy Song of Greeting" (both setting the vocables *hega* as given above), are unfailingly duple. They invite performance in the quick style, with drum beat on each quarter note in a duple pattern. These would suit the needs of the Welcome Dance formation.[15]

Frank Speck included three versions of "the formal Penobscot Greeting Song" in *Penobscot Man*, transcribed by Jacob Sapir (cylinders 5081, PR 66b; 5086, PR 72; and 5063, PR 18, in Speck [1940] 1997:293, 294). The last of these is described as the song sung by the host *Sakom* to visitors.[16] The basic melody of these three songs is the same and is similar to the modern Passamaquoddy song. They all consist of three different phrases; PR 18 features a varied iteration of the first phrase, which Sapir wrote out as the beginning of a subsequent verse. This is the longest and slowest rendition; the singing is broken up by two speeches. I have inserted Speck's translation of the speeches into my transcription from his recording (example 5).

The melodic outline of the modern song's three phrases resembles that of these examples, as diagramed in Example 6. The differences in the pacing of Speck's recordings are significant. PR 18, the *Sakom*'s greeting to the visitors, is sung more slowly and with more repetitions than the others. This recalls the slow pace of contemporary Passamaquoddy performances and the way that the *Sakomak* often slow down the Greeting Dance by adding to the dance step as described above.

These features suggest that length may be a contextual marker of political status. Historical accounts of formal speeches evidence that the leaders' ability to make elaborate and eloquent speeches was a crucial characteristic of their status (Maillard 1758; Lescarbot [1618] 1907–14; A. H. Morrison 1976).

The lyrics of these three examples from Speck's collection are similar, and they are clearly related to those of the modern *Qanute* songs. In his book Speck gives the texts in summary only, without noting the variations that are included in my transcription (example 5):

> He ga hwa nu de, He ga hwa nu da (repeat)
> Gwɑn ha li ya ho, Gwɑn ha li ya he (repeat)

The quality of Speck's recordings is not very good; consonants particularly are obscured. It is probable that "hwa nu de" is *qanute*, which is how I have transcribed it.[17]

The slow songs recorded by Speck are melismatic, similar to the Election Dance Greeting Song as sung by Delia Mitchell and her niece Deborah Brooks (see the Election Dance discussion in the following chapter).[18] Although PR 66b is included in the section on Greeting Chants in *Penobscot Man*, in the notes accompanying Speck's recordings it is labeled an "Election Song" (cylinder 5081). It was probably a Greeting Song used during the election ceremonies, but whether it was sung as a greeting to arriving guests or as the greeting to or by the new *Sakom* is not clear from Speck's notes. Likewise, PR 72 is labeled a Wedding Dance Greeting Chant. It could still be a Welcome Song used in the context of weddings—or an example of the same piece of music used for two functionally different songs.

Speck also included a song "belonging to the second part of the Greeting Ceremony" (PR 74 in Speck 1997 [1940]:295). It is a quick song with two short phrases, sung to syncopated vocables; the phrases are repeated with slight variations several times. It suggests the type of quick dance song used in contemporary Passamaquoddy ceremonies to celebrate the formal exchange of greetings between *Sakomak*. The melody and lyrics of this example are very similar to other quick dance songs found in Speck's collection, suggesting the same generic treatment of fast dance songs that operates today in the Passamaquoddy community.

In summary, analysis of the melodic materials of Welcoming and Greeting Ceremony Songs from the past century of recordings reveals continuities at several levels. Similar melodies and signal words are found in recordings separated by decades and from different communities sharing the Wabanaki Confederacy protocols. These similar songs are used for similar functions.

The historical descriptions cited in the opening section of this chapter confirm that Waponahkewiyik have employed such protocols when visiting each other since at least the first period of extended European contacts in the seventeenth century. Similarities in the dance choreographies are evident from the earliest descriptions to present-day observations. The mimetic quality of the dance formations is constant: in the Welcome Dance lines of dancers form a "house" figure even when performing outdoors. This may be a metaphor for the council longhouse of the Confederacy. In the Greeting Dance, the *Sakomak* symbolically approach and greet each other.

The striking similarities between songs recorded in the first decade of the twentieth century and songs sung by contemporary Wabanaki singers a century later reinforces the connection of present performance practices with the past. Analysis of the recordings and transcriptions also reveals a continued compositional process of varying and recombining basic melodic materials in any performance. The use of melodic formulas such as are found in different versions of the Greeting Chant reinforces the connection between these songs and their ceremonial function. This suggests that the compositional and performance procedures of variation and recombination have served to preserve the tradition while allowing a high degree of individual expression by singers in performance situations. A flexible aesthetic system is revealed, one that is able to maximize the effect of minimal materials and adapt to a variety of circumstances.

Contemporary Reinterpretations of Welcome Songs

The significant position of welcoming ceremonies in the community life of the Wabanaki nations is evidence that hospitality is a core cultural value. In the history of the Passamaquoddy Tribe, cultural concepts of sharing, including welcoming and gift-giving, are crucial to understanding the complex relations between Natives and the European immigrants who tried to take control over their lands and livelihood. Native sharing has been misunderstood, and this has led to betrayal. Recent examples include New Age entrepreneurs who have "sold" knowledge shared with them in personal situations. Even ethnographers—who for nearly two centuries gathered information, made recordings, and took them away to archives—have not always reciprocated properly.

This dilemma is keenly felt by Native people. One Elder cautioned me, "It is very difficult for Native people to say No, and they don't protect themselves" (the point, as I understood it, being that outsiders should not ask for intimate knowledge).

The Dawnland Singers were a folk music group involving members of the Bruchac family, of the Abenaki Nation. They expressed the complicated history of Abenaki hospitality and European abuses in their song *Awanikia* from their album *Alnobak* (1994):

> *Awanikia dokahkwiyun?*
> Who are you, and what do you know?
> *Alnombayi* way, the way of this land
> And from the beginning we took you in our clans
> Another *alnombay missiskoway*, Indian man.
> (Refrain): he, kwa nu de, he kwa nu de, he he kwan, he he kwa nu de
> . . . .
> *Awanikia dokahkwiyun?*
> Who are you and what is this that you have planned?
> After giving our lives to you, you're saying this is not our land?
> *Alnombayi* way—I'm still living so here I'll stand
> On *alnombayi missiskoway*, Indian land.

The refrain uses an Abenaki Welcome Song similar in text and melody to the Passamaquoddy Greeting Chant, *He, Qanute*. Its use here is symbolic: the entire song references multiple significances of the act of welcoming outsiders, poetically combining them so that their contradictions are revealed.

These contradictions were evident in July 2004 as the 400th anniversary of the de Monts expedition to Passamaquoddy Bay was marked with an international celebration.[19] A reenactment of the French ship's landing was held at St. Croix Island, where a new International Park historical site had been erected the previous fall.[20] A delegation of Passamaquoddy leaders from Sipayik, Motahkomikuk, and St. Andrews, New Brunswick, welcomed representatives of the French, U.S., and Canadian governments to the site. Blanche Sockabason sang the slow chant used for the Greeting Ceremony, *He, Qanute̜*, accompanying herself with a hand drum. The French delegation gave the medal of the French Legion of Honour, Commander Rank to the Passamaquoddy Tribe collectively in recognition of their aid to the 1604 expedition. Elder Hugh Akagi, leader of the Schoodic Band of the Passamaquoddy First Nation of Canada, acknowledged during the ceremonies that tribal members had debated whether the arrival of Europeans was an event they should celebrate. He had decided to do so to honor his ancestors who had helped the French. His participation was all the more notable because at the time of the commemoration, the Passamaquoddy First Nation he represented had not been granted recognition by the federal government of Canada.[21]

The traditional welcoming ceremonies employed in the Sipayik Indian Day also have multiple layers of meaning. On one level, they extend welcome; on another, they demonstrate the continuous practice of traditions; on yet another, they are a statement of political status. They do other things as well (unify the community, teach younger generations, contribute to the status of singers, etc.), and an attempt to catalogue all their meanings would be futile. This is a living tradition, and meanings will continue to be produced around these songs and dances. The songs themselves can become symbols bearing the weight not only of tradition but of historical events.

SIX

Ceremonies of Peace
and War

Historical records of European interactions with Peskotomuhkatiyik and their
allies indicate that ceremonies of welcome, alliance, and warfare were related
as part of the protocols for political conferences. They appear together in the
Wampum Records of the Wabanaki Confederacy. Connections between the
welcoming ceremonies and those of peace and war are explicitly made in
contemporary performances of the wampum protocols by using the Greeting
Chant to accompany the War Club Dance. Other less obvious connections
linking these ceremonies emerge from the detailed analyses to be presented
in this chapter.

Recent work interpreting North American pipe ceremonialism provides a
suggestive parallel to analysis of the Passamaquoddy versions of the wampum
protocols for alliance and warfare. Robert L. Hall (1997) and Jordan Paper
(1988), arguing from archaeological evidence, historical records, and present
practices, have suggested a uniform cultural layer among prehistoric Amerindian peoples that links ceremonies of alliance to those of mourning and earth
renewal. Passamaquoddy ceremonialism was influenced by the introduction
of the Calumet to political negotiations in the seventeenth century and, in the
last century, by protocols associated with "pan-Indian" cultural movements.

Although the wampum protocols are characteristic of the Wabanaki Confederacy, they include elements common to First Nations with whom the
Confederacy has had contact. Because they have been a medium of interaction
between cultures, the political ceremonies of alliance and warfare particularly
show evidence of intercultural influences.

Two contemporary Passamaquoddy dances directly address the topics of
war and peace: the War Club Dance and the Peace Pipe Ceremony Dance.

The Passamaquoddy Tribe today does not pursue its political goals through armed conflict. Contemporary ceremonies that reference conflict thus have largely symbolic value. Much like commemorations of military action in the larger United States—Memorial Day, Veterans' Day—they are reminders of past sacrifices and of the responsibility to maintain peaceful relations at all social levels.

These dances also represent a political function that is absolutely crucial in the struggle of First Nations to achieve recognition. Because warfare is intimately bound up with the concepts of statehood and nationhood, the recognition that a tribe or First Nation has waged war confers on it the status of a state or nation. Thus ceremonial protocols for conducting warfare, even though not in the spirit of current goals for Native community renewal, acquire a terrible significance. Evidence that these protocols have been continuously practiced—even in an adapted format—maintains the conception of political self-determination.

Protocols for warfare and for making peace were especially important in the historical context of the Wabanaki Confederacy. During the period leading up to its constitution around 1700 and during its first century of existence, the threat or outbreak of warfare in Waponahkik was constant. Alliances shifted dramatically, in response to the volatile politics and economy of the Maritimes region. The ongoing conflicts between European groups in Wabanaki territories—the French and English; the loyalist English and the colonists—and the constant disruptions in the trade partnerships that bound European and Native peoples together pulled Wabanaki communities in different directions.

These ceremonies operated in domains other than the merely political. The symbolism of a Peace Pipe Ceremony would clearly mark the intentions of participants, at least for a period of time. A public display of weapons of war and recitations of the bravery of ancestors would inspire fighters. Elaborate ceremonies made these events memorable and probably helped to rationalize them. Historical descriptions of Wabanaki warfare protocols are consistent with the ritual displays of power characteristic of tribal societies (Nordstrom 2001).[1]

The Wampum Records of the Confederacy are distillations of perhaps centuries of practice. When compared with the historical record, certain significant actions emerge that can be related directly to the modern War and Peace Pipe Dances. But the context of smoking the Peace Pipe is much broader than the Wabanaki group; the practice was, and remains, widespread in Native North America. The Wampum Records also show the influence of French Catholic practices, with the priest being required to perform certain actions. The Peace

Pipe itself was an object of concern to many missionaries but had been shared with French exploring parties since the sixteenth century.

After Maine became a state in 1820 it also imposed requirements before it would recognize the legitimacy of Passamaquoddy leaders. The sources for contemporary political ceremonies thus cover a great range, culturally and historically.

The Peace Pipe Ceremony

The Peace Pipe Ceremony is included in the demonstration of traditional dances at the annual Indian Day. On those occasions it is called the Peace Pipe Ceremony Dance, and it follows the Greeting Dance. These dances are linked by their formations: the Welcome Dance forms groups of hosts and visitors into lines facing each other; the Greeting Dance formation has the lines of participants seated, with the *Sakomak* moving between them; the Peace Pipe Ceremony Dance has the Pipe Bearer moving down the lines of seated participants, carrying the Pipe to the visiting *Sakom* and all of that party, then to the host *Sakom* and all of that party. The Peace Pipe Ceremony Dance as it is performed at the Indian Day may include everyone participating in the Welcome Dance.

The Peace Pipe Ceremony Dance is related to two different uses of pipes. In the context of the wampum protocols it is demonstrably related to smoking protocols carried out during peaceful visits of delegates from one community to another. Clear evidence of ceremonial tobacco smoking by the Etchemin ancestors of Peskotomuhkatiyik is provided by European accounts from the seventeenth century on, as smoking was an important feature of meetings between Native and European delegations. The dance as performed at the Indian Days is a version that functions equally to teach about these protocols.

The choreography of the Peace Pipe Ceremony Dance also relates it to calumet ceremonies found across North America in which a pipe is danced with. In the Passamaquoddy ceremony the action of smoking and of offering the Pipe to spiritual entities, to the four directions, are similar to protocols in Plains ceremonies such as the Hako, and in contemporary intertribal Pipe ceremonies. Historical European accounts suggest that calumet ceremonies reached the Northeast from the Mississippi Valley and upper Great Lakes region as a result of French negotiations with First Nations of the interior.[2]

The Peace Pipe Ceremony Dance as it is performed at Indian Days was taught by Mary Moore in the 1960s to Joseph A. Nicholas and the group of dancers he organized. Nicholas explained that Moore learned it from her grandmother (AMS 28.Feb95). In its current form, the dance shows accretions of cultural contact and individual innovations that the following analysis aims to clarify. It is a complex combination of all of these elements.

The Pipe itself is an entity of great significance and power. In his summary of pipe ceremonialism, Jordan Paper compares the Pipe to the Torah or the Koran: "It is the primary material means of communication between spiritual power and human beings" (Paper 1988:13). Many of my Native consultants use Catholic religious beliefs and practices as points of comparison, and thus I prefer to compare the Pipe to the Host in a Christian Communion ceremony. Like the Host, the Pipe binds together in a mystical union all who share it. It has transformative power, connecting human beings with spiritual beings. The English words "community" and "communion" have the same root; the sacrament binds individuals together. A Penobscot explanation of the origins of tobacco in sacrifice suggests another point of comparison with the Christian Host: the First Mother directed that she be ritually killed, and her body became corn and her bones tobacco (Nicolar [1893] 2007:134–39; Curtis [1923] 1968:4–6). All these European ideas are analogous to the power of the Pipe in Native cultural systems, but they do not convey its full meaning.

The form of pipes used in ceremonies is important: those that are all of one piece may be used for smoking but are not of the same ritual significance as pipes in two separable parts, the stem and the bowl. The stem is considered male, and the bowl female, and their union has cosmological significance. When the two parts are joined, the Pipe is potent. The precise ritual use and significance varies from culture to culture, but this basic underlying scheme is found across Native North American cultures.[3]

Some scholars reserve the term Calumet for a pipe in two parts, of which the stem is most important (Hall 1997; Paper 1988). Ceremonies in which the stem plays an important part seem to have originated in the Plains cultures (Brown 2006:377; Hall 1997; Blakeslee 1981).[4] In some of these, the Calumet is not smoked, and the stem may not be tubular but solid (Hall 1997:57). Robert Hall distinguishes solid flat stems, which he relates to the *atlatl* (spear thrower); and stems that are round, which he relates to arrow shafts (Hall 1997:118–19).

The earliest accounts of Passamaquoddy pipe ceremonies emphasize smoking tobacco, rather than choreographed actions with the Pipe or pipe stem. As noted, smoking was an important opening action in political ceremonies and councils. Passamaquoddy ceremonial pipe bowls were carved from stone, often steatite, as well as formed from clay; figures could be created on the bowl in either process.[5] Where the figures face away from a smoker, a pipe can be inferred to have been used to make offerings rather than for personal use (Paper 1988:78, 90).

After European contact, pipes made for trade were devised, their bowls formed of metal with a blade on the opposite side, symbolizing peace and war.[6] Ritual use of these pipes is unclear, but some were used in treaty-making.[7] Some pipe bowls carved of wood have been found in the Wabanaki cultural area, and although these also had an attached stem, they are considered to have been not ceremonial but rather made for personal use (Speck [1940] 1997:196, Smith 1957:77).

The Pipe used at the Indian Day for the Peace Pipe Ceremony Dance is of a different stylistic type. It was made by the contemporary Passamaquoddy artist Richard Keezer, who carved the bowl from one point of a deer antler; feathers are attached to the other points. The stem is of wood wrapped in buckskin decorated with the lettering PASSAMAQUODDY. This Pipe belongs to the office of the *Sakom*. It has been consecrated as a ceremonial Pipe, but at the Indian Day, to protect it from potential misuse in the context of a public demonstration, it is not actually smoked (AMS 14May 07; 12Aug.07).

Contemporary Description of the Ceremony

I have observed two versions of the Peace Pipe Ceremony Dance. One is as an extension of the Greeting Dance between the two leaders, involving all the participants in the Welcome and Greeting Dances at the public Indian Days. Recently this version has not included actual smoking or tobacco, not only because young children were participating but also to prevent the mishandling of sacred tobacco.

On other occasions, the Peace Pipe Ceremony Dance was restricted to prominent men in the host and visiting communities. I observed this at the Indian Day in 1994 and on a videotape of the 1972 Indian Day in the collection of the Waponahki Museum. (Illustration 9 diagrams the dance as I observed it in 1994.) In the past, participants in the Peace Pipe Ceremony were members of the tribal council of each community, according to David A. Francis and Joseph A. Nicholas. Women now serve on the tribal councils, though a woman has not yet been elected *Sakom*. On all the occasions I have observed, however, the Pipe Bearer has been a young woman. At recent Indian Days she has led all the dancers in the Grand Entry to the dancing area, carrying the Pipe and reserving it until this dance (illustration 7).

In both versions of the Peace Pipe Ceremony, the participants were seated in two lines facing each other with the host and visiting *Sakomak* at either end facing each other, in a rectangular formation. The Pipe Bearer presented the

Pipe first to the visiting *Sakom*, who smoked it, offered it to the Four Directions, and then handed it to the bearer to take to the host *Sakom*, who did the same (illustration 8). In the dance with many participants, the Pipe was then passed along to each participant's left, with each free to offer a prayer or reverence as she or he wished. (This choreography is similar to a modern intertribal Sacred Pipe Ceremony, but in that, participants often sit in a circle.)[8] The mimetic aspect of the Welcome Dance, resembling the formation of a longhouse, is also evident here.

On the occasions when the dance was restricted to prominent men, the ceremony was held in a field at one end of which were rocks overlooking the water of a cove. This ceremonial ground has since been built over, though the rocks are still there. In this instance the Pipe was returned to the host *Sakom* after all participants had smoked it. The host then took the Pipe up on the rocks and offered it to the Four Directions again. He returned to the seated dancers, and the ceremony was concluded with a fast dance of general celebration. The gesture is beautiful, and significant in that it ties the landscape into the ceremony. The rocks and the shoreline in this area are considered a special or spiritual place by many in the community as the home of the *mihkomuwehsisok* (Little People).[9] Melvyn Francis was the first to follow this procedure when he was governor, according to Joseph A. Nicholas.[10] The image was captured by a local photographer, Leslie Bowman.

This part of the ceremony has been accompanied by a drum beat alone, with no singing—or singing only to accompany extended movements of the participants—which allows prayers to be spoken aloud at certain points, similar to the use of antiphons in Catholic rituals, with pauses for the prayers.[11] After all the seated dancers have smoked or offered the Pipe, the Peace Pipe Ceremony Dance is concluded by a fast dance. On the occasions when the ceremony was limited to a few men, all rose from their seats and formed a line; they danced clockwise in single file and were joined by women traditional dancers.

The dance songs used are from the usual stock of quick dance songs, with extemporized words that often praise those participating, refer to the Pipe, to the tribal councillors (*putowosuwin*) or to the Great Council Fire (*putuwosuwakon*). Example 9 gives an excerpt of the concluding Peace Pipe Ceremony Dance songs on one occasion, discussed in chapter 8.

Historical Sources

The form of the Peace Pipe Ceremony Dance as practiced today is similar to historical accounts of ceremonial smoking when envoys arrived for council in Wabanaki communities. Wabanaki use of pipes and ceremonial smoking as a symbol of unity between different parties is apparently quite ancient. It is documented by Samuel de Champlain ([1603] 1922:100) and succeeding generations of ethnographers. The Etchemins and Souriquois smoked ceremonially in situations of alliance, war, and councils. Champlain's description of his first encounter with the western Etchemins shows how the Peace Pipe was used within the ceremonies for welcoming and alliance. The host at this meeting was Bessabez (Bashaba), a leader whose territories were along the Penobscot River.

> Bessabez also came to see us with six canoes. As soon as the Indians on shore saw him arrive, they all began to sing, dance, and leap, until he had landed, after which they all seated themselves on the ground in a circle, according to their custom when they wish to make a speech or hold a festival. Cabahis, the other chief, also arrived a little later, with twenty or thirty of his companions, who kept by themselves; and they were much pleased to see us, inasmuch as it was the first time they had ever beheld Christians. Some time afterwards I landed with two of my companions and two of our Indians who acted as our interpreters.... Bessabez, seeing us on shore, bade us sit down, and began with his companions to smoke, as they usually do before beginning their speeches. They made us a present of venison and waterfowl.... [T]hey signified that they were well satisfied, declaring that no greater benefit could come to them than to have our friendship; and that they desired us to settle in their country, and wished to live in peace with their enemies, in order that in future they might hunt the beaver more than they had ever done, and barter these beaver with us in exchange for things necessary for their usage. When he had finished his speech, I made them presents... [and] then we separated.(Champlain [1603] 1922:294–96)

Marc Lescarbot describes a protocol very like the modern Peace Pipe Ceremony with which councils between Etchemins and Souriquois opened: "As for the compliments that they use one to another coming from afar... we have seen strange savages arrive at Port Royal [a Souriquois encampment was established near the French settlement] who on landing went without a word straight to Membertou's cabin, where they sat down, and began to smoke; and when they had well smoked, they gave the tobacco-pipe to him who seemed most prominent, and then in turn to the others; then some half an hour later they would begin to speak" ([1618] 1914:204).

Historical sources suggest that the use of ceremonial pipes and tobacco was ancient and widespread among the First Nations of northeastern North America. The excerpts above indicate that in Wabanaki communities, smoking protocols paid respect to leaders. They were part of greeting ceremonies and used to open councils where leaders discussed affairs and made decisions affecting their communities.

Descriptions of ceremonial smoking in Peskotomuhkatik and other eastern Wabanaki communities suggest parallels with calumet ceremonies that are recorded among Abenaki communities and farther west. Calumet ceremonies were elaborate ritual greetings with which prominent visitors and emissaries were received, alliances sealed, and treaties signed. The extent to which these ceremonies extended into Waponahkik is not clear, but William D. Williamson in his account of the First Nations of Maine states that the Calumet was in use and was distinct from other pipes in the early nineteenth century (Williamson 1832(1):507).

Father Jacques LeSueur, a Jesuit missionary to the Abenaki between 1716 and 1759, recorded that they had received the Calumet and associated ceremonies from the *Renards* (the Fox nation). He followed the precedent of previous missionaries at his station in prohibiting the use of the Pipe among his communicants. LeSueur noted eight features of the Calumet Ceremony that indicate its spiritual efficacy, the connections between protocols of peace and war, and also give early evidence of its widespread use:

> 1. That this [Calumet] dance was a true religious cult... among almost all the upper nations [i.e., residing north of the St. Lawrence]; that it was called the Dance of the Spirit; that one was said to be dancing not at all with the calumet, but to be dancing in honor of the calumet; in a word the calumet was the god of this nation. 2. That the words which are used in the song of this dance are an invocation of the spirit. 3. That when in the councils this calumet is smoked, any man whose wife was pregnant must refrain from smoking this calumet inasmuch as his wife would not bring her fruit happily into the world, and it would undoubtedly perish. 4. That this dance is employed to summon the souls of those against whom they are going in war, and by these means to kill their enemies without question. 5. In order to conciliate foreign nations and enemies and to make a good peace with them. 6. In order to obtain good weather and rain in accordance with the needs of the earth. 7. In order to have favorable winds for navigation. 8. That, finally, it was a specific to keep away every kind of evil and to obtain every kind of good. (LeSueur 1952:10–11)

Cultural Dynamism in the Peace Pipe Ceremony

George Heriot's *Travels through the Canadas* contains a lengthy discussion attesting to the widespread ceremonial use of smoking and of Peace Pipes in North America, even extending to Carib peoples (Heriot [1807] 1971:474–76). In interpreting the Wabanaki ceremonies, one must distinguish smoking and calumet ceremonies: different cultures had different smoking technologies, and the Calumet in many of the documented ceremonies was not a pipe that could be smoked but one that had a solid stem. In calumet ceremonies it was the stem that was principally important; it was symbolically decorated, and various movements with it were part of the Calumet Dance.

European documents from the first contacts with the Etchemin ancestors of Peskotomuhkatiyik indicate that they smoked ceremonially before counseling with each other and with newcomers. They also used various wampum adornments as symbols of leadership status (Lescarbot [1618] 1914:159). The use of wampum belts as described in the Wampum Records was probably derived from these earlier practices.[12] Descriptions of the "Grand Peace" negotiated at Montréal in 1701 mention ceremonial use both of wampum and of Calumets (Havard 2001).[13] It thus appears that the introduction of calumet ceremonies coincided with use of wampum but did not displace it in Wabanaki communities.

William Turnbaugh (1979) suggested that the adoption of the Calumet and its ceremonies by the western Abenaki was part of a nativistic movement devised in response to French pressures for trade, alliance, and territory. Donald Blakeslee (1981) believed that the Abenaki took up the ceremony for more practical reasons of facilitating trade. As the French moved into the interior of North America, this ceremony was shared between First Nations and adopted as a guarantee of peace, spreading eastward. In his analysis of the Calumet Ceremony in the Southeast, Ian W. Brown (2006) presents archaeological evidence supporting the idea that the Calumet was brought into that region by the French.

Blakeslee argued that one of the defining features of calumet ceremonies is that they "establish a fictive kinship relation between individuals of different clans, bands, or ethnic groups" (1981:759) and are thus similar to the ritual welcoming ceremonies that Peskotomuhkatiyik practiced even before the Wabanaki Confederacy was constituted. A number of scholars accept that calumet ceremonies are related to adoption ceremonies, and that adoption ceremonies through the substitution of the adoptee for a deceased person are related to mourning ceremonies. Through symbolism connected with the earth, employed in adoption and mourning ceremonies, these are all related ultimately to ceremonies of renewal. Hall (1997) finds the basis for all these ceremonies in the archaeological evidence of Mound Builder practices: the mounds recreated the earth and honored the dead. In the contemporary Pipe Ceremony, many participants use the phrase "All my relations" when offering the Pipe. As Paper (1988:38–40) explains, this refers to the social, spiritual, and cosmological implications of the ritual actions.

If ceremonial tobacco smoking is accepted as a base layer of ancient Amerindian culture as proposed by Hall, based on archeological evidence, and by Paper, based on ceremonial features, it was followed by a process of cultural diversification, documented in the historical records. During the twentieth century, a process of consolidation around intertribal culture is evident.

The contemporary Passamaquoddy Peace Pipe Ceremony Dance is also informed and influenced by intertribal culture. The way that individuals handle the Pipe and tobacco and the prayers they offer during the Passamaquoddy ceremony are often similar to intertribal uses. The Pipe Carrier in the Passamaquoddy dance, however, is a temporary role, an honor given to someone suitable. The designation Pipe Carrier outside of this dance context has a different meaning, understood in the intertribal cultural context. A Pipe Carrier in this sense is an individual who is deemed worthy to carry a ceremonial Pipe and to lead pipe ceremonies. He or she is leading an exemplary life based on Native principles, described by some as "following the Red Road." Drawing another analogy to Christian tradition, a Pipe Carrier is like a minister. Although not directly connected to the powwow, the Pipe Carrier tradition similarly spread across Native North America. At present, several individuals in the Passamaquoddy communities are Pipe Carriers. Tobacco is used to prepare powwow Drums, and many singers, drummers, and dancers undergo fasting, sweat lodges, and smoking before participating; thus the services of Pipe Carriers are required at many powwows and also at Native gatherings, including meetings of the Wabanaki Confederacy.

The creation of the contemporary Passamaquoddy Peace Pipe Ceremony Dance, then, appears to have resulted from the combination of several layers of cultural influence and stylistic innovation that have accrued to the original practices. These range across several centuries and different expressive domains, from the exchange of the Calumet between First Nations in the Great Lakes region and Wabanaki nations in the late seventeenth century as part of an alliance to the changing form of the Pipe itself, to the inclusion of an offering to the Four Directions as part of greetings between *Sakomak*, and down to the extemporization of songs for each performance. The Passamaquoddy Peace Pipe Ceremony Dance today may be adapted to a public demonstration or a sacred ceremony. These innovations have not altered the essential ceremonial use of tobacco and pipes in Passamaquoddy culture. The historical records cited give evidence that ceremonial smoking was practiced in Peskotomuhkatik at the time of first contact. The changing style of pipe ceremonies is a small-scale but crucial manifestation of the cultural dynamics that surround them.

The War Club Dance

Dances with weapons are documented in the earliest historical sources of Wabanaki life. Such dances are related to calumet ceremonies, where the pipe stem is iconic of the shaft of an arrow or an *atlatl*. Connections between such ceremonies and dancing with flutes are suggested in other culture areas (Brown 2006:230), but all the evidence suggests that Peskotomuhkatiyik did not use flutes in traditional public ceremonies.[14]

In the contemporary Passamaquoddy War Club Dance the *Sakomak*, accompanied by the lieutenant governors (or other men representing the convening tribes), step out to meet each other as in the Welcome Dance. When they meet, they form a circle, join hands in the center or raise ceremonial weapons, and step clockwise in a circular movement. The elaborately carved war clubs that were a specialty of the Francis family from Sipayik are often used, but it is not always necessary to have actual weapons; on some occasions, men who are asked to participate will simply raise their fists (see illustration 10). This segment of the dance symbolizes unity, as the MC pointed out at the 1994 *Sakomawkan* at Sipayik (AMS 26Nov.94). The dancers raise weapons as a reminder of the tribes' decision to share power rather than to turn it against one another. The inversion of mimesis that operates here also recalls Frank Speck's interpretation of the lines of the Welcome Dance as a modified gauntlet formation ([1940] 1997:290).

After circling several times in this formation, the drummer and singer (who may be one person) will signal a change. The beat increases in speed, and a fast celebratory dance song is begun as the men break apart and begin dancing freestyle. This second part of the ceremony affirms and celebrates the action completed in the first part.

The War Club Dance today does not have an independent genre of accompanying songs. Different melodies from the repertory of general dance songs are used on different occasions, and words are extemporized. The first segment may be accompanied only by drumming, as I have heard it performed on some occasions.

The choreography of this dance has been maintained for at least a century. Joseph A. Nicholas and David A. Francis remembered it from election ceremonies in their youth. Similarly, Mechling's Maliseet consultant in 1911 mentioned War Dances as being among the group dances performed by men at the inauguration of a new leader but no detailed description is given (Mechling 1958–59:150). The formation of the War Club Dance is similar to historical descriptions of dancing with weapons in ceremonies preparing for warfare.

From these sources two different genres emerge: a group dance, and a solo dance. The group dance has the more complex symbolism.

Historical Sources: Seventeenth- and Eighteenth-Century Accounts

Judging from the historical accounts of Etchemin and Passamaquoddy life, going to war was a serious decision that required many meetings in council. Historical descriptions of the ceremonies involved in warfare indicate that if conducted formally, there were several marked stages: councils to decide on a declaration of war; preparations for the departure of a war party, including songs, dances, and feasting; and celebrations of their return, either in mourning or in victory. Related to the conduct of warfare is the treatment of captives, who were subjected to physical abuse in the context of group dances. Death songs are frequently mentioned; ostensibly they signified bravery, but they also marked a change in state of being (from living to dead, or from outsider captive to insider adoptee). Although historical accounts often aim to convey only a sense of the ferocity, bravery, and cruelty of Native warfare, ethnohistorians have shown that many of the features described can best be interpreted symbolically.

Bernard Hoffman's analysis of seventeenth-century sources suggests that prestige and display were the motivations underlying warfare among the Souriquois and Etchemin of Passamaquoddy Bay. Leaders went to war either to gain prestige or to avenge a slight (Hoffman 1955:649). He argues, however, that warfare was conducted in large degree symbolically. William Mechling agrees, stressing the determinant role that the presence of a *Kinap* (war leader) had among the Mi'kmaq and Maliseet: "A war party, no matter how numerous, is entirely helpless before a much less numerous enemy if it loses its *ginap*" (Mechling 1958–59:142). These ideas conform to current anthropological theories of warfare in tribal societies generally (Nordstrom 2001).

The frequent references in historical accounts to songs and recitations praising the exploits of individual men in war further attest to the symbolic function of warfare as a measure of status. Lescarbot considered it similar to European customs of singing praise ([1618] 1914:182–83). In the contemporary War Club Dance, the implements displayed (as well as the singing) may have symbolic functions. They are often part of a man's traditional regalia, given as a gift, presented in recognition of his good character, or handed down as a family hierloom.

Both historical accounts and oral traditions indicate that ritual torture of war captives was practiced historically by the ancestors of Peskotomuhakatiyik. Although many of the accounts try to emphasize the notion that torture was administered simply out of innate cruelty, the resulting apparent irrationality

7. Carrying the Peace Pipe, Sipayik Indian Day 2006. Photograph by Roger Spinney.

8. Offering the Peace Pipe, Sipayik Indian Day 1988. Photograph courtesy of the *Quoddy Tides*.

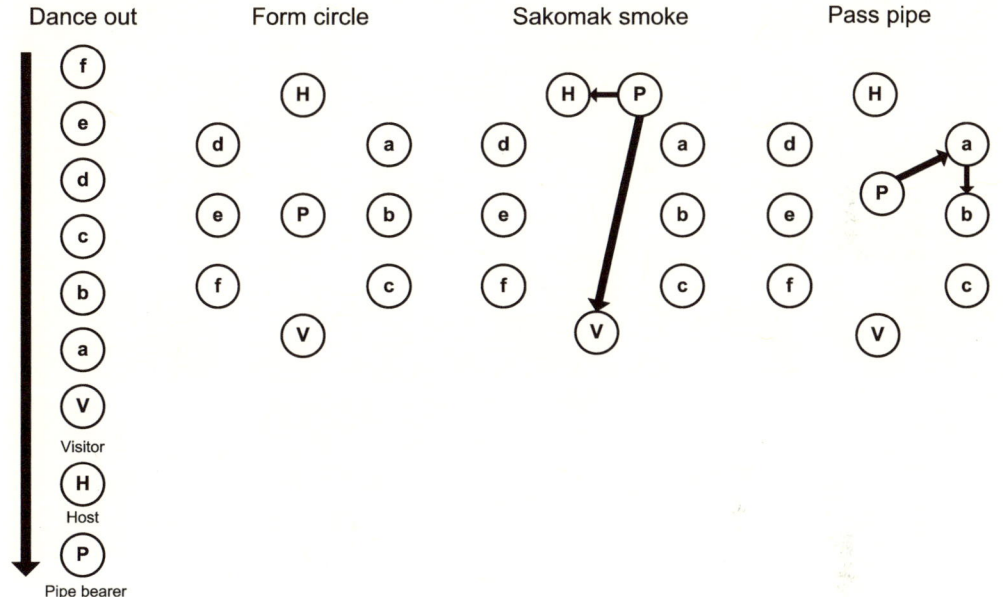

9. Choreography of the Peace Pipe Ceremony Dance.

10. War Club Dance, Sipayik Indian Day 1993. Photograph courtesy of the *Quoddy Tides*.

of all the actors is unconvincing. It makes more sense to interpret these rituals symbolically. Physical trials were *rites de passage*, important markers of the status of captives within the communities that adopted them.

English colonists John Gyles and Captain William Pote described victory dances performed by Wabanaki women which included the torture of captives. Pote became the prisoner of a band of Hurons in King George's War (the third French and Indian War). He was taken, he said, through "Micmac" and Maliseet territory, during which he observed how the Micmac women came out to greet their returning men and danced around with their prisoners. Upon arriving at a French fort, the Indians spent two days celebrating with feasts and contests: "running, wrestling, Eating and drinking and Dancing &c." Pote went on to describe how he was tortured by women in victory dances at two St. John River villages, one being Meductic (Pote 1896:25, 28, 57–58, 62).

John Gyles's account of his life in a Maliseet band gives many more details of torture by women in Maliseet victory dances during the first days of his captivity. He was not yet able to understand their language and found his experiences at the village of Madawamkee altogether incomprehensible.

> At Home I had ever seen Strangers treated with the utmost Civility, and being a Stranger, I expected some kind Treatment here: but soon found myself deceived, for I presently saw a Number of Squaws got together in a Circle dancing and yelling; and an old grimace-Squaw took me by the Hand, and led me to the Ring, where the other Squaws seiz'd me by the Hair of my Head, and by my Hands and Feet, like so many Furies: but my Indian Master presently laid down a Pledge and release'd me (1736:5).

At Meductic he faced similar treatment, and the presence of prisoners taken months before among those being tested underscores the transitional function of the process. Gyles believed that the Maliseets had learned these tortures from Mohawks. This is possible, as the same procedures were described by the Jesuits working among the Mohawk and other Iroquois nations.

Gyles was tortured again in the second year of his captivity as a recompense for atrocities perpetrated by English fishermen on Cape Sable Mi'kmaqs. He and another Englishment were used symbolically as scapegoats, and after being struck with the blunt side of an axe Gyles was made to dance and sing while holding a tomahawk (1736:12–[13]).

The torture of captives seems to have been a test to select those individuals able to make the transition into a new life. Gyles was ransomed but never adopted by the Maliseet, and he lived under the epithet "Captive" until his final ransom by French settlers.

131

DEATH SONGS

Father André Richards, a missionary to the Gaspesians (Mi'kmaq) in 1661–62, provides another instance of torture leading to adoption. A boy captured during warfare was stabbed in the arm by the wife of the chief to whom he had been ransomed, then "forced to sing as he beheld his own blood" (Lalement [1662] 1896(47):231); the boy was eventually ransomed again by Father Richards.

The singing here may have been significant as a "death song." There are countless references in European writings to the bravery exhibited by Native captives who sang as they were put to death (Lalemant 1896(4):199). Some early accounts of the Souriquois and Etchemins describe individuals on their deathbed singing their own death songs (Biard [1611] 1896(1):166–67). Singing appears to have marked the transition from life into the state of death, or from life as outsider to life as insider.

Among Death Songs recorded from singers in several Wabanaki communities, there are two repertories: songs that seem more traditional in style, and songs that are specifically connected to Catholic rites of death and burial. The Catholic songs have been analyzed elsewhere (Spinney 2006; A. Morrison [Spinney]) 1996a).

Frederic Gleach has detailed the same basic principle of marking the passage into a new life with a symbolic death in the treatment that John Smith received from the Virginia Powhatans, eastern Algonquians. "Pocahontas...was acting her proper part as a young Powhatan woman in a ritual situation that was part of an adoption of Smith and the English colony....[T]he threat of death by clubbing may seem excessive for a ritual of adoption, but it is precisely what one might expect, structurally: a symbolic ending of one existence, and the beginning of a new existence." Gleach argues that this form was based on the *huskanaw* ceremony, which marked the transition of boys to adulthood through a symbolic death (Gleach 1994:177–78). He goes on to analyze the removal of Captain Smith from peripheral to central villages as the symbolic incorporation of the English group into Powhatan's realm (1994:179–80).

WAR SONGS: PASSAMAQUODDY

Today, the ceremonial Passamaquoddy War Club Dance is associated with alliance—celebrating or furthering alliance through collective performance. Fitting this function and significance, it is a group dance and uses songs associated with the Welcome and Greeting Dances. Tradition and historical accounts in Waponahkik also reference another genre: songs sung by individuals when declaring their intent to join a war party. This important stage of preparations for war could involve sending a delegation to another community to ask for assistance, requiring welcoming and greeting protocols. Potential warriors were invited to a feast where dogs were ceremonially eaten; the heads of the sacrificed dogs were singed in the fire to form a grimacing effigy and then mounted on a stick, which the warriors would hold while announcing their intentions. They would extemporize songs during this ceremony, referencing their past exploits, the provocation they were responding to, and other contextual factors (Maillard 1758:18–19, 27)

Analysis and Interpretation of War Songs

J. W. Fewkes's recordings provide the only extant Passamaquoddy examples of the War Song genre. He listed three in his collection, including one "ancient War song, said to have been sung in the old times when the Passamaquoddies were departing for war with the Mohawks" (Fewkes 1890a:259; 1890b cylinder 4260). He said these three songs were "typical of a large number known to the Passamaquoddies" and reported that "the words of many are improvised, though there is no doubt that the tunes are ancient." He published only the translated text of one song, without its tune:

> I will arise with tomahawk in my hand, and I must have revenge on that nation which has slain my poor people.
> I will arise with war club in my hand, and follow the bloody track of that nation which killed my people.
> I will sacrifice my own life and the lives of my warriors.
> I will arise with war club in my hand, and follow the track of my enemy.
> When I overtake him I will take his scalp and string it on a long pole, and I will stick it in the ground, and my warriors will dance around it for many days;
> then I will sing my song for the victory over my enemy. (Fewkes 1890a:264–65)

The form of this translation is similar to that of the "Song of the Drum." Lines begin with a parallel expression ("I will arise...") and are similar in length, until the conclusion summarizes, without formal constraints, what has gone before.

Songs and dances that are suggestive of war are to be found in various sources for all the Wabanaki nations. Natalie Curtis's transcriptions include a Penobscot War Dance ([1923] 1968:8, 18), which was sung by Bedagi "Big Thunder" (Frank Loring), a former vaudeville performer. Since he fooled Frank Speck with a contrived War Bow (Siebert 1941:278–80), this War Song too may be of questionable authenticity. The text is only the word *qanute*, which he translated for Curtis as "no real words...I wish that you were dancing, too." As it has been established that *qanute* is an expression of welcome, this translation is not literal; however, the use of this text fits the hypothesis that ceremonies of alliance and warfare are linked.

William H. Mechling recorded War Songs from both Maliseet and Mi'kmaq men.[15] All the Maliseet songs are in quick time and feature the shifting rhythmic emphases characteristic of the old Passamaquoddy song style described in chapter 3. All but one are accompanied by drumming and feature "whoops" at the end of verses. They are all composed of short phrases, in clear antecedent-consequent relationships, that are varied and recombined; the words may well have been extemporized as Fewkes described. Example 10 exemplifies the style of these songs.

Frank Speck also recorded several solo War Songs from Maliseet, Mi'kmaq, and Penobscot men.[16] These songs are strophic, with whoops at the ends of verses. The recordings are of such poor quality that it is impossible to tell if there is any accompaniment. Speck included no transcriptions nor even a mention of this genre in *Penobscot Man*, the book summarizing his Penobscot research.

Nicholas Smith observed a Tomahawk Dance at the Western Abenaki village of Ôdanak in 1960, and he previously had recorded one at Indian Island (1962:17). The Abenaki dance was accompanied only by drumming and exclamations. Smith testifies that the Penobscot dance had words that were identical to the recording made by Speck in 1910 at Tobique Maliseet Reserve (Smith 1955:29), but he does not give the words, and they are now impossible to recover from the recordings.

Peskotomuhkatiyik currently do not perform solo War Songs or War Dances in public, and the record of this genre from the last century indicates that it is vestigial. The Hunter's Dance, a mimetic dance in which a man adopts postures of scouting for and ambushing an animal, is close in style to the old War Dances, however, and Passamaquoddy men currently perform this in public to the accompaniment of a drum only. Nicholas Smith describes personal Hunter's Songs that were never performed in public and closely guarded by individuals (Smith, personal communication). It seems possible that public solo War Dances and private Hunter's Dances may have merged in the present Passamaquoddy repertory. There is now no public context for solo War Dances, so the related men's genre could have taken its place. This hypothesis accords with Thomas Vennum's analysis of changes in Ojibway song repertories: "Reservation life...encouraged singing as a group activity by diminishing the contexts when an individual's songs would be performed; by juxtaposing sacred and secular events it also contributed to a blurring of musical styles" (Vennum 1989:15).

All the sources suggest that there are, or were, two different genres of dance connected with warfare in the Passamaquoddy tradition. First, there is a solo dance that an individual may do, miming his past exploits or what he hopes to accomplish in the future. This solo genre may be performed in a group context, such as the councils described in historical sources. With regard to the solo dance, Mrs. W. Wallace Brown's description of Passamaquoddy election ceremonies notes a "Mohawk Dance" that was "more properly a War Dance . . . executed with much energy and very fatiguing" (Brown 1893:59). It is possible that the "wild Micmac Dances" done by the Penobscot and Maliseet in the early twentieth century were similar acknowledgments of the markedly different culture of their former adversaries (Speck [1940] 1997:285–88). A Passamaquoddy consultant, in discussing how significant their cooperation in the Confederacy is today, stated that between Peskotomuhkatiyik and Mi'kmaq is "bad history" (AMS 24Jun.95).

Second, there is also a group dance that in its choreography mimes or demonstrates group cohesion. Today the group dance known as the War Club Dance demonstrates the unity of the Wabanaki Confederacy. At one time the same choreography could have demonstrated a short-term alliance between groups pledging to support each other in warfare against a common foe.

Contemporary Passamaquoddy performances of the War Club Dance are accompanied by songs and drumming according to the needs of each occasion. I have observed the War Club Dance set to the slow Welcome Song *He, Qanute* or accompanied by drumming without singing. Thus the Abenaki Tomahawk Dance that Smith observed in 1960 may not have been degenerate because it did not have lyrics, as he implies.

Over the centuries, War Dances seem to have been incorporated into different contexts and thereby reinterpreted. Speck's conception of the formation of the Welcome Dance as symbolically running the gauntlet like war prisoners emphasizes that reinterpretation of such elements of warfare was an active principle in establishing protocols of the Wabanaki Confederacy. The ceremonies of warfare can be viewed as an alternative manifestation of the same overriding concern with defining allies that motivated welcoming ceremonies.

War Dances may have been used also as displays of potential prowess. The Tomahawk Dance that Nicholas Smith observed at the Abenaki community of Ôdanak in 1960 (Smith 1962:16–17) seems to have been employed as an expression of power at this 300th anniversary celebration. But the ultimate message of the importance of alliance remains: This community is powerful; therefore it is best to be allied with us. Undeniably, War Dances play into stereotypes of "warlike Indians." The tomahawk, however, is a traditional

Wabanaki implement, the English word being derived from cognates of *tomhikan*, cutting tool.

The Sakomawkan (Election) Ceremony Context

The installation of tribal government officials is an important present-day occasion. It is an act of community sovereignty, a statement of existence as a political entity. Yet self-described traditional Peskotomuhkatiyik express conflicting feelings about the way tribal government is accomplished. Elections were imposed on their communities, and the whole apparatus of government—with a written constitution, laws, executive sessions, and registration of tribal members—is foreign to the Native cultural system. Significantly, older practices of choosing and installing leaders were never completely abandoned: erratic coverage in newspapers and by ethnographers proves that ceremonies continue to be held up to the present day.[17] The current way of managing tribal elections combines the traditional and legally required procedures. It is a fascinating blend, evidence of the flexibility of the cultural template.

It is only since 2002 that historical descriptions of the *Sakomawkan* have been explicitly referenced by participants. Previously, experience passed down from the older generations was the source. The new historical consciousness can be attributed to the circulation of ethnographic materials within the Passamaquoddy community. The process of incorporating these materials has been fascinating in itself, and is discussed as an aspect of repatriation in the analysis below.

From the time of the first Wabanaki Confederacy until the establishment of European-style elections in Maine in the mid-nineteenth century, the selection and installation of leaders was undertaken with the assistance of a committee of visiting delegates from other member tribes. Today, elections for the tribal offices are held like those for positions in other municipalities, and the inauguration occurs several weeks later.[18] Inaugurations continue to be attended by delegates from other Wabanaki communities, and thus protocols similar to those outlined in the Wampum Records are followed. The *Sakomawkan* (Inauguration) extends only over one evening but includes Welcoming and War Club Dances. Thus, the indigenous ceremonial complex overlaps with introduced election ceremonies that might be found in any Maine community: a church service, a public supper, a dance with a disc jockey.

The Wampum Records

The Wampum Records describe the events surrounding the choice and installation of new leaders, an occasion that was necessitated when the leader of a band died. The description begins with mourning: the leader's flagpole (symbol of office) had to be cut down, and his belongings burned. He was mourned for one year. Then the councilors met and began to talk about a new leader, and sent messengers out to call delegates from the other tribes to council. The elaborate greeting ceremonies employed on such occasions, when a leaderless tribe would have been most vulnerable to attack, have already been dwelt upon above. The protocol seems to require that the events would not take place in winter, yet the state of Maine later established election procedures for the Penobscot and Passamaquoddy Tribes that did take place in midwinter.

The delegates from the other tribes met with the band's council and selected a new leader. Their decision was then announced to the people in a ceremony with delegates from the other tribes officiating. The leader was installed in office with speeches directing him and his people to respect each other, he was given medals as insignia of his office, and wrapped in a deer hide by one of the visitors' wives to the accompaniment of a drum. Then there was dancing to commemorate the occasion (Leavitt and Francis 1990:45–46).

Introduction of State-Style Elections

The election and installation of Passamaquoddy and Penobscot Tribal Governors was established soon after Maine became a state in the nineteenth century. The state later clarified procedures in order to resolve disputes that had arisen over the practice of making a *Sakom* governor for life. The state-sponsored election process retained many aspects of the old system, however, and governors were still chosen for life terms simply by reelecting them repeatedly until they died. In the 1950s William Neptune was alternating terms in the offices of governor and lieutenant governor, having first been elected in 1926 (N. Smith, personal comm.). Reelection is common today: Motahkomikuk *Sakom* John Stevens held that post for over thirty years, from the mid-1960s to the mid-1990s except for one term; and the Sipayik community has reelected several men to more than three terms.

Historical Sources
WILLIAM WILLIAMSON

William D. Williamson gave a general description of the election of John Aitteon[19] as Penobscot governor and John Neptune as lieutenant governor in September 1816. This was the last election of a governor "for life" and is a firsthand account. Williamson lived in Bangor from 1806 to 1846 (Eckstorm [1945] 1980:145). He states that among the Maliseet, Passamaquoddy, and Penobscot, the candidates were chosen by the individual tribes but installed in office only with "the presence and assistance of a delegation from each of the other Tribes." The men of the Penobscot and Maliseet tribes sat in rank order in a *wikuwam* (traditional house), with the Passamaquoddy men arrayed outside. No women were allowed in this part of the ceremony. Wampum belts and engraved silver medals, the insignia of office, were presented to the new Penobscot governors by men of corresponding rank in the other tribes; as each was installed, the Passamaquoddy delegation raised and lowered the flag and shot off a cannon. Inside the *wikuwam* a priest (Father Romagne) read appropriate passages from scripture in Latin, with homilies in Penobscot, and the men sang a psalm, during which he and the Maliseets processed outside to join the Passamaquoddy delegates. Outside, they sang a *Te Deum*, then the priest retired. All but the Penobscot men had been dismissed from the *wikuwam*. Penobscot women in full regalia now entered the *wikuwam* to dance the Installation Dance—a round dance—while the Penobscot men observed. The women left, and the other men reentered the *wikuwam*. The Maliseet officers in turn then sang solo songs, to which the new Penobscot officers responded with songs. All then attended a feast, presumably held outside the *wikuwam*, which was followed by "rude dances and wild sports in the evening" (Williamson 1832(1):495–98).

Frank Speck's oldest Penobscot consultants added that before the Installation Dance, seven women led by a woman Elder had danced a special dance once around the dancing circle. This was called *mowia'wegan*, which Speck translated as Chief's Dance. The women were rewarded with blankets placed across their shoulders by the new tribal officers (Speck [1940] 1997:243).

FANNY HARDY ECKSTORM

Clara Neptune gave her reminiscences of the Penobscot election ceremonies to Fannie Eckstorm in 1917, when Neptune was elderly. According to Eckstorm, it is in part historical, probably based on information told to Clara by her grandmother. This places the events described in the middle of the nineteenth century (Eckstorm [1945] 1980:172). Neptune's references to Eastport and Quoddy show that Peskotomuhkatiyik and Penawahpskewi assisted each other according to the protocols of the Confederacy.

> Used to be when we make Governor then two men go down there Quoddy, get whole lot of people Eas'po't way, invite 'em. When come back, 'bout two weeks afterward, come four canoes, Governor, his wife, all dose high ones.
>
> When see comin' all dose Injuns got guns down shore, big gun.
>
> White folks other side lookin' on. Little flags, white one. Five canoes, one in middle, dat's Governor.
>
> Come 'shore. Dis Oldtown Injun singin' old song; all sing. Guns goin'. Singin'. Guns goin, jus' like war.

Den Oldtown Governor [Elect or retiring] took his hand dis [visiting] Governor, took him out of canoe. Whole lot of people go get his canoe. Den go other ones.

Den womans go down shore, took dose womans, took canoe ashore. Dancin'!

Den we make Governor. Great time. Women silver, evryding silk all round—silk shirts, ribbands, stiff hats, silver round it.

When Eas'po't Injuns make Governor we go down dere.

Last time make trouble, fightin', everythin', don't go dere now. Dose Eas'po't Injuns come here, make trouble, till Bangor folks send letter: "If Eas'po't Injuns make trouble, send soldiers, kill whole of us."

Yes, 'fore I was married this happen. (Eckstorm [1945] 1980:172–73)

Salient points of Neptune's description are her focus on what the women did, and the emphasis on singing old songs. Fine dress marked it as an important occasion. Silver was at one point the material of the medal of office worn by the *Sakom*.

This special emphasis on women is found in all accounts of the Passamaquoddy installation ceremonies. It would seem that although women were excluded from the council meetings, they expressed their approval of the candidate through this dance. There are no records that women ever refused to perform this dance.

MRS. W. WALLACE BROWN

In 1892 Mrs. W. Wallace Brown, wife of the Calais-based state Indian agent for the Passamaquoddy, published a description of the election and installation ceremonies at Sipayik which she personally had observed. Since she published this article just as the tribe became involved in a lawsuit challenging their sovereignty (*State v. Newell*, 1892), it is likely that she intended it to bolster their case.

The ceremonies she described are similar to those described in the Wampum Records. A candidate for chief was chosen, elected, and inaugurated in five days, "though the festivities often last for one or even two weeks." Visiting officials from other Wabanaki nations attended the inauguration. The actual installation took place inside a *wikuwam* that only the elder men and tribal officers were allowed to enter. After this, a feast centered on a moose, caribou, or beef stew was brought into the *wikuwam*. The feast was so important that the meat had a special name: *Ges-a-ta-ga-ben*. Leftovers were taken by men to their individual houses. The chief sang a song of thanks for the feast (*Sachem-sca-wint-wagen*), and the officers followed suit. Then a group of women dancers burst in, were given shawls, and did a type of shawl dance; Brown gives its

139

name as *moeee-mayic-hapijic*, "women thanking for the chief," again suggesting that women had a crucial role in reminding the leader of his responsibilities toward the community. Next, the new leader went out to the people and sang "a long salutation," after which everyone was invited to join the dancing. The dances included "tribal dances, the Micmac, the Mohawk, and the Snake Dance," though Brown admitted it was "difficult to see where one ends and the next begins." Those she mentions by name are all social dances. A council meeting was held on the fourth day; on the fifth, more general feasting and dancing took place, after which the hosts decided how much longer to detain the guests (Brown 1892:57–59).

Nicholas Smith observed and recorded *Sakomawkan* in the 1950s. In 1953 he was lent a tape recorder to take to Motahkomikuk, but the weather was so cold that the machine did not function well. His recordings are nearly inaudible, but his notes contain many observations that give evidence of the continuity of these ceremonies in the Passamaquoddy community (Smith 1955 and personal communication).

Contemporary Descriptions
1994 SIPAYIK *SAKOMAWKAN*

The inauguration (*Sakomawkan*, literally "Sakom dance") was held the day after Thanksgiving of 1994, and officially installed in office the governor (*Sakom*), lieutenant governor (*Leptenent*), tribal councilors, and state representative (*Lehposenti*). The occasion began with regular evening Mass at Sipayik St. Ann's, followed by a special Blessing ceremony, which was attended by at least half of the Tribal councilors. (There were more people at the Blessing than at the Mass.) At the Blessing, the group that sang regularly for Sunday services sang appropriate songs from the congregation's special collection of hymns in Passamaquoddy, a booklet made for a Tekakwitha Gathering in 1988.[20] The Blessing was presided over by the resident priest at Sipayik St. Ann's, Father John Caskin S.J. Steve Nicholas, the Saturday Eucharistic minister and son of the previous governor and state representative, Joseph A. Nicholas, accompanied the opening procession to the altar by slowly beating a hand drum. One of the tribal councilors smudged the altar, priest, and governor-elect, and gave the first prayer in Passamaquoddy.

A chair had been set up to the right of the altar for the governor. Father Caskin blessed the governor's insignia with holy water, after which the singers sang "The Healing Song" from *Glory and Praise* (the standard American Catholic hymnal), a song that asks for guidance. There were Prayers of Intercession for the tribal leaders, followed by the Lord's Prayer in Passamaquoddy, as it is usually done for Masses. This ended with the attendees extending a greeting of peace to one another, accompanied by the song "*Sankewitahasuwakon* [Peace is flowing like a river]," translated into Passamaquoddy by David A. Francis. Finally, the priest blessed all with the Sign of the Cross.

After the Blessing a potluck supper, sponsored by the tribal government, was held in the reservation school cafeteria. The Elders were waited on first, then adults and children formed lines to be served.

After the supper the *Sakomawkan* proper (i.e., the Inauguration Dance) was held to commemorate the installation of officers. Two Drum groups were present, one identified as a "traditional Drum" and one made up of young men. Wayne Newell, who grew up at Sipayik but now lives at Motahkomikuk, helped lead the singing. A country-and-western band from Nashville, which were in the area, had also been hired to perform after the Native dances.[21] The dancing opened with the honor song "Red Sky" sung by the traditional Drum, which included several women. The majority of the Native dances on this occasion were by and specifically for women dancers: the *Tuhtuwas* dance, shawl dances done to old songs, and a Two-Step for which the women dancers chose partners from the men in the audience. Many of the elderly women danced to the *Tuhtuwas*, fewer to other songs. Their participation recalls the role of elderly women in this ceremony as described in historical sources.

After several dances, Wayne Newell called for a traditional dance, part of the old protocol for inaugurations. His announcement spoke to the past, present, and future of the tradition: "This is the way all ceremonies used to start, years and years ago. When visitors came they were accorded this honor; and this chant went with it. So, you young ones, you listen to this chant, because we don't want it to die" (AMS 25Nov.94). Wayne sang an extremely slow version of *He, Qanute*, accompanied by the traditional Drum group (example 7). The dance was a variation of the War Club Dance, performed by Governor Dore, Lieutenant Governor Fred Francis, Governor Stevens from Motahkomikuk, and his lieutenant governor. Although the song was organized to a duple meter drumbeat, the men stepped out to meet each other in a triple pattern: two stamps with each foot before stepping onto it. From a four-square formation they came together in a circle, both arms outstretched to clasp hands in the center, a spoked wheel formation. They moved clockwise around, stepping very slowly.

After two verses of the song, Wayne stopped singing and pointed out the significance of this dance: "If you want a symbol for unity, you are watching it right now—the Tribes of the Wabanaki Confederacy represented by our four people, and the Four Directions." He continued with one more verse before moving into a fast dance song with the call: "Now that everybody's greeted each other!" The song was a common melody, adapted with textual references to the occasion.[22] After two verses, he called for everyone to join, *Psite wen!* and several women did (example 7 continued).

The 1994 inauguration ceremonies contained other significant links with the past. The Blessing ceremony at the church harks back to the Wampum Records, which mention the delegates visiting the church as part of the election proceedings. The congregation of the parish was formerly synonymous with the tribe, but this is not so today. In the emphasis on women's dances and the inclusion of the War Club Dance, important aspects of the older form of the ceremony were carried forward.

Wayne Newell told me afterward that he had not rehearsed with the Drum group, and its members said that they had not known what they would do beforehand, either. At that time, none of the singers or dancers knew about Mrs. Brown's article. Wayne said he had approached the governors and said, "Let's do this the way we were taught." On this occasion he was very concerned with emphasizing traditions, as his speech so eloquently made clear. Watching the Drum group continue afterward, he remarked to me that the powwow style Drum groups were "a prelude, a way of getting in," of getting the young people interested in the old traditions. He remembered listening to dance leader Sabattus Tomer (recorded by Smith in 1953) and emphasized, "We're damn lucky to have anything to go back to" (AMS 25Nov.94).

2007 SIPAYIK *SAKOMAWKAN*

The 2007 *Sakomawkan* held at Sipayik closely followed the protocols described by Mrs. Brown. Her article was referenced by the MC, who introduced and explained different elements and segments of the ceremonies to those attending. At the opening, Elder David A. Francis explained in Passamaquoddy the importance of the ceremonies. As an editor of the published edition of the Wampum Records, Francis could draw on these for his remarks in addition to his own experience of the ceremony in years past.

Analysis and Interpretation of Election Songs

The songs used for contemporary *Sakomawkan* are similar to those used in the Greeting Dance and the War Club Dance outside of this context. The election ceremony features the Welcome Chant *He, Qanute* in its most complex setting. Its use for elections is documented by a century of recordings, from Speck's to my own, and was corroborated independently by all my consultants.

This chant is the most formal part of the ceremony. It is sung extremely slowly; singer Delia Mitchell remembered the slow style as proper to election ceremonies (AMS 28Oct.95). The complex rhythmic grouping in the 1994 performance—resetting the familiar syllables of *He, Qanute* and taking three dance steps to duple drum rhythms—may also be a marker of older style. The performance recorded at the 1994 *Sakomawkan* is very close to the version singer Peter Dana recorded in the mid-1960s for the Waponahki Museum (example 8).[23] Rhythmic complexity and slow tempo may be analogues of the rhetorical skill required of the *Sakom*, who governed by persuasion rather than by force.

Formerly, the Election Greeting was performed in two parts: one section was addressed to the new *Sakom* as a greeting, and the second was his reply. Both used the same melody and repeated iterations. Peter Dana's version follows this form. One of my consultants indicated that the greeting was supposed to be sung by an old woman, to remind the *Sakom* of his responsibilities to care for the elderly, women, and children (AMS 25Oct.95). The *Sakom*'s reply could be sung by a proxy, as Speck noted of the Penobscot election ceremonies.

David A. Francis and Joseph A. Nicholas remembered that in their youth the tribal council (then men only) used to keep time for the War Club Dance without a drum, by exclaiming "Heh-heh-heh" in guttural tones. This practice was remarked on by Champlain ([1607] 1922:102) and Lescarbot ([1618] 1914:184) in the early seventeenth century and mentioned by Williamson in his description of the 1816 Penobscot Inauguration, "throughout which [the officers' songs] the whole assemblage uttered, at almost every breath, a low-toned emphatic guttural sound, not unlike a hiccup—the singular way by which they expressed their plaudits and pleasures" (Williamson 1832:498). Mrs. W. Wallace Brown also mentioned that the men provided this style of accompaniment to the women's dance of thanks (1892:59).

Women's Roles in Election Ceremonies

In the 1990s the role of women in the ceremonies was less obvious than it is now that Mrs. Brown's article has been accepted as a source. Nevertheless, the emphasis on women's dance genres and the presence of a Drum group led by women made their role prominent in the 1994 ceremony. This was perhaps a balance to the fact that no woman has yet been elected Passamaquoddy *Sakom* or *Leptenant*, though other Wabanaki nations have been led by women. The historical role of women as dancers and singers in election ceremonies also recalls the prominent role of women as dancers, singers, drummers, and orators in the war preparations of the Maliseet as described by the missionary Maillard (1758). Women's genres are clearly marked in Wabanaki musical culture, but the markers may be either functional (as in the old woman's role in greeting the *Sakom*), or stylistic (as in the *Tuhtuwas* Shawl Dance). Stylistic markers are discussed in more detail in chapter 7.

Repatriation of Ethnographic Materials

The explicit use of historical ethnographic materials in the recent *Sakomawkan* at Sipayik is part of a process of repatriation. It is not merely that the materials have become accessible and widely distributed. At the time I was resident in the area in the mid-1990s, I became part of the process of distribution; I shared historical materials with Waponahki Museum staff and other consultants. In many cases these sources were already known to them, and it may be that my interest in the sources piqued the interest of other people.

The process of repatriation is not simply returning materials to their original communities. The materials must be acknowledged as useful by influential community leaders, and the community must accept them as well. There must be a value in referencing them, for there is also the risk that if they are depended upon, the community will be seen by outsiders as having lost traditional sources. My observations from the mid-1990s and those of Nicholas Smith in the 1950s show that continuity was maintained in practice even without these sources.

Many of my consultants expressed the opinion that traditional knowledge was given to ethnographers in order to preserve it, so that later generations of the community would have access to it. The community has decided to incorporate ethnographic materials now in order to deepen their connections with their ancestors.[24]

SEVEN

The Marriage Ceremony and
Social Dances

The Marriage Ceremony Dance and the Wampum Protocols

Protocols for marriage are included in the Wampum Records of the Wabanaki Confederacy, underscoring the interpretation of marriage as a kind of alliance. Historically, this was often the case. Marriage was at the least an alliance between two families, creating bonds of honor and ultimately of blood between them. Since political allegiance within the Wabanaki communities for centuries has tended to be formed along family lines, marriage can be understood as having a political aspect. This interpretation is borne out in the historical record with examples such as that of Jean Vincent d'Abbadie, Baron de Saint-Castin, a lieutenant at the French fort of Pentagoet who married Etchemin *Sakom* Madockawando's daughter (Bourque 2001:155; McBride 1999:1–37, 139–43).

The Passamaquoddy Marriage Ceremony as represented at contemporary Indian Days is an exhibition, and therefore a shortened version of the prescription in the Wampum Records. The dance is the focus and thus becomes a synthesis. It is used in hybrid ways in real life practice as well.

The Passamaquoddy Marriage Ceremony differs from contemporary weddings designated Traditional that borrow from other Native traditions.[1] Contemporary Traditional weddings may include parts of this ceremony, however, and some performances of the Marriage Dance at the Indian Day have been the public commemoration of the legal marriage of a man and woman performed privately (*Quoddy Tides*, 22Aug.1986, 1; AMS 13Aug.93). Joseph A. Nicholas expressed his wish that because "it is such a beautiful ceremony, it could be incorporated into the modern wedding" (AMS 28Feb.95). In the two formulas described in Louis Mitchell's transcription of the Wampum Records, it is the Catholic liturgy that is incorporated into an older ceremony.

At the heart of the Marriage Ceremony is a group dance, in which the choreography symbolizes the union of two families. The terms "Marriage Dance" and "Marriage Ceremony" are used by my contacts interchangeably; perhaps because like the *Sakomawkan*, the dances confirming the *Sakom* in office, the whole event of speeches, singing, dancing, and feasting can be understood as a long, multipart ceremony. In the early twentieth century Frank Speck reported that Penobscots used the term "wedding dance" similarly to designate the "occasion for performing a group of dances rather than any one particular dance" (Speck [1940] 1997:257). In the contemporary Passamaquoddy context, however, the specially choreographed group dance is symbolic.

Marriage proposals historically involved the presentation of wampum strings by the groom to the bride. These were woven with mnemonic symbols of the protocols being followed, like the wampum belts and collars used to commemorate other alliances. The efficacy of the ceremony is thus reinforced on several levels: in the movements of the dance, which represent the blending of families; in the visual cues of the wampum strings; and in the words of songs and speeches.[2]

Contemporary Description

The Marriage Ceremony Dance presented at the Sipayik Indian Day incorporates all these protocols into a dance. The bride and groom, each with a man and woman representing their parents (sometimes their actual parents), dance toward each other. The two "mothers" talk. Joseph A. Nicholas explained, "The groom's mother asks to be accepted. The bride's mother takes that message back [to the bride]. The bride's mother conveys acceptance to the groom's mother, [who conveys it to the groom]" (AMS 28Feb.94).

The groom then dances toward the bride, places a necklace on her, and stands next to her. The groom's mother dances toward the couple with a blanket or shawl and covers their shoulders to signify their union. Then the party dances in a circle, the new couple followed by their parents. The parents form a squadron, facing each other. As they dance around, the partners cross over to signify the blending of the families: first mothers, then fathers (illustration 11).

Historical Documentation

Historical documentation of Passamaquoddy Marriage Ceremony protocols is scarce. However, Europeans recorded their own marriages to Native women and men, and marriages performed in the Catholic churches.

The Wampum Records

Louis Mitchell gave two versions of marriage ceremonies when he transcribed the Wampum Records at the end of the nineteenth century: "the marriage custom of olden times" and "the marriage custom as it has been put together in recent times" (Leavitt and Francis 1990). The description of the ancient rite is very brief; the modern rite is more detailed, with provisions for including the Catholic ceremony. It is not possible to date the "old" and "recent" marriage ceremonies with any precision. Mitchell's terms are relative. It is possible that the "recent" ceremony developed around the time of the formal constitution of the Wabanaki Confederacy: that is, circa 1700. The ceremony followed today most resembles the one Mitchell gives as recent.

The old ceremony had the prospective groom notifying his family and seeking approval for his choice; if he received it, his father gave him a new bearskin, deer hide, or beaver skin to take as a gift when he went to the family of his chosen bride to make his request. (He might himself have procured such skins, but they were the property of his father if he lived in that household.) If his request was granted, the marriage was celebrated with "feasting, eating together, and dancing and greeting. Sometimes it went on for weeks" (Leavitt and Francis 1990:47).

The more recent ceremony recorded by Mitchell involved elaborate presentations of wampum in the form of beaded strings. The prospective groom appointed a man to negotiate with the bride's family on his behalf. The negotiator carried the wampum as an indication of the groom's intentions. Frank Speck had reproductions of Passamaquoddy marriage wampum made for his study.[3] His collection included a string representing the proposal, from which a somewhat formulaic request was "read" by the groom's messenger. The bride's response, whether affirmative or negative, was also made by a negotiator with wampum, and there was a different string to represent each option.

According to Mitchell, if marriage was agreed upon, a Catholic priest could then marry the two if they chose.[4] The marriage was celebrated "in the traditional way" with two special greeting ceremonies (*natolasihkuwan*): first from the bride and her party to the groom, and then the groom and his party to the bride. After this, a feast was held, and then guests were led to a long house (*qanotuwan*) with another ceremony. Here, the bride and groom danced toward each other in a dance given the special descriptive term *astukaniya*. At midnight there was another feast for the guests; the newlyweds were counseled in the ways of married life; and then the bride was escorted to her new home with her bedding (Leavitt and Francis 1990:48–49).

Marriage Ceremonies in Other Wabanaki Communities

The disputed letter attributed to the Abbé Maillard dated 1755 contains a description of marriage protocols in the Mi'kmaq communities he served, before they adopted Christianity (Maillard 1758:53–60). Although many of the details in this account are fanciful—Maillard represented the speeches of the groom, the shaman who advised the couple, and other protagonists—the basic structure of the ceremonies accords with Louis Mitchell's description in the Wampum Records. Although Maillard stated that he was describing marriage customs of Mi'kmaq people in "their unconverted state," there are many parallels with Christian ideas in Maillard's account, an indicator of the syncretic worldview of its author and perhaps of his subjects.

MALISEET

In 1914, William Mechling published a collection of Maliseet oral traditions that includes a description of the marriage ceremony. In this version, "the bride and groom never saw each other"; the negotiations were conducted on behalf of the groom with the prospective bride's parents. If they approved of the match, she was consulted, and then the groom would be notified of her decision. If accepted, the groom presented to the bride's father a wampum string and furs or blankets (Mechling 1914:25 n1).

PENOBSCOT

During the twentieth century the Marriage Ceremony Dance was documented in Passamaquoddy and Penobscot communities. Frank Speck believed that at Penawahpskek in the early twentieth century it had become a social dance and because of the influence of the Catholic Church was no longer ceremonial.

Speck observed that when a wedding was celebrated the Round Dances were performed first, then other styles of dancing might ensue. In his description the Wedding Round Dance is similar to the Marriage Ceremony Dance performed at Sipayik Indian Days, except that the squads of dancers are formed as two rows of three or four persons facing each other rather than two rows of two parents, and the squadrons were not confined to the parents of the bride and groom. All the dancers taking part might form squads. I also observed this in the 1994 and 1995 Indian Day performances, but only the squadron of parents changed places to signify the union of their families.

In Speck's description of the Penobscot Wedding Dance, "the groom is flanked on one side by the leader and a companion while another friend takes position at his other side. Facing these are four women," including the bride positioned opposite and facing the leader; her chosen friend faces the groom.

Speck noted that instead of women facing the four men, there could be "a quartet of male friends and relatives." In either case, this was the leading squad. The next squad behind this one comprised "four females facing four males in the same way," including the bride if she were not in the first squadron. The number of partners in each squad varied "from three or four to as many more as could conveniently circle abreast inside the hall." Speck noted that except for the presence of the bridal party, "there are no particular differences between wedding dances and the ordinary round dances performed on all social occasions" (Speck [1940] 1997:256–57).

The step for this dance was the simple scuff and step. As in the usual Penobscot Round Dance, periodically the rows in a squadron would reverse position. Speck noted that the Round Dance was the most generic Penobscot dance, being designated *alnigan* or *alnoba'gan*, "person's dance." He reported that the songs, a dozen of which he had recorded from various singers, formed a set of dances; these were interspersed with promenading or intervals of rest (Speck [1940] 1997:273). This form is very similar to that of the other ceremonies associated with the Wabanaki Confederacy.

Analysis: Comparison of Indian Day to Historical Sources

The contemporary Passamaquoddy Marriage Ceremony Dance is a shortened version of the ceremony described in the Wampum Records, perhaps analogous to the *natolasihkuwan* greeting ceremonies between the bride's and groom's parties described in the protocol that Mitchell gave as recent. It does not leave time for any real discussion of the proposal by the bride's family but is not necessarily a token reenactment of the old ceremony; that too may have been abbreviated. One example of Passamaquoddy marriage wampum discussed by Speck is a single long string in five sections that incorporates "the whole procedure" in its symbolism (Speck 1919a:50–52, fig. 9). Marriage proposals are sometimes expected, and discussions may take place beforehand; this string would seem to stand for such cases.

The Use of Wampum in Arranging Marriage

According to oral traditions, strings of wampum beads represented all the ceremonial protocols of the Confederacy. In addition to crafting strings to represent specific events, communities convened yearly for a public reading of the wampum belts. Although the marriage ceremony has less to do with the operations of the Confederacy per se, the use of wampum is as clearly integrated into the efficacy of this ceremony as it is in the ceremonies of alliance, warfare, and chief-making.

The function of the wampum in marriage protocols is related to its use in alliance. Penobscot Elder Joseph Nicolar indicated that wampum was not intended for use as money (Nicolar [1893] 2007:181, 192) but was "a pledge of honor" (Speck 1919a:47). Frank Speck categorically denied any association of the use of wampum in negotiating marriages with a bride price function in Waponahkik (Speck 1919a:47). Significantly, the wampum strings were not kept within families; Speck documented the reuse of one string of wampum over several generations (1919a:48) This accords with Maliseet traditions documented by Mechling, that the wampum string was kept by the *Leptenant* "until another young man in the tribe wants to get married" (Mechling 1914:25; cited in Speck 1919a:53).

Such practices of communal reuse underscore the mnemonic function of wampum in Wabanaki cultures generally. Wampum strings used to negotiate marriage recorded only the outlines of the procedures. Communal use also suggests the primary importance of the community—which marriages construct—since the strings were not associated with specific unions or families. Wabanaki use of wampum strings in negotiating marriages thus contrasts with Euro-American wedding bands, which are frequently unique and when reused evoke specific familial relationships.

Marriage Dance Songs

Nicholas Smith recorded Wedding Dance Songs from Wabanaki singers in the 1950s. His principal consultant was Andrew Dana (Penobscot), who told him there were "twenty-one variations of the Wedding Dance" (Smith 1955:34). Some of the Wedding Songs that Smith recorded are very similar to each other, partly because other singers had learned from Dana how to sing for this occasion. Smith also recorded the Wedding Dance Songs known by Gabe Polchies, a Maliseet who had married into the Penobscot community (1955:34); only one appears on the tape deposited with the Canadian Museum and the Northeast Archives (Smith 1959, track 8).

The songs Smith recorded are similar to the Marriage Dance Songs recorded by Speck and Mechling. Speck admitted, "Just how many distinct [wedding] songs were known I never could determine." ([1940] 1997:256). There appear to be "families" of related songs for this ceremony, sharing similar tunes and texts.[5] The melody of Speck's cylinder 5098 resembles Polchies's version (Smith 1959, track 8).

Wedding Dance Songs as a group share several distinguishing stylistic features. Those recorded by Mechling and Smith are characterized by antiphonal performance between the leader and chorus, a feature also noted by Speck

([1940] 1997:166–67), though not all his recordings are performed this way. The structure of the Marriage Dance Songs is ideally suited to antiphony, being pairs of parallel antecedent and consequent phrases: however, contemporary Wabanaki singers most often reserve antiphonal performance for new Intertribal songs. They generally sing historically established dance songs solo or heterophonically. Even in intertribal songs the antiphony is scanty: the leader sings the first phrase of each verse and is answered by the other singers in chorus. Gertrude Kurath (1956) noted that antiphonal performance is characteristic of other Algonquian social dance songs, particularly those in which both men and women take part. It is possible that antiphonal singing carried connotations of sociality which have since been overwritten by its association with powwow style songs.

The Marriage Dance Songs collected by Speck and Mechling are among the most rhythmically complex of the social dance songs. The recordings demonstrate the old style of drumming the equivalent of an eighth-note subdivision while singing in additive triplets or sixteenth-note rhythms. A further level of complexity is created by the alignment of melodic phrases over the pulse. The texts of these phrases are chant syllables, and they fit syllabically with the melody. The beginning of each phrase is aligned with the beat; then the singer moves apart with syllables that last 1, 2, 3, or 4 subdivisions, creating the phrase from subphrase units, or motives. But the last motive in each phrase is also aligned with the beat, thus providing a "boost" into the next phrase.

There are also words particular to the Marriage Dance, notably the exclamation *matama oliye*! made at the end of a song. In Passamaquoddy this means, "s/he can't get out," or "s/he doesn't go anywhere." Speck reported that "it is asserted jokingly [by the Penobscot] that the cry is a corruption of French, *madame mariée*!" ([1940] 1997:257)—apparently a bilingual pun, since marriage in this Catholic culture restrains the parties from certain kinds of socializing. Exclamations are a feature common to social dances, used to comment on the dancing, urge the dancers on, or direct them. Insofar as they are made by the leader, exclamations may be considered a manifestation of the antiphonal performance style.

The songs used to accompany the Marriage Dance at the Indian Days I have observed at Sipayik utilized melodies also sung for other dances, but the songs were adapted to the particular occasion by obvious changes in text and subtle changes in rhythm and phrasing. In 1994 Blanche Sockabasin sang and drummed for this ceremony. As in the Peace Pipe Ceremony, she did not sing continuously but strung several dance songs together, keeping the drum going to accompany the action. She sang seven repetitions of a short piece with the text *qey heya hey*, which generally is used to accompany dance songs, as the bride's and groom's parties moved into the center of the dancing circle to meet and negotiate, and the couple and their parents danced around in the marriage formation. Then she switched to a fast dance song as the wedding party was joined by other dancers (example 11).

Interpretation of the Marriage Dance

The Marriage Ceremony Dance signifies meaning on several levels at once. As in the Welcome Dance, its function is manifested in the choreography. The wampum belts visually symbolize the stages of the ceremony. The dance that celebrates the union requires suites of songs, with extemporized lyrics that make each performance unique.

In the Passamaquoddy version of the Marriage Ceremony Dance today, participants may find both Christian and traditional significance. This dance is a primary site of cultural blending and mixed meanings.

In 1993 the Indian Day marriage dance was the formal celebration of the marriage of a couple who had not had a church wedding. My consultants mentioned other couples who had made this their only ceremony (AMS 13Aug.93). The Marriage Dance has also been performed at the Sipayik Indian Day by a bride and groom who *have* been formally married in a prior ceremony (AMS 8Aug.93). Some members of the Sipayik community today have only church *or* civil ceremonies. But most often at the Indian Day the Marriage Dance is performed by persons not related to each other, as in 1996 when the "bride" was actually celebrating her anniversary to her real husband, the police chief, away on duty.

The role of the bride in the proposal process is strikingly similar to the role of women in the selection of a new leader. After a man has identified himself as her suitor, she can confirm or reject the "candidate." Speck cites oral traditions that women and girls were sometimes pressured to accept an offer. As the mainstream culture trended toward love marriages between partners, however, the protocols for negotiation may have been simplified, as reflected in the single-strand marriage wampum noted above.

The multiple levels on which meaning is signified in this ceremony leave room for humor and sometimes, as in a verbal pun, the symbolic association slips. Performing the Marriage Ceremony Dance as an exhibition at the Indian Day is the subject of jokes when it is not the confirmation of an actual ceremony. This sort of metaphorical play is characteristic of Passamaquoddy song performances (see chapter 8).

Social Dances

Several dances with ostensibly social functions are closely related to the ceremonies described in the Wampum Records by being regularly included in the celebratory segments of the various protocols. These social dances are not generally presented as ceremonies in themselves, but they reveal essential Passamaquoddy concepts that illuminate the function of dancing.

Peskotomuhkatiyik participate in a large repertory of contemporary intertribal social dances, associated with powwows and intertribal events called Socials. The focus here is on social dances that are specifically identified with the Wabanaki cultural group. In Peskotomuhkatik today, dances from both traditions may be performed at intertribal events such as powwows. Differences between old and new as well as gender distinctions are maintained.

Gender in Dance Styles

Men's and women's dance styles are very clearly marked in Passamaquoddy tradition. Comportment, choreography, and dress are all employed in making the distinction obvious. A frequent joke is to dance in the style of the opposite gender. Whether dressed in regalia or casual clothes, women who consider themselves Traditional[6] do not wear pants for ceremonial dancing; many even eschew pants for dancing at intertribal Socials. Furthermore several dance genres are restricted to men or to women. The War Dance discussed above was a men's dance, though historical accounts indicate that women sang War Songs as well as men. The Hunter's Dance, mentioned as a corollary of the War Dance, is another men's genre still performed. In traditional Passamaquoddy culture, women have a particularly important genre, a type of shawl dance known as *Tuhtuwas* (little pine tufts).

The gender differences in Passamaquoddy musical culture parallel those in intertribal powwow culture. In the Powwow there are several men's genres, and men's dance styles in general emphasize athleticism; this is rewarded by judges in competitive dancing. Women's genres and styles emphasize grace, although the movements may also be athletic. The different dance genres associated with intertribal powwows also have distinctive regalia, different for men and women, such as the Men's Fancy Dance, the Women's Fancy Shawl Dance, and Jingle Dress.[7] Many powwow dances have developed within recent memory (Jingle Dress is one) and reflect common features of the many different Native North American cultures. Clear distinction between male and female dance style and genres is one of these shared traits.

153

Tuhtuwas: *The Quintessential Women's Dance*

The *Tuhtuwas* Dance is a shawl dance, a women's genre found throughout North America. *Tuhtuwas* means "little pine tufts," and the dancers' movements evoke pine needle tufts gently tossing and turning at the ends of branches (illustration 12). This is perhaps the preeminent Passamaquoddy dance today, almost symbolic of the musical tradition and often demonstrated for public teaching occasions. Although today it is strongly associated with Peskotomuh-katiyik, Frank Speck's consultants in the early twentieth century described it as a Penobscot dance (Speck [1940] 1997:299), and Nicholas Smith recorded it in 1953 at Indian Island, Maine (Smith 1955:33). In the Penobscot community, the dance is related to a game in which pine needle tufts are placed points down on a board and the board is tapped to make them "dance." Speck found that the Penobscot had ceased performing the actual dance and only the game was in current practice ([1940] 1997:183). The songs used were those for the men's *Nawadawe* or *Mi'kmaq* Dance. The *Nawadawe* Song examples given in *Penobscot Man* are quite different from the Passamaquoddy song used today for the *Tuhtuwas* Dance (Speck [1940] 1997:286–88).

Peskotomuhkatiyik use one melody consistently for this dance (example 12). It is a strophic song, with each verse consisting of one pair of phrases directing the dancers, followed by two parallel phrases of vocables. The texted opening phrases of each verse allow the singer to extemporize.

The dancers respond to verbal commands given by the singer: "Have it dance proudly," "have it dance sideways," "have it dance turning around in circles," "backwards," "dance faster." The commands given are not direct, but rather ask the dancers to create an impression. This mode recalls the ceremonial language of the "Song of the Drum" (example 1), expressing what is wished for.[8] The words are adapted to fit each situation but usually end with "dance faster."

The movements are very sedate for the most part but can get energetic. A humorous incident occurred at a public demonstration when the female dancers complained to the (male) singers that although they were singing "have it dance faster" (*kakawtehkomusic*), they were not increasing the speed of their drumbeats. So the singers continued for two more verses, working up to a wild speed for a final *kakawtehkomusic* verse that left all the dancers gasping and laughing (AMS 22Apr.95). Usually the dance is more controlled. The footstep is the touch-and-step movement, alternating feet, that is used for other dances. One contemporary dancer who often leads this dance has a very beautiful, clearly placed, and delicate step; other dancers follow her style in this dance.

With the dancers turning and their shawls swinging, *Tuhtuwas* is a very attractive dance to watch. Another factor contributing to its popularity with the public is that the text consists mainly of "real words" in the Passamaquoddy language (AMS 11Sep.94). To dance well, the dancers must understand the language, so this song and dance are used in the Passamaquoddy schools.

The current song melody for *Tuhtuwas* is employed to set a variety of extemporized texts for other functions, probably because it is so familiar and requires only one new text phrase per verse. This same tune is also found in other Wabanaki communities: it sets the Mi'kmaq song *Kitpu* (Eagle), and a similar melody is given by Speck as a comic song, lullaby, or dance song used by Penobscot singers (Speck [1940] 1997:170).[9] The melody's origin and original function are thus unclear, despite its current strong identification as Passamaquoddy.

Reconstructing the history of this dance is difficult. Records of special women's dances in intertribal councils go back to the earliest accounts written by Europeans. As noted in chapter 6, historical records indicate that a women's dance was part of the protocol of the *Sakomawkan*. Women performed the dance to signal their acceptance of the new leader that the all-male special council had chosen.

Mrs. Brown (1892) was the first to mention shawls as a specific part of women's dance regalia at a *Sakomawkan*. But recordings of the melody and text of the *Tuhtuwas* Dance date back only to Frank Speck's work in the early twentieth century, collected between 1905 and 1911. The *Tuhtuwas* Dance that Smith recorded at the Penobscot governor's inauguration in 1953 unfortunately is almost inaudible on the tape, and pitches cannot be discerned (Smith 1959).[10]

Tuhtuwas is the quintessential women's dance, enacting many of the important ideas about gender found elsewhere in traditional Passamaquoddy culture. The movement is focused on graceful carriage of the whole body, with subtle footwork. The dancers' dress is supposed to be modest: to achieve the imitation of pine tufts, fringed shawls or buckskin tunics are usually worn, but even in their absence the focus is on the women's interpretation of the commands and not on their physiques, lending an aura of dignity. Older women are especially appreciated in this dance and generally participate even if they do not otherwise dance at an event. Some consultants have suggested that one contemporary singer's version of *Tuhtuwas* is "like an Honor Song" for women.

Older consultants described the way women used to dance in general as similar to the way *Tuhtuwas* is performed today. This style of comportment is also parodied when a man wishes to imitate women, for a joke. On one occasion a man donned a shawl and danced with exaggerated stiffness, turning slowly from side to side. Where gender roles are marked in Passamaquoddy dances they are very clear, and switching roles can easily evoke laughter. Dance regalia also clearly mark gender.

Many of the social dances now performed do not mark gender roles, however, and anyone can be anyone's partner. In powwow dancing, women have copied some movement styles from men. The popular Fancy Shawl Dance—a genre invented less than fifty years ago—copies the jumping and kicking footwork of the men's Fancy Dance. Although gender remains an important division in powwow culture, it is marked with different style features than in traditional Passamaquoddy dancing.

The Snake Dance: A Social and Medicine Dance

A Snake Dance is usually used to close the Indian Day ceremonies at Sipayik. This is an intertribal dance, and since a circle is not formed, anyone can participate. All the dancers join hands and move in a long single line, following the leader to create an overall serpentine form that coils and uncoils (illustration 13).

Documentation for the Snake Dance genre covers about a century and represents all of the five Wabanaki nations: Abenaki, Penobscot, Passamaquoddy, Maliseet, and Mi'kmaq. Snake Dance songs were among the famous recordings Jesse Walter Fewkes made in 1890, and have been a topic of great interest more than a century later in Peskotomuhkatik. Taken altogether, the sources—which include written descriptions by outside observers, recordings, and orally transmitted information—present a complex history for this genre. Questions arise concerning its origin, transmission, and function among the Wabanaki communities.[11]

Several of the sources suggest that Snake or Serpent Dances were associated with medicine and spiritual power, yet they are often performed today as a form of entertainment. Contradictions between the sources are resolved by assuming that there are two genres distinguished by function, both commonly referred to as Snake or Serpent Dance. The primarily social Snake Dance is a group dance performed in public. The songs used for this dance, historically and at present, share features of the song genres associated with the wampum protocols and political alliances in the Northeast. The second genre seems to have been a solo dance, performed in private contexts for purposes including gathering medicine, healing, driving away snakes, seasonal propitiation, and personal protection. The two genres could have originated as two portions of one ceremonial dance, as described in some of the earliest sources. Such a bipartite division would accord with other Wabanaki dance genres.

11. Marriage Ceremony Dance, Sipayik Indian Day 2007. Photograph by Ann Morrison Spinney.

12. Tuhtuwas Dance, Sipayik Indian Day 1997. Photograph courtesy of the *Quoddy Tides*.

13. Snake Dance, Sipayik Indian Day 1993. Photograph courtesy of the *Quoddy Tides*.

The mystery surrounding the origin and multiple meanings of the Snake Dance demands consideration of ideas about the power of dancing. This dance was so important in the nineteenth century that it was one of only two dance songs among the first field recordings ever made (Fewkes 1890b), and it was danced by Wolastoqewiyik (Maliseets) for the Prince of Wales at St. John in 1860 (Sable 1998:331). Stanislas Hagar reported in the early 1890s that among the Mi'kmaq nations of Nova Scotia, the Snake Dance had been "suppressed by missionaries" and was no longer used (1895:36).

Fundamental to understanding the history of this dance is the concept, currently maintained in Peskotomuhkatik, that dancing can be spiritually powerful and also healing for participants. When Native people dance together, unity is achieved, and the effects of diaspora, degradation, and decimation are abated. When Native and non-Native dance together, unity is achieved, and the history of conflict between them is abated. Dancing is considered medicine, and a means to generate or access spiritual power. Further, in some accounts the Snake Dance specifically is associated with gathering materia medica, with the changing seasons, and with healing.

CONTEMPORARY DESCRIPTION OF THE SNAKE DANCE

The Snake Dance performed today is a group dance. Participants join hands in a single line and, stepping to the beat of singing and/or drumming, follow a leader who moves across or around the dancing space in a zigzag. The dance features a coiling and uncoiling of the line of dancers; sometimes this is the culmination of the dance. Sometimes the zigzagging is rough, making the dance into a game designed to throw dancers out of the line; Nicholas Smith described it as being like the children's game "Crack the Whip" (Smith 1955:34).

This dance is unquestionably a social dance: amusing, encouraging mingling, and a lot of fun. It is used at intertribal gatherings, and at the Sipayik Indian Day the public is encouraged to participate. On that occasion it is not rough, and I have observed more than a hundred people of all ages dancing.

Currently, the songs sung for this Passamaquoddy Snake Dance are ad hoc. Singer Blanche Sockabasin typically strings several dance song melodies together and extemporizes words in the Passamaquoddy language directing the dancers or describing what they are doing (see example 13). Drum groups singing in the intertribal style have even used Two-Step songs, although some participants consider these unsuitable because the iambic triple meter of this genre does not match the rhythm of the Snake Dance step, the same touch and step movement used for other dances.[12]

The Snake Dance as performed at Sipayik today is similar to performances described by Nicholas Smith in the 1950s and 1960s, except that Smith was told that it was used to start—rather than conclude—an occasion of dancing by Penobscot singers. I have observed (and participated in) Snake Dances midway through an evening of social dancing during intertribal gatherings. Joseph A. Nicholas chose the Snake Dance to end the Sipayik Indian Day when he was the MC, because he thought it was a nice way to connect with the audience, whom he asked to participate.

THE SOLO SNAKE DANCE

Passamaquoddy traditions suggest that there may be two genres of Snake Dances, perhaps with different origins. Evidence for this was provided by David A. Francis, Passamaquoddy language specialist. In the 1930s an Elder took him aside and showed him a special Snake Dance, along with a Hunting Dance [Hunter's Dance]. This was a pantomime of following a trail around the ground, then pouncing on the prey and dancing in exultation of achievement. This dance is still done today by Dwayne Sockabasin and his son. The Snake Dance that the Elder taught David Francis along with the Hunting Dance may also be a pantomime. It is a solo dance, completely unlike the group snake dance described above. David described it as "like the Highland Scots Sword Dance." He suggested that it could be imitating a person trying to step out of a tangle of snakes; "it would get you out of it," he noted in one consultation. He pointed to possible seasonal connections to spring, when tangles of snakes are found lying in the sun. Analyzing the implications of a similar seasonal association for the Mi'kmaq Serpent Dance, Trudy Sable concluded that that dance had associations with the gathering and administration of medicine (Sable 1998).

Unfortunately, David Francis cannot remember the song that went with this solo dance; and according to consultants no one in the Passamaquoddy community has performed the dance since. If it was a personal dance, done for protection against snakes, it could have been closely guarded like the Hunting Songs sung for personal protection that were described to Nicholas Smith.

HISTORICAL DESCRIPTIONS

Jesse Walter Fewkes was the first to record any information about a Passamaquoddy Snake Dance per se. He recorded songs along with a description of the dance in 1890, while testing the new Edison cylinder recording machine. The dance described to him by Noel Josephs, Peter Selmore, and Mrs. W. Wallace Brown is the same as that described by Speck, and observed later by both Nicholas Smith and me:

The leader or singer... begins the dance by moving about the room in a stooping posture, shaking in his hand a rattle made of horn, beating the ground violently with one foot. He peers into every corner of the room, either seeking the snake or inciting the on-lookers to take part, meanwhile singing the first part of the song recorded on the phonograph [example 14]. Then he goes to the middle of the room, and, calling out one after another of the auditors, seizes his hands. The two... dance around the room together... [and] others join until there is a continuous line of men and women, alternate members of the chain facing in opposite directions, and all grasping each other's hands. The chain then coils back and forth round the room and at last forms a closely pressed spiral, tightly coiled together, with the leader in the middle. At first the dancers have their bodies bent over in a stooping attitude, but as the dance goes on they rise to an erect posture. They call on the spectators to follow them, with loud calls intermingled with the music. (Fewkes 1890a:262)

Fewkes recorded several Snake Dance Songs that he was told were different, but he considered them all to be variations of one song and presented only one transcription (Fewkes 1890a:261). As published, it contains an obvious layout error, the end of each staff line having been cut off, so I have transcribed it again from a copy of the recording (example 14).[13] On the published recording of the song, Josephs prefaced his singing with an invitation to dance and a description of the good time to be had (Spottswood 1978).

Information on the song's use was given by singers Noel Josephs and Peter Selmore, and reported by Fewkes in his article as the basis for some ethnological speculation. The dance always occurred at the end of the Passamaquoddy dances, though it might be followed by other dances. Perhaps this could be glossed as occurring at the end of the Passamaquoddy ceremonial dances, followed by intertribal social dances. Fewkes noted that the description given in the article was obtained from Mrs. W. Wallace Brown (rather than a transcription of Josephs's words) and that he himself had never seen the dance. Fewkes, however, thought that this song and the dance were extremely ancient: "Although the ceremonial element has now disappeared from this song, it may be presumed that it originally had a religious importance similar to that of the Snake Dances of the Southwest, since the extent of the worship of the snake among North American Indians is known" (Fewkes 1890a:261).

His cross-cultural connections in this article are not well supported—he reaches as far as Italy on occasion (Fewkes 1890a:260)—but they are symptomatic of the time. Proceeding more cautiously to probe the intercultural connections of this dance, we note that his description of the choreography shows similarities to Iroquoian and southeastern line dances led by a man accompanying himself with a shaker.

THE SNAKE DANCE IN OTHER WABANAKI TRADITIONS

A few years later, Stansbury Hagar published a description of a Mi'kmaq Serpent Dance, based on the recollections of Elders Newell and Adam Glode. This dance was performed by men and women, with a male leader, and was in two parts. In the first, the dancers formed circles around the leader, who stood in the center. They circled around him twelve times: three times facing him; three times with their backs to him; and six times with their backs to each other. In the second part of the dance, the leader emerged from the circle and the dancers formed a line following him, coiling and uncoiling the line. Hagar did not record any songs, as the dance was no longer performed and his sources could not recall the songs; but they described the use of a shot-horn rattle for accompaniment (Hagar 1895:36).[14]

Hagar indicated that the Serpent Dance was associated with spring and with gathering medicine but was also "a proper feature at the election of a chief" (1895:37) . Several points made by his consultants suggest the spiritual power of this dance: that its original purpose was to gather venom for medicine; that from dancing it too much, Ancestors had been turned into serpents; and that it had been suppressed by missionaries. Hagar drew connections from the cultural associations of this dance to ideas about serpents in other Native American traditions.

Trudy Sable followed up Hagar's research one hundred years later with further contextual and linguistic research. She found that oral traditions in the Mi'kmaq community affirmed the origin of the dance in intercultural exchanges (1998:331). Sable's research also confirmed the dance's association with spiritual power, medicine, and the changing seasons.

In the early twentieth century, Frank Speck noted that the Snake Dance, *(pə)matagi'posi*, was performed for weddings at Indian Island by Penobscot singers and dancers. It followed the Wedding Round Dance, a special dance whose squadron formations represent the families involved in the wedding. The name described the movement: he gave the literal translation "coming creeping along the ground" ([1940] 1997:257, 283). Speck provided conflicting information about this dance. He noted that there were two names for it: the one given above, which is descriptive, and *Yuneha* after its predominant syllables. When first introducing *pəmage'wintowa'gan* Dance Songs, he described their effect as hilarious, but he later suggested that "anciently," the Snake Dance was done to imitate the movement of a serpent constellation ([1940] 1997:166, 284).

Speck recorded six Penobscot Snake Dance Songs, but only two transcriptions appear in his book, and they are not cross-referenced with his recordings.

Both of the transcribed songs appear to be fast dance songs. At several points, Speck described the complexity of the rhythm in this dance: "The song is entirely independent, in time, of the rattling [accompaniment] and stamping [of the dancers]" ([1940] 1997:284). The quintessential accompaniment for this dance was the shot-horn rattle, *halonossis*. On Speck's recordings, one can hear a lot of noise over the singing. Although presumably this is partly the noise of the recording machine, one Penobscot Elder and several Passama-quoddy singers have told me that this noise sounds like the way dance leaders used to beat the rattle for this dance: it is rhythmic, setting a pulse of sixteenth notes under the uneven duple and triple groupings of the sung melody.

I have tentatively identified cylinder number 5046 as the source of the transcription on page 284 of Speck's monograph *Penobscot Man*; it is at least a close variant. I have retranscribed the song following current conventions (example 15, Speck Collection, cylinder 5046).

Analysis

The division of the Snake Dance Song recorded by Fewkes into a slow section followed by a fast danceable tune is typical of many of the Passamaquoddy ceremonial songs, as has been shown. The Teaching (previously noted) from an Abenaki consultant that the first part is supposed to get everyone focused on the ceremony is helpful in understanding why they may have become separated. The slow first section may be "proper" to the ceremony as in other wampum protocols, with the second section employing stock dance tunes as needed.

Fewkes believed that the Snake Dance Songs he recorded were an old genre. He does mention that "the boisterous finale may be of modern date." Perhaps it was only this "finale" that Speck was describing, though he was cognizant of the division into slow and fast sections of other ceremonial songs; compare his discussion of the Penobscot Greeting Chant ([1940] 1997:292–95). Historical sources before Fewkes do not contain evidence of this kind of serpentine dance among Wabanaki people, though other social and ceremonial dances are described in detail in European accounts from the seventeenth century on.

CROSS-CULTURAL QUESTIONS

This Snake Dance form is not unlike the Friendly Dances of the intertribal Powwow, an event that has origins in the ceremonial traditions of First Nations brought together in reservations in the nineteenth century. The Oklahoma powwows began in the late nineteenth century; it is possible that there is a connection between the popularity of Friendly Dances and the documented public performances of Snake Dances in Passamaquoddy, Mi'kmaq, and Penobscot communities.

On the other hand, if at the time Fewkes made his recordings people in Mi'kmaq communities were doing a similar dance, it is possible that the social serpentine form dance may have come from the East to the Passamaquoddy and Penobscot communities: It could be an imitation of the Mi'kmaq dance described by Hagar's consultants. Another vigorous Penobscot social dance that Speck recorded and described was attributed to the Mi'kmaqs: the *Nawadawe* or "Micmac Dance" previously mentioned. This dance used songs of a type that Speck thought were set apart from other Penobscot songs, and he noted that only four of the song leaders knew them in 1912 ([1940] 1997:286–88). It was a freestyle men's dance with a strong uneven rhythm supposedly imitating Mi'kmaq dance style. Some of my older Passamaquoddy consultants found the idea of "dancing like Mi'kmaqs" very funny—an example of intertribal humor. Speck noted, "The dance seems to be purely for amusement, a conclusion to festivities; the noise and exuberance of the occasion culminating in a grand finale." He gave two translations of *Nawadawe*: "Micmac Dance" and "War Dance" (Speck [1940] 1997:286, 257, and Speck Collection notes).

A third possibility—not excluding of either of the previous two—is that this particular form of Snake Dance dates from activities of the Wabanaki Confederacy and related alliances. From this perspective, the similarity of its choreography to that of various southeastern ceremonial dances is particularly interesting. Wabanaki adoption of calumet ceremonialism from the Plains and Prairie culture area in expanding alliances during the seventeenth century has been noted; the Snake Dance could be another instance of building bridges on basic cultural commonalities. According to Cherokee ethnomusicologist Charlotte Heth, a document from the early nineteenth century describes a Snake Dance among the Eastern Cherokee, the majority of whom were relocated to Oklahoma in 1838–39 (Heth 1982:75). Willard Rhodes noted that the Cherokee ceremonial Stomp Dance "was a serpentine line dance in which the dancers follow the leaders as they wind the line into an ever-narrowing circle" (1987:14). Victoria Lindsay Levine reports similar choreography in other Southeastern ceremonial dances and emphasizes that all these dances predate the Powwow (personal communication).

LINGUISTIC EVIDENCE

The Passamaquoddy word for "snake" is *athusoss*; the Penobscot, *athossis*. David A. Francis suggests a relation to words meaning "wriggle, wave, or wrinkle" in the morpheme *ath-* or *atk-* (from *-atoke-*?): related words include *atkuwessos*, a water bug that makes waves; *atkiqe*, "wrinkles on his face"; *wolatokehlal*, "he straightens it out." The Mi'kmaq words for "snake" and "snaking" are quite different (Sable 1998:332). Blanche Sockabasin employed the word *athusoss* in her extemporized Snake Dance Song text as she directed and responded to the dancers in August 1994 (example 13, an example typical of her artistic approach to accompanying the dance).

The text *al-la-de-gee-eh* that Nicholas Smith found on the Speck recording of Maliseet singer Jack Solomon (1955:34) was recognized by David A. Francis as a typical Passamaquoddy Snake Dance Song refrain: *wolatokiye*, "they are straightening out."[15] This word suggests a connection to the Penobscot Green Corn Dance, as the second section of the song proper to that dance also uses this text. Green Corn is a seasonal ceremony celebrated by Iroquoian, Cherokee, and some Algonquian nations farther south. The presence of this word thus may be another link to Southeastern ceremonials or the Longhouse tradition; see the discussion of *Qanute* Songs in welcoming ceremonies in chapter 5. Sable (1998) noted that the Mi'kmaq word for 'crawling around' is similar: *alatejiey*, though the sound j has been substituted for g.

The texts of Noel Josephs's Snake Dance Songs recorded by J. W. Fewkes consist of the word or vocables *Yuneha*, repeated throughout the second part (Fewkes 1890a:262). This text is described as an archaic "chant word" by all my Passamaquoddy consultants. It is in the same category as the text of the ceremonial Passamaquoddy Greeting Chant "*He, Qanute*," discussed in chapter 5.

Some of my Passamaquoddy consultants speak of "*Yuneha* songs" as an old and important genre. Speck noted that this was another term applied to the Penobscot Snake Dance Songs, though in the notes to his collection of recordings he lists both "Snake Dance" and "*Yauniho* Dance" as though they were not interchangeable categories (Speck 1911).

MELODIC ANALYSIS

Analysis of the melodies and texts of the available historical Snake Dance Song recordings supports the tentative conclusion that this dance originated as a distinct genre with ceremonial associations.

The well-preserved Fewkes recording of Noel Josephs (example 14) will serve as the exemplar, recalling that Fewkes declared all the Snake Dance Songs the same. The song is in two parts, suggesting an antiphonal performance style; the first section is slow, less rhythmically regular, less markedly rhythmic, and less tuneful than the second; it is more like a call, and ends with an exclamation, whereas the second section is tuneful, rhythmically regular, and repeated. The southeastern and Iroquoian dances to which a connection has been posited use antiphonally sung songs. Noel Josephs's solo performance here could have been due to the limitations of the recording equipment, which required a singer to face directly into a cone.

The melodic contour of Noel Josephs's first phrase is a falling fourth, made up of a second and a minor third. In the melody of Speck cylinder 5046, "Snake Dance," the first phrase features a rising fourth, including a minor third and a second (example 15). This is the inversion of Noel Josephs's motive.

Five Snake Dance Songs sung by Maliseet singers were recorded by William Hubbs Mechling around the same time as Speck made his recordings (Mechling 1911). Three of these share a similar melodic outline in what seems to be the second of their multiple sections: cylinder 8 (example 16, part 2); cylinder 13 (example 17, part 2); and cylinder 25 (example 18, part 2). In cylinders 8 and 25 these sections share the range of a sixth; cylinder 13 emphasizes this range except for the intermediate phrase endings on low C#. All three segments share the same pentatonic scale form of tonic, minor third, two major seconds, with the subtonic a major second below.[16]

The tunes are close enough to be related and perhaps are variants of a melodic family. All three examples emphasize the opening interval of the major third; the tonic is a minor third below the opening. In scale structure, they are similar to Speck's cylinder 5046 (example 15). Even if the structures of these opening phrase motives are vestiges of an archaic pentatonic melodic system, this in itself is interesting, given the presence of other pitches outside the pentatonic scale in these songs. The recorded versions could be elaborations of an older basic melodic type. The texts are similar to the first section of Noel Josephs's Snake Dance Song (example 14).

Of the other Snake Dance Songs in the Speck and Mechling collections, Mechling cylinders 19 and 35 (example 19) share melodies and texts; the melodies are similar to that of a War Dance Song in the collection, cylinder 38 (example 10). They are fast and consist of short phrases, repeated.

Speck cylinders 5060, "First Dance," and 5061, "*Yauniho* Dance," share the text *yuneha, yauniho* and have similar melodies. The second phrases of these melodies are similar to the closing phrase of the Greeting Chant "*He, Qanute.*" A feature is the play with emphasis between the syllables of the text: *yuNEha, YAUniho.* Both songs were sung by a Penobscot singer and are followed by a Wedding Dance of the social type.

Speck did not include a description of a "*Yauniho* Dance," nor any analysis of this type of song in his book. I suspect that these are the fast segments of Snake Dance Songs as done at weddings, a usage Speck does discuss. "*Yauniho*" is the first of the *pemege'wintowahgan* 'Dance Song [*sic*],' refrains Speck presented in discussing social dances in *Penobscot Man* ([1940] 1997:167). The contiguous presentation of these recordings in the Speck collection—"First Dance" and "*Yauniho* Dance" sung with a Wedding Dance

Song—and their use of the archaic vocables Speck later transcribed as *Yuneha* both suggest that they are all connected to the marriage ceremony.

Nicholas Smith recorded Andrew Dana singing a Penobscot Snake Dance Song in the 1950s. Dana's song is also in two parts, the first slow and the second fast (Smith 1959, track 27).[17] The opening of the slow part shares the melody of Speck cylinder 5046 (example 15), rising a minor third plus a second before falling back by thirds to a fifth, one step below the starting pitch.

Smith also recorded singers from another family singing a Snake Dance Song that is a version of this same slow melody, which, a Penobscot Elder indicated, is a very old song. A variant of this version is today sung for healing and for prayers on various occasions in the Sipayik community. According to one Passamaquoddy singer, it was taught to the women of Sipayik by a Mi'kmaq Elder. This suggests that the tune is known in all three communities, and the healing property attributed to it agrees with Sable's analysis of the Mi'kmaq Serpent Dance. (Given its current use, a transcription of the song would be inappropriate.)

A commercial recording by the Kitpu Singers of a Mi'kmaq Snake Dance Song (*Mte'skmuey*) has an opening phrase that also follows the melody type of a minor third plus a second, descending like the Fewkes recording but with the intervals reversed (example 20). It is sung first by a leader, answered by the chorus of drummers, and accompanied by the large, stationary Dance Drum used for intertribal powwow songs. The fully antiphonal style of this performance is similar to that of Cherokee Stomp Dance Songs, rather than typical powwow songs, which feature alternation only at the opening of each verse.

Summary Interpretation

The evidence from recordings suggests that Passamaquoddy, Penobscot, and Maliseet Snake Dance Songs formerly were two-part pieces: the first part slow and unmeasured; the second fast with a strong beat and a polyrhythmic relationship between drumming, dancing, and text declamation. This two-part form—slow song for ceremonial action plus fast song for celebratory dancing—is typical of the Wampum Records ceremonies and suggests a connection, even though the Snake Dance is usually described today as a social dance.

The melodies of Snake Dance songs, in particular the slow sections, appear distinctive: structured around five tones, without semitones (anhemitonic pentatonic), they have a prevalent motive of a fourth comprising a minor third plus a major second (or vice-versa), whether rising or falling in pitch. This interval structure is found in Passamaquoddy, Maliseet, and Penobscot Snake Dance Songs recorded between 1890 and 1911, as well as in a contemporary

Mi'kmaq recording and a contemporary song used for healing in the Passama-quoddy and Penobscot communities.

Over the past century, it seems that the two parts of the Snake Dance Songs became separated: the slow segment with its characteristic melody used for healing, and the fast segments incorporated into the group of those used for ad hoc accompaniment to social dancing. Since many of these fast segments are tunes used for other dances on the historical recordings, they may already have been part of this group. The Kitpu Singers' Snake Dance Song differs from other singers' use of "generic" dancing songs for the Snake Dance.

Another element distinguishing both slow and fast Snake Dance Song segments within Passamaquoddy and Penobscot repertories are the syllables *Yuneha*, found in the examples recorded over a span of nearly 110 years. These syllables are considered archaic by consultants, and in this regard the songs are like others associated with Wabanaki wampum protocols. The texts are not apparently related to words for the creature "snake'" or "snaking" motions.

The use of the Snake Dance in association with the wampum protocols is documented by Hagar and Speck, and reinforced in the public presentation devised by Joseph A. Nicholas. Fewkes, Hagar, Speck, Sable, and others have suggested symbolic associations with this dance formation that go beyond sociality into the realm of medicine, healing, and spiritual power.

For Waponahkik, the descriptions published by Fewkes and Hagar seem to be the earliest documentation of the serpentine social dance. If it emerged from the solo dance associated with power, it may have been guarded previously. This dance could have been old before the 1890s, even though we have no earlier descriptions, since the descriptions of other Wabanaki dance genres existing in the late nineteenth century are surprisingly similar to those from the eighteenth and even seventeenth centuries (see chapters 5 and 6). The persistence of melodic formulas associated with this genre throughout its functional permutations argues for the integrity of its distinct status.

Whether the origins of the Snake Dance go further back in time, to an archaic cultural period (i.e., 10,000 to 3,000 years ago), is an intriguing speculation but cannot be proved.[18] The symbolic associations of the movements and similarities with ceremonial dance traditions of other eastern peoples hint at deep levels of connection. As proposed in the discussion of Peace Pipe Ceremony Dances, ceremonial elements may date to a period before the cultural differentiation so evident in seventeenth-century European accounts of eastern Native Americans. The prominence of snakes in Native iconography and in healing and religious traditions across the Americas is suggestive. Commonalities with other Eastern Woodlands cultures are especially interesting in light of archaeological evidence of contacts during the Ceramic period with Mississippian culture and trade networks along the East Coast (Bourque 2001:92–100). Like Peace Pipe ceremonies, the contemporary Snake Dance may be a return to common cultural themes.

In any case, the obvious connections of the Passamaquoddy Snake Dance to medicine make explicit the power that dancing adds to ceremonies. Power is present in the other dance genres associated with the wampum protocols as well, harnessed to specific ritual functions.

The Round Dance

A feature of contemporary Wabanaki socials and powwows is the Round Dance, an intertribal dance that makes use of the circle as a symbol of unity. This is one of the dances that bystanders are encouraged to participate in. At powwows, I have heard many of the Native participants express that one goal of the event is to get everyone dancing together. I have also observed dancing used as a tool to combat conflict at events, with dancers positioning themselves in the circle to "dance against" a perceived troublemaker (AMS 24Jun.95). On one occasion of social dancing, an unsupervised child ran across the dance circle while an intertribal round dance was in progress, and although the dancers did not stop, suddenly the drummers lost control of a beater. This was used as an occasion for teaching by the master of ceremonies, who related the power of the circle to the bonds of community and admonished that it should not be broken (AMS 23Jun.95).

It requires many individuals to make a full circle around the drummers, if they are positioned in the center; but a Round Dance can also be done with an arc of dancers. The "grapevine" step most commonly used is similar to that of the Israeli *hora* and other Mediterranean and central European line dances (one steps with the leading foot in front of the other foot, with which one then steps sideways; then one steps with the leading foot behind the other foot, with which one steps sideways again). The leading foot may be changed whenever the singers move to a bridge section of a traditional song or the antiphonal opening section of an intertribal powwow-style song. During this, the new leading foot is moved forward and back in place (usually eight times) before the singers pick up the verse again. When I have observed this dance in Waponahkik, the step across front with the leading foot has always been the stepping-off point (*contra* Burton 1993:63). An easier version is simply to slide-step alternately with each foot sideways, changing direction after the bridge section of the accompanying song.

Wabanaki Drum groups use a variety of songs for this dance, some from traditional local repertories and some modern powwow-style songs. Sometimes,

169

songs associated with other dances are employed. The beat is usually straight, iambic; but sometimes the triplet pattern associated with the Two-Step genre is used. This is difficult to fit the steps to, and one consultant said a song of this type was not a correct choice for this dance (AMS 13Aug.95).

As previously noted, the Round Dance genre described in Speck's ethnography of Penobscot life is close to the modern Passamaquoddy Wedding Dance. Speck noted that this dance was "the most general," being designated *alnigan* or *alnoba'gan*, "person's dance," and he describes its use as ubiquitous.

Round Dances are one of the basic group dance formations performed around the world, so it is not possible to state definitively the origins of this Round Dance. Differences consist of whether the dancers move in a single line, in couples, or in larger squadrons; and whether there are any movements within the basic circular progression of the dance, such as switching directions or trading places. The Round Dance genre performed in Passamaquoddy communities today could be indigenous. It is similar to the intertribal variety but may be related also to French folk dances. Many of the French who settled in Acadia came from Brittany, and there are several Breton Round Dances that are strikingly similar in form and choreography to the those that Peskotomuhkatiyik perform today. A single line of dancers moves clockwise with a step that crosses the feet as described above, and there are variations in arm movement, footwork, and additional choreography. Thus, this dance may predate the influence of the Powwow in its "intertribal" function as well as specific elements of its choreography. We know from accounts of Passamaquoddy public ceremonies and social occasions that dancing has long been an activity shared by Natives and non-Natives.[19]

Dance Music as a Site of Cultural Interaction at Sipayik

At Sipayik, Euro-American social dances have been included at events along with traditional dancing since at least the early twentieth century; Speck noted this also at Penawahpskek ([1940] 1997:245). Joseph A. Nicholas remembered his grandparents playing piano and other Western instruments for European dances held in the same dance hall as traditional dances. Music was taught at residential schools and in the military. Several members of the Sipayik community attended the Carlisle Indian School in Pennsylvania and learned to play orchestral instruments there. Jazz cornet player Bennie Francis had a celebrated career in dance bands, even touring Europe. David A. Francis believes that Bennie learned the instrument at the Carlisle School. He led Francis's Famous Orchestra, which toured extensively around Maine and New Brunswick (Tomer n.d.). Sipayik had an excellent marching band from the late nineteenth century, as did Motahkomikuk (Walker 1973); both were all-male organizations. The bands participated in local parades, accompanied the reservation baseball teams to away games, and were often photographed; they disbanded some time before World War Two.[20]

At present, many Peskotomuhkatiyik are involved with different styles of music. All my contacts firmly distinguish Native music from Western, even though some singers accompany traditional songs with guitar and other non-Native instruments. Generally speaking, current popular music is felt to lack the spiritual significance of Native songs, chants, and instruments. The Native American flute has become popular, and Rolf Richter from Sipayik has established himself as an excellent and respected flutist. The adoption of this instrument so much later than powwow-style drumming is most likely due to the difficulty of playing it well. This type of flute requires players to formulate an individual style, requiring much practice.

The differences between older Passamaquoddy drums, songs, and singing styles and styles adopted more recently are openly discussed in the community. Adaptation and creativity are thus open to social control, but the prevailing attitude has not been one of exclusion. Accommodations are made in ceremonies for the inclusion of different repertories and styles. This is another manifestation of the aesthetic of adapting preexisting materials. It also articulates respect for the power of singing, drumming, and dancing. The borders of the tradition are clearly marked, but there is room for all that is honorably offered.

EIGHT

Aesthetics and Survival

Performances of the ceremonies of the Wabanaki Confederacy at the Sipayik Indian Days are contrasted throughout this study with performances of the same protocols in other contexts. The Indian Day presentations differ from other contemporary performances in that they are reconstructions for a general audience, with a primary purpose of educating outsiders about Passamaquoddy and Wabanaki traditions. Adaptations are made for this purpose and to accommodate the public.

Some elements in the Indian Day context, however, are similar to the primarily ceremonial tribal occasions on which the same protocols are used, and there are demonstrable connections between the Indian Day and traditional contexts. The event takes place during the prime summer season in Peskotomuhkatik, a time when Waponahkiyik customarily camped on the seacoast, family bands gathered together, and allies visited each other. The contemporary Sipayik Indian Day still contains the component of welcoming visiting tribes and leaders to a gathering on the shore. The presentation of the ceremonial protocols by a master of ceremonies recalls the historical tradition of a Wampum Keeper publicly reciting Confederacy protocols from the wampum belts that encoded them in mnemonic symbols.

The Indian Day can thus be understood as an important component in the process of transmitting these traditions to younger generations within the community. The transmission of traditions today is both frustrated and mediated by the conditions under which contemporary Passamaquoddy people live. This chapter will consider how the ceremonial protocols have been maintained under these circumstances, analyzing the social factors that have influenced the adaptations noted in previous chapters.

Modifications of the ceremonies have kept them functional in changing social circumstances. When analyzed all together, these adaptations appear as part of larger processes involved in the survival of Passamaquoddy culture and of Peskotomuhkatiyik as an identifiable group. An aesthetic is revealed underlying these processes which is based in traditional practice and can be understood as a cultural theme. The principle animating extemporization and recombination of stock melodies in song performance (discussed in chapter 3 and noted in the analyses of individual ceremonies) can be related by analogy to other domains of Passamaquoddy culture; parallel techniques for adapting to circumstances are evident in the traditional political system and in the language.

The Transmission of Song Style

The wampum protocols are public events, even when they are restricted to Native people or to members of the tribe. Those who lead them are mostly adults whose experience and skill is recognized by the community. These events transmit the traditions from generation to generation and are occasions of learning for younger people. All participants acquire skills, whether they sing, dance, give a speech, or just listen and observe.

Transmission is essential to the maintenance of any tradition. Among Peskotomuhkatiyik today, transmission may be through face-to-face contact, through recordings, and through formal instruction in schools or in adult study groups. But the contexts in which songs and dances are learned shape the meanings that they carry. Up to this point, the discussion has focused on specific ceremonial uses of songs and dances; the significance that these elements convey is multiplied and enriched by associations that extend outside ceremonies. A brief consideration of these is needed to support the analysis offered in concluding this study.

In the past fifty years the Passamaquoddy communities have emphasized cultural transmission in public situations, including school classes and extracurricular drumming and dancing groups. But transmission within families remains strong, as many of my contacts emphasized in interviews. Seemingly insignificant private genres such as lullabies and game songs acquaint children with musical and linguistic principles of pronunciation, syllabification, and pitch inflection.[1] These short songs, which like the dance songs exist as recognized "core" stanzas that are then varied to suit any occasion, appear among those recorded over the last century by collectors. They are well known in the community, passed from generation to generation, aural evidence of the intimate contact – and stability – that living together provides.

The Role of Grandmothers

Most of my contacts recalled that someone in their families had taught them the songs and dances that they knew. Grandmothers were identified as principal teachers of language and also of songs, which help to teach the language. In addition to the knowledge itself, the value of passing it on was transmitted, as one consultant attested:

> [My grandmother] really has had an influence on my life—I was encouraged to be proud of who you are, and to continue on the traditions that she learned from her mother and her grandmother....Actually she's had an influence on many people's lives, really. It's real important that we not forget that she wanted us to pass it on, from one generation to the next.

He felt that the recent shift in reservation communities toward having their schools teach Native culture was no excuse for parents to neglect teaching language and culture at home:

> It's really important that individuals take on that responsibility. Because this is the responsibility of each and every one of us. It isn't the responsibility of the school, it isn't the responsibility of the tribal government, it's not the responsibility of all these different organizations. The responsibility is each and every one of us that are on this earth and on the reservation. Their Ancestors have influenced them to keep passing on some of those traditions and customs. So it really stems from the home. (AMS 22Feb.95)

In the past as well as today, if young families faced economic hardship, it was often the grandmothers who cared for young children while both parents worked. Thus grandmothers were often the first person a child communicated with, and it was often in the Passamaquoddy language. Children watched while grandmothers pursued traditional tasks such as sweetgrass braiding and basket weaving, and listened while they said their prayers in "Old Passamaquoddy." Many older women are addressed as "Grandmother" by children who are only distantly related to them, because they fulfill these teaching roles in the community.

Several of my adult consultants at Sipayik remember that the dance group Joseph A. Nicholas started was important in their cultural development. A group of women, contemporaries of Joseph's son, clarified that they felt especially grateful to Mary Moore; she was Joseph's collaborator, of the same generation as their grandparents, and the person who taught them the dance steps (AMS 25Jun.95). Another Elder was remembered for having taught her own sons, daughters, and successive generations of young people to dance before Joseph's group was founded, often taking informal groups to the Penobscot Reservation at Indian Island for social and ceremonial occasions (AMS 22Apr.95).

Joseph A. Nicholas pointed out that he was raised by his grandmother, Fanny Nicholas, and that she had also raised his cousin Blanche Sockabasin, another prominent singer in the Passamaquoddy community today. Joseph remembered that his family members were all very musical: one played piano, another violin, another drums. His grandfather Horace kept the instruments of the Sipayik marching band and played several of them himself (AMS 28Feb.95).

The consultant quoted above points out an important shift in the contexts of song and dance transmission from private to public, the home to schools and youth programs administered by the tribal government. The teachers in these new institutions are very often women, however; so their role is preserved even as their status as teachers has changed. Similar changes were noted by Beverly Diamond in Abenaki and Montagnais-Naskapi communities in the 1980s (Cavanagh 1989:60–61).

Children's Songs

The songs sung in childhood seem to have made great impressions on my consultants. All could remember the game songs, pastimes, and lullabies that they learned and sang in the context of family and social life. The examples shared with me serve the process of cultural transmission in several capacities: the rhythm and cadence of the language is emphasized by melodic pitches; typical melodic organization patterns are learned in the phrase structures; and cultural values are conveyed by the texts.

Passamaquoddy lullabies are called *Baylo baylo* songs. David A. Francis remembered that parents used to string up ropes across a corner of the one-room houses, and drape a blanket over the ropes to make a cradle. A cord was attached to the ropes so that a baby resting in the blanket could be rocked, even when the attending adult was across the room, engaged in some other activity. He remembers his mother cooking at the stove, working the cord to keep the baby quiet, singing and humming songs.

Baylo baylo melodies are simple, following the intonation of the language (example 21). The importance of "baby talk" syllables for the development of linguistic pattern recognition is important, however.

Pastime Songs

"*Mahqankatik*" (Example 22) is sung casually for amusement, to pass the time. The lyrics describe how people used to take canoes down the coast in the early spring when the maple sap was running. They didn't have much food at that time of the year, but made do by chewing dried fish skins (*nuhkomeqotekon*).[2] According to David A. Francis, the word "*Mahqankatik*" here means specifically New Hampshire.

Another family reported that every spring people from Peter Dana's Point used to go across Big Lake to a sap place (also mentioned by another consultant from Sipayik), and that the codfish skin was a treat given to the kids for fun on this occasion. They insisted it was not a hardship—they had loved it!—and the song, often sung for children, reflects this attitude (AMS 29Oct.95). Whether the words encode a memory of hard times or not, this song teaches an important aspect of the traditional yearly life cycle. The late winter sugaring was the break with winter's solitary hunting and the beginning of the gathering and planting season. Further, the song fits the physical rhythm of paddling a canoe, and if the refrain words are pronounced "upiye-wi-he-ye" may refer to the paddle dipping in and out of the water.

The melody of the song verse exactly fits the intonation and stress of the words it sets except for the syllable *nuh-*, which is set to a low tone but stressed durationally so that its meaning is clear. Tonal inflection is the hardest aspect of the Passamaquoddy language to learn for persons who have not grown up surrounded by it. Songs like this help to reinforce the feel of correct intonation, and both this and the following example are used in the bilingual program in the reservation schools. Other verses have been added to this tune that have no connection to maple sugaring.

The game song "*Liwisu*" (S/he is named, example 23), is performed by children, frequently in school, where it serves both to introduce everyone's name and to teach children to extemporize words to song melodies. This ability is highly valued in song leaders, who must keep dancers going by linking songs together (as discussed in previous chapters); extemporizing words to preexisting melodies also encourages the adaptation of "traditional" tunes to new contexts.

"*Liwisu*" is frequently sung by adults as a joke and is ubiquitous in William Mechling's recordings of Maliseet singers. It is unclear whether the endearment *nitapehsis welaqik* (my little friend whom I met last night) is associated by adults with the very adult pastimes of flirting, sexual encounters, and drinking. Similar phrases occur in the two Lonesome Songs (love songs) recorded by Frank Speck, one of which he labeled a Drinking Song (1928:197). Song texts on this combination of subjects, full of innuendo and ironic humor, are found in many twentieth-century Native American repertories. A powwow genre called Forty-nine Songs is one example, reflecting the human realities of reservation life.

The joking "Priest Song" on Speck's cylinder 5075 uses "*Liwisu*" to represent the scenario of a priest having attractive company. In a Penobscot version recorded by David McAllester, the singer states, "Don't anyone be jealous, I am just like a priest," before launching into "*Liwisu*." This seems to have been a running joke throughout Waponahkik, though it could be black humor in light of the sexual abuses uncovered in residential schools (see chapter 1).

176

Generic Dance Songs

Short songs used for dancing and not proper to specific ceremonies have been noted throughout the previous chapters. In most cases these short songs appeared in the celebratory second section of a ceremonial procedure. Singers refer to them as "just dance songs," and the classification *generic* seems appropriate. Joseph A. Nicholas emphasized the distinction between these and songs proper to ceremonies when he distinguished a "core" of Passamaquoddy songs and remarked, "The others you hear around here are very short" (AMS 28Feb.95). On recordings made in early decades of the twentieth century, singers and their audiences often giggle through renditions of these songs, and one singer on Nicholas Smith's tapes apologizes "That's all!" after singing one.

Nevertheless, these short songs sung and learned in casual contexts were a means of preserving musical traditions under external, colonial pressures. Their apparent insignificance did not attract attention, yet they could provide coded references and jokes and otherwise undercut the appearance of the situation in which they were deployed. These and other songs are used similarly today.[3]

A subgenre of the short generic dance song melodies is made up of those associated with lyrics that make historical references. "Historical songs"—as we may call them to distinguish them from others—serve to transmit information about the past events and life of the Passamaquoddy people. I have heard only adults sing historical songs, and although they are sung for children, they also serve important functions in adult social life. Two historical songs are melodic cognates of songs sung to accompany ceremonial dancing today. It is arguable whether ceremonial use made these melodies prominent choices to set historical texts; or whether song melodies associated with these particular texts are now being used symbolically in ceremonies. Different consultants make different claims. In any case, once learned, the associations provide subtexts that add interest by reinforcing or conflicting with the overt meaning of the ceremonial activity.

The short lyrics of *Qonasqamki monihkuk* (Example 24) refer to the departure of the Passamaquoddy people from St. Andrews, New Brunswick. This was one of the original settlements of the tribe, but dispersed in the eighteenth century when Loyalists from New Jersey moved there from the rebel colonies. There is historical evidence that Peskotomuhkatiyik—coastal Etechemin—did not abandon the Canadian side; the U.S. Indian Agent Nutt mentions in his 1860 report that members of the Passamaquoddy Tribe were sick with smallpox near Magaguadavic, New Brunswick. But today that third Passamaquoddy Tribe, headquartered at St. Andrews, is not recognized by the Canadian federal government. Peskotomuhkatiyik continued to reside primarily on that side and

177

visits over the border were common. Many elderly people remember winters when Passamaquoddy Bay froze over and people from Sipayik walked across the ice to visit family in St. Andrews. They made the trip by canoe at other times of the year.

St. Andrews can be seen across the bay from Sipayik, and Joseph A. Nicholas recalls that his grandmother used to sit on her porch and rock in her rocking chair, singing this song while looking over toward St. Andrews (AMS 28Feb.95). The lyrics ensure that the connection to St. Andrews will not be forgotten but encode the reference in a cryptic fragment and in the Passamaquoddy language so that outsiders will not understand. When teaching me the song, Joseph A. Nicholas joked, "Say it was sung by a man of few words!" a double entendre because as a public figure he spent so much time talking.

The tune of this song is the same as that to which the lyrics *kakawtehkomusic* (dance faster) also are sung. The question of which came first proved to be both unanswerable and irrelevant to my consultants; the association of the St. Andrews lyrics with this melody is established in their minds. The version given was transcribed from a cassette recorded by Joe Nicholas and features in the final phrases the kind of flexible rhythm for which singers are prized.

The second of these historical songs, "*Qayuwa*," takes its title from the refrain, which means "they are angry" (example 25), though it does not name a specific object of or reason for the anger. The lyrics may well refer to injustices the Passamaquoddy people have suffered, but only one consultant agreed with this interpretation. Delia Mitchell, a highly regarded singer from Motahkomikuk, has sung it several times for the Sipayik Indian Days, and it is sometimes danced to. It is the briefest of all the dance songs, and does not seem to have a ceremonial association; according to consultants, it is used merely to accompany dances. The transcription is from my recording of the 1994 Indian Day; a version of the song has also been published by the Wabanaki Bilingual Education Program.

The close relationship between ceremonial and nonceremonial versions of such songs is a crucial element in their symbolic function within contemporary ceremonies, for the outside referands can create a coded subtext to the public ceremonial action. In the case of "*Qayuwa*," many interpretations are possible. It may be a reminder of the centuries of oppression the Passamaquoddy people have endured, and the anger that led them to their land claims case.

Contrafacta

Additional subtexts also emerge when Passamaquoddy singers extemporize new song texts to preexisting melodies, creating *contrafacta* with layers of references.[4] A new text may refer to the event in progress or a current situation, whereas the tune it is sung to carries associations from other contexts. The effect is similar to that of a linguistic pun but is not necessarily humorous. A few melodies are used over and over, acquiring a multiplicity of meanings. These will be especially rich for listeners familiar with the tradition and with older generations of singers, who have heard the songs on many occasions. As argued above, performance contexts are an important source of meaning in the Passamaquoddy musical system, and the generally evocative quality of song melodies and lyrics is supplemented by specific strategies of extemporization that are part of the aesthetic of Passamaquoddy singing style.[5]

Since the vocal inflections of lyrics must be matched to melodic contours, some newly composed texts are carefully worked out in advance of performance. Two examples of such *contrafacta* written by David A. Francis and Joseph A. Nicholas address social issues faced by the tribe. They set words exhorting Waponahkiyik to come together in unity to the tune of the dance song "*Aliyaha, Aliyaqanute*" (example 2). Their new text uses metaphors of dancing, which work in concert with the *Aliyaha* melody associated with dancing, to convey the message on several levels simultaneously (example 26).

Another of their songs, "*Nil te nkason weciyuki*" sets a comment about first-cousin marriage (and other perceived social problems) to the *Tuhtuwas* Dance Song melody (example 27); still another they have set to this tune warns against drinking alcohol ("*Musa kotuhsomihkoc puktewick*," example 28). The refrain used in these two songs, "*Sami motoweyu*" (isn't it a shame), is often sung in the context of dancing even without the verse lyrics.

The Aesthetics of Song Performance

I asked a Passamaquoddy singer to describe how he had made up words to a song to make it fitting for an occasion I had observed. He noted, "There's one way of doing it that works. You can't just use any words, you have to use certain rhythms.... It's the *form* you have to stay loyal to.... It's not necessarily *rhyming*, more *timing*. It's got to end on the right inflection" (AMS 12Oct.96; emphasis original). He thinks that this way of singing, extemporizing new words, is the way singers traditionally approached performance but noted, "It's just my personal opinion, I can't *prove* it." The approach has broad musical style implications, as it requires an extremely flexible rhythmic sense, and the song melody often must be stretched to fit the new words. This is not possible if the accompaniment is the powerful powwow drum played by several drummers in unison, but it accords with historical evidence and traditional Passamaquoddy singing style (as discussed in chapter 3). Short, slight songs such as "*Mahqankatik*" and "*Liwisu*," to which new words are constantly added for games and pastimes, train young people to appreciate and excel in extemporization. Thus, despite their low position in the culture, these songs fulfill a core function in the transmission of tradition.

The multiple layers of reference and coded references in songs used to accompany dance ultimately serve as techniques of reinterpretation. For example, the appearance of the refrain *sami motoweyu*, associated with two new songs about social problems (first-cousin marriage and drinking) in the extemporized songs accompanying the Peace Pipe Dance at the 1995 Sipayik Indian Day, seemed to complicate the meaning of that dance. The Indian Day, was taking place after months of community division. There had been a recall vote on one tribal governor, and a federal investigation of nepotism in the other tribal government represented at the Indian Day. The presence of this refrain associated with songs propounding what are considered traditional values could be interpreted as affirming those traditions in the face of problems exacerbated by the outside administrative structures that tribal governments must assume.[6] This interpretation is consistent with the notion of the Indian Day context as a reworking of the wampum recitation—yet the singer, when queried on the songs she had chosen to sing, replied, "They're just dance songs, *tuss* [hon']!" Earlier, however, she had used the melody and refrain associated with the historical St. Andrews song to accompany the fast dance between *Sakomak* in the concluding section of the Greeting Dance.

These juxtapositions create a counterpoint of messages, whether or not the singers intend them on any given occasion. Many consultants firmly believe that singers traditionally have exploited the multivalent potential of songs: "They hid things in the songs," insisted one consultant, discussing older generations of Passamaquoddy singers. And in discussing the song "*Qayuwa*" Delia Mitchell's niece pointed out the poetic inversion that occurs when songs referencing unhappy events are used to accompany dancing: "In dancing to them, the people found joy" (AMS 28Oct. 95). Thus irony becomes a means of resisting oppression.

Analogy to the technique of irony is made possible by the multiple levels at which signification is possible in the wampum ceremonies. Choreography, melodies, and lyrics all carry meaning. The mimetic nature of the choreography can convey the ostensible function of a dance, while song melodies add historical references, and lyrics relate the performance to the specific occasion. These can also be inverted and played with, as shown. Such techniques are skillfully deployed by all participants, and singers especially are valued for their ability to make extemporaneous meaning. Thus, the short, even fragmentary, nature of the Passamaquoddy musical repertoire appears to be an aesthetic choice that accords with principles of a musical style system.

This conclusion is bolstered by 117 years of recordings in which the same performance practices appear consistently; however, this finding contradicts those of previous researchers in Waponahkik. Frank Speck described the Penobscot repertory as fragmentary and degenerate in the early twentieth century ([1940] 1997:270–71; 303–5), and Philip Bock similarly noted at midcentury that Mi'kmaq musical traditions had almost disappeared (Bock 1966:85–86), replaced by Western genres. These observations can of course be true if the listener tries to fit Wabanaki repertories to the standards of Western European folk music systems. Neither Speck's nor Bock's study was focused on analyzing songs or discerning a musical system, and the traditions certainly have been altered by sociocultural factors. But I argue that in the Passamaquoddy community, at least, core principles were maintained because extemporization is at the heart of them.

Dance Song Construction, Linguistics, and Political Organization

This argument can be supported with reference to other domains of Passamaquoddy culture. An analogous situation exists in the Passamaquoddy language, which is characterized by compound words. Words are created by combining lexemes into long strings of meaningful parts, using inflections.[7] There is a large stable vocabulary, but new words can be improvised for a given situation, and there are many local variations. The construction of words is like the performance of dance songs: analogous to the lexemes there is a certain set of musical motives; like the inflections on lexemes, these are matched in a certain order by rhythmic-melodic cadences; these motives may be extended by repetition, or cut, or varied with addenda. Whole songs are also strung together to accompany a period of dancing.

The analogy between musical and linguistic repertory can be extended when the adaptive essence of both is considered. The words formed in Passamaquoddy are frequently descriptive, as demonstrated in the discussion of terms for musical instruments (chapter 4). This allows new words to be generated, as for "hair curlers": *topuwuhutikonok*. The principles organizing compounding also allow for the importation of words from other languages as lexemes, fitting them with Passamaquoddy prefixes and suffixes, as in *npenom*, my pen: the English word *pen*, affixed with the Passamaquoddy first person singular possessive *n-* and an animate noun ending *-om*.[8] The result is a vibrant language that allows for considerable variation from speaker to speaker and for adaptation to changing semantic needs while maintaining intelligibility, much like the personal variations that singers make to songs in performance.

Another analogy to the formative principles of song performance can be drawn in the traditional political organizations in Waponahkik. Historical sources refer to different organizational units: families, bands, tribes, nations, and confederacies. The formation during the colonial period of synthetic communities, of refugees or Christian converts, is also evident (as discussed in chapter 1). During the seventeenth and eighteenth centuries rapid changes in social alignments were occurring in response to invasion, colonization, trade, warfare, and disease. Although the situation was fluid, recent ethnohistorical research has demonstrated that Native responses followed discernible principles that lent organization to a potentially chaotic scene. The formation of the Wabanaki Confederacy was one response.

To understand the dynamics of the response and its relation to musical composition requires a brief review of social structure. Migratory winter hunting bands formed around the smallest social unit, the family. Some of these included more than one generation, as men commonly provided for their wives' parents for a time. Larger encampments, long- or short-term, might include adult siblings and their families. Men took as many wives as they could support, but excessive numbers are not documented. When warfare was necessary, messengers were sent to gather potential warriors from different encampments. They would pledge to join war parties, but allies do not seem to have been compelled always to support each other in war, as shown by their different allegiances during the War for American Independence.

In characterizing Wabanaki social bonds, A. H. Morrison has noted that leaders were chosen, that individual family heads could choose to belong to the community or not, and that the alliances leaders made were fluid (1976:4–8). Comparing both French and English sources to anthropological models, Morrison points out that "*tribe-level confederations* can be considered the norm for the seventeenth-century Wabanaki. These seem to have ranged between simple and complex extremes, apparently depending a great deal upon the personal influence of individual leaders therein" (1976:2; emphasis original).

The English tendency to identify Native people by the place names where they settled, sometimes temporarily, reflects these subgroups but does not reflect the fluidity of the situation. The French tended to distinguish larger groups based on language differences.

Charismatic leaders united different bands into confederacies, an example being the Mi'kmaq *Sakom* Membertou. These confederacies on some occasions combined forces in warfare, as when a large expedition under Membertou attacked the "Almouchiquois" settlement at what is now Saco, Maine, in 1607, as documented by Champlain and Lescarbot. A. H. Morrison models Membertou's alliance as a "superconfederation." The early eighteenth-century Wabanaki Confederacy is a "super-superconfederation" in Morrison's terms, bringing together the opposing superconfederations involved in the 1607 attack, and other groups as well. (See the diagram in A. H. Morrison 1976.)

The presence of people Father Sebastian Rale called *Amalingans* near his Catholic settlement at Norridgewock, Maine, evidences the blending of formerly far-flung Native groups in mission stations by the first quarter of the eighteenth century. Individuals by this time might migrate far in the course of their lives, as in the case of the charismatic leader Wattanummon, whose career was analyzed by Evan Haefeli and Kevin Sweeney (1994). Other examples include Paugus (Eckstorm 1939), Nescambiouit (Bourque 2001:180), and Kancamagus (Calloway 1990:82–94. The settlement at St. Francis/Odanak in Quebec was nominally Abenaki but included Huron/Wendat people (the writer Peter Paul Wzokhilain is a prominent example). Western Etchemins, such as the Wawenock descendants interviewed by Frank Speck (1928), also resided at the nominally Abenaki community of Beçancour (Wôlinak), Quebec.

At least two principles appear to have operated in these situations. First is the principle of choice: leaders were chosen to hold the responsibilities of overseeing communal welfare and could command large groups, if they were persuasive enough, when the need arose. Individuals could choose where to place their allegiance, and many migrated when the smaller community social structures began to break down in the late seventeenth and early eighteenth centuries. The second principle that emerges is adaptation to changing circumstances. This is not to argue that Waponahkiyik were fickle or disorganized but rather that they were habituated to making judicious alliances and were not subservient to a fixed hierarchy.

When these different cultural domains are compared, an underlying aesthetic principle is revealed which is comparable to Ruth Benedict's concept of a cultural configuration (Benedict 1932, 1934; Bateson 1958).[9] While broad essentialisms must be used with caution, as there are always exceptions, synthesizing what is needed from preexisting parts appears to be a characteristic Passamaquoddy cultural theme. The aesthetic may be considered characteristic of Wabanaki culture and can further be extended to their quick adoption of European trade goods, some replacing technologies that were inferior (iron kettles for wooden trenchers) and others adapted for Wabanaki purposes (tall silk hats for women's headdress), as Ruth Whitehead (2001) has demonstrated.

The techniques used by singers and others in performing the ceremonies, and by audiences in interpreting them, are drawn from a repertory that has its basis in past experience. This recalls Pierre Bourdieu's concept of the *habitus* as a repertory of ideas and practices, shared by a group, from which individuals draw when living their lives (1977:72–95). Bourdieu's intuition of the flexibility of cultural systems distinguishes his theory, and makes it especially helpful in understanding how Passamaquoddy culture has survived.

Adaptation as Resistance

The reworking of Passamaquoddy ceremonies into public contexts such as Indian Day has served to maintain the traditions, while at the same time the public exposure has opened the ceremonies to innovations in style and even content. As in the spiritual traditions sheltered under the rubric of Catholicism (Spinney 2006), taking on European features has made possible the continual practice of ceremonies that otherwise might have been banned. In the nineteenth century, some of the Indian agents disapproved of the annual summer celebrations at Sipayik as too expensive (Erickson 1982:171–72); but the public Indian Day inaugurated by Joseph A. Nicholas in the 1960s as an educational event receives sponsorship from a variety of local and state corporations. The adoption of an election process for governors, wherein leaders have been reelected and maintained in office as they might have been under the preexisting system of charismatic leadership, is another example of this accommodation.

The Indian Day, and the program of wampum protocols that is its centerpiece, can be described as "touristic culture" (Picard and Darling 1996), but it arguably fulfills community needs. The ceremonies have been adapted, in all the various ways previously described (no tobacco, using the powwow drum, breaking formation between the Welcome and Greeting Dances for intertribal dances), specifically to appeal to outsiders. A significant feature of "touristic culture" as social scientists have defined it is that practitioners are consciously performing traditions. It is difficult to ascertain that this was not already the case—the protocols of the Wabanaki Confederacy traditionally were recited at least once a year at gatherings to ensure they would remain in practice. Further, under the gaze of outsiders for several centuries, very little of Passamaquoddy culture remains unconscious in Pierre Bourdieu's sense that "it is because subjects do not, strictly speaking, know what they are doing that what they do has more meaning than they know" (1977:79). This consciousness is often a burden, as expressed to me by one participant in a powwow: "I got sick of people coming up and asking me what tribe I am."

This is not to say that the Indian Day versions of the wampum protocols are simulacra of Passamaquoddy ceremonies. Rather, they are authentic expressions of identity for the majority of Peskotomuhkatiyik, who participate in them as dancers, singers, vendors, or audience. The Indian Day can be framed as an appropriation of traditions, or simply a selection from traditions, by members of the culture itself, for new purposes. The Indian Day fulfills needs that were not being met in traditional internal tribal contexts: principally, the necessity of interacting with outsiders to signal cultural presence and to correct stereotypes.

The interaction that occurs at touristic cultural events is not unidirectional. Events such as Indian Day are enriched by cultural mixing. Native visitors add *their* traditions when asked to lead a dance or song; their regalia is different, their drumming, singing, and dancing styles differ from locally preferred styles. Non-Native visitors, especially researchers and journalists, who brought audiovisual recording equipment to the Indian Days, have prompted members of the tribe to make their own documentation as well.

But the ceremonies described in the Wampum Records were created as hybrids around 1700, as the analyses of individual dances has shown. They were consciously constructed combinations of Wabanaki, Iroquois, and French Catholic protocols and rituals. In the case of the Peace Pipe Ceremony Dance, the sources may be even broader, including traditions from the Northern Plains area.

Thus from their historical source to their current instantiation, the wampum protocols as presented at the Sipayik Indian Day are the site of intertribal accommodation. This is evident on many levels but perhaps most obviously in the schedule of dances. The specific protocols of the Wampum Records, originally linked, have their own logical sequence. At an Indian Day event they are combined with intertribal genres following another logical sequence that begins with a powwow-style Grand Entry, followed by the Welcome Dance. The Greeting Dance would come next in a traditional context, but is sometimes displaced by an intertribal Veterans' Dance and Flag Dance at the Indian Day performances. As noted, the Peace Pipe Ceremony Dance can be connected to the Greeting Dance or be convened separately after an intertribal dance. The War Club Dance is usually convened separately at the Indian Day, but on ceremonial occasions I have seen it emerge from the Greeting Dance or follow the Peace Pipe Dance.

Accommodating Passamaquoddy ceremonial traditions to contemporary Native American intertribal style has been a community process, during which differences of opinion and of taste have surfaced and been smoothed over. Several points emerge from observing the Sipayik Indian Day from the early 1990s to the time of this writing. The problem created by Passamaquoddy women drumming in intertribal contexts has been one of the more serious divisions. The style differences between Passamaquoddy and intertribal sing-ing and dancing are also marked, generally aligning with different generations.

Older people often objected to the vocal tone of intertribal style singing and to the primacy of the propulsive drumbeat. Many also pointed to the use of vocables instead of lexical texts in the song lyrics as a potential loss of Pas-samaquoddy identity. Vocables, though, allow people from different nations to sing and dance together. And younger people, especially those whose families had returned to the reservations after the land claims resolution made doing so economically viable, have stressed that the language was being used to exclude tribal members from other aspects of their own heritage.

One older consultant emphasized differences in the choreography of dances: the intertribal dances emphasize individual expression instead of the group formations of the wampum protocols. He also objected to the strophic forms of the songs, saying he could not follow them, and to the vocable lyrics, which he felt did not distinguish the sections of dances.

The accommodations made in the Indian Day events reflect contemporary Passamaquoddy life. Many participants in ceremonies did not grow up on the reservations or in close contact with a Passamaquoddy community and so do not otherwise practice their heritage. Many have a blended cultural heritage that may include other Native traditions or non-Native traditions. Most criti-cal for the maintenance of the traditional ceremonies is the Passamaquoddy language, and not all participants are fluent speakers, even those who grew up on the reservations.

Accommodations also reflect the educational purpose of the Indian Days. They allow people who are not Passamaquoddy to participate. Many guests come from all over Native North America, wearing their own styles of regalia, dancing in their own style, sometimes leading a dance or song to share their traditions. Sharing is a feature of the "Socials" that are held in the evenings after the scheduled events of the Indian Days.

The Indian Days fall into a category of contemporary Native American practice that is related both to traditional ceremonialism and to popular enter-tainment. In the Indian Days, Peskotomuhkatiyik perform the wampum pro-tocols for several purposes: among them, to maintain traditional practices, to emphasize the community's presence as a political entity, to educate the public about their specific traditions, and to combat stereotypes of Native Americans.

Such hybrid performances have been criticized as self-stereotyping, "re-constructed ethnicity" formulated according to tourists' expectations (Peers 1999:45). There is some evidence of this in the Sipayik Indian Day: some men still wear war bonnets in the style of Plains cultures, and two totem poles by the late Passamaquoddy artist John Francis are erected at the roadside entrance to the public area. Ribbon shirts are worn by many of the dancers; a ubiquitous adaptation to European trade goods across North America, these were not commonly worn in Waponahkik until recently.[10]

Dean MacCannell's discussion of similar performances of village traditions in Africa argues that such performances constrict traditions so that they cease to evolve naturally (1984:388). A similar concern was expressed by a young Passamaquoddy consultant who was frustrated that older people had canonized the wampum protocols: "They did the same songs and dances over and over at the Indian Day and that to them *was* Passamaquoddy music" (AMS 29Nov.94; emphasis original). But as Laura Peers points out in her analysis of Native interpreters at historical sites and Native pageants such as Indian Day, Native people have agency in choosing this modality of presentation: "Although I would agree that there is a 'tourist gaze,' that tourists interpret foreign cultural sights through deeply ingrained stereotypes, I would also argue that there is a Native performers' gaze. Native performers have, for centuries now, been quite aware of what outsiders expect to see from them, and why, and they are quite capable of manipulating these dynamics for their own ends" (1999:46).

The role of the MC is crucial in shaping interaction with outsiders and to the educational function of the Indian Day. He speaks in both Passamaquoddy and English, translating Passamaquoddy when required. He can point out details and contextualize information, sometimes with jokes that play with stereotypes to disarm any sense of unease. He explains protocols, such as removing hats and not recording during Honor Songs, and encourages audience participation in dances where appropriate.

The people chosen to be MC at the Indian Day have had extensive experience dealing with the public. Joseph A. Nicholas—the original MC—represented the Passamaquoddy Tribe in the state legislature for several terms, worked for Catholic Charities, and served as founding director of the Waponahki Museum at Sipayik, where he worked with generations of researchers. John Francis served as MC for several years when Joe's wife was ill; he was a well-known and often interviewed artist who also held positions in tribal government. The current MC, Wayne Newell, has held several positions in tribal government and is a prominent educator, serving on the Board of Trustees of the University of Maine system.

A subset of contemporary tourism practices is heritage tourism (or cultural tourism), broadly distinguished by a goal of learning about cultural roots. This is not restricted to tourists seeking to connect with their family heritage, although that is a primary motivation for many. Heritage tourism is often suspected of manipulating culture for economic gain, for the exchange is often patterned on former colonial relationships. Patrick Duffy observed of heritage tourism in Ireland, "The ultimate aim of the industry is to match Ireland's heritage and landscape opportunities with Europe's tourist and leisure needs" (1994:80). Yet as Betty Duggan showed in her analysis of the Qualla Arts and Crafts Mutual, Inc., in the Eastern Cherokee community, cultural tourism does not necessarily imply manipulation; in the Qualla cooperative she found "traditional Cherokee values, responses to cultural crisis and change, and historical patterns of crafts production and exchange" (1997:33). Patricia West's extended analysis of Seminole involvement in tourism demonstrated that even in spectacular exhibitions and adopted traditions such as alligator wrestling, Native people were active participants in their own representation, and West concluded that "cultural tourism . . . serves to reinforce a tribe's group identity" (1998:xv).

The Indian Days differ from other touristic events in that the ceremonies they present are based on protocols that are still practiced in other contexts. Arguably, the Indian Day context in turn adds meaning to the cumulative effect of the ceremonies. This conclusion is based on the emphasis placed on experience in constituting meaning, and on the social functions that the Indian Days fulfill. Despite differences of opinion about the inclusion of powwow elements, even in times of political division the Passamaquoddy Tribe comes together to host this event for the public.

Many of the participants in the Indian Day ceremonies live some distance away, and return at this time. Some are asked to fill special roles, such as a Visiting *Sakom* in the Greeting Dance if no one currently in that position is present; others are publicly introduced. Several times in the last two decades, returning individuals have performed a solo dance; many more fill the audience. The Indian Days thus function as a kind of Old Home Week, keeping returnees in touch with their heritage.

Outsiders are welcomed as tourists to the Indian Day, and much is made of their presence. The MC typically announces the presence of visitors from far away, encouraging others to announce themselves. Participants take pride in having attracted foreigners to their cultural event. The presence of visitors from around the world indicates that Passamaquoddy identity is recognized around the world and is an affirmation of the culture's significance in the global economy.

Dancing and Singing as Resistance

In many ways, Passamaquoddy maintenance of the Wabanaki Wampum Protocols has functioned to resist political and cultural domination. The historical

Wabanaki Confederacy originated as a response to catastrophically changing circumstances, and as has been shown, its protocols reflect an accommodation of Iroquois, French Catholic, and Wabanaki traditions. Native leaders resisted European-American pressure to make decisions by insisting on consulting each other in matters affecting the larger community. The ceremonies of the Confederacy persisted among Waponahkiyik in Maine even after the historical Wabanaki Confederacy could no longer function as originally constituted.

When the Confederacy was reconstituted at the time of the Maine Indian land claims, the protocols encoded in the Wampum Records had only recently emerged from private tribal contexts to public adaptation in the Indian Day at Sipayik.[11] In this new touristic exhibition context they have served to signify to the world the distinct cultural heritage of Peskotomuhkatiyik. The adaptations made to accommodate intertribal participation have served to meet contemporary needs, resisting historicization and arguably maintaining Passamaquoddy heritage within a new context that otherwise could, with its popular appeal, have obscured older styles.

Within the songs and dances themselves, resistance is encoded in the multiple layers of meaning, the possibility for double meanings, and contradictions inherent in the extemporized style of performance. This style has maintained its core principles over centuries of documentation. While changes are inevitable, these principles have proved adaptable enough that it seems likely they will be retained in the near future at least.

The persistence of Passamaquoddy identity over five centuries of the tremendous structural pressures that obscured other First Nations is an achievement that inspires deep respect. By analyzing the dances and songs of the wampum protocols I have attempted to reveal the depth of Passamaquoddy tradition, and the rich implications of its underlying aesthetic. In the maintenance of these ceremonies, all *skicinuwok*, all humanity, is enriched.

Appendix
Transcriptions

Example 1. Song of the Drum (Transcribed by Louis Mitchell)

Nil nulopin naka ntotolitehmen pokuhulakon.
Nil ntotoli wiqtahan weyossisok . . .
pemotonek naka ona peciw wucowsonol n'ciksitmakon n'pokuhulakon.

Nulopin naka ntotolitehmen pokuhulakon.
Peciw mecikiskak petagik ntasitemgok pokuhulakonok
naka na kci Apolahsomwehsit cenisu 'ciksotomon npokuhulakon.

Nulopin naka n'pokuhulakon.
Nitte Cipelahq naka n'ciksotomakun npokuhulakon.
Eltaqak pecite kci Wocawson 'conekehla unoski
Naka 'ciksitomon eltaqak npokuhulakon.

Nulopin naka n'tokotomon npokuhulakon.
Peciw te Lumpeqinuwok moskapasuwok naka 'ciksotomoniyia npokuhulakon
naka na Atwosskonikess conaqtihike naka 'ciksotomon n'pokuhulakon.

Nulopin naka ntokotomon npokuhulakon naka kci Aputamkon
muskessin tehna nekom 'ciksotomon npokuhulakon.

Pesahqetuwok, petakiyik, wucowsonol, mecikiskakiyil,
Atwosskonikess, Apolahsomwehsit, Lumpeqinuwok, Cipelahq,
mpsiu mace petapasuwok naciciksotomoniya eltaqahk npokuhulakon.

Translation (David Francis and Ann Morrison Spinney)

I sit down and I am beating the drum.
I am drawing[1] them in . . .
and even the winds listen to my drum.

I sit down and I am beating the drum.
Even storm clouds,[2] and thunder, reply with their drums;
and more, Apolahsomwehsit the great whirlwind stopped and listened to my drum.

I sit down with my drum.
And Cipelahq (that great monster) listened to my drum.
The great Wind-Bird, making noise, suddenly stopped moving its wings
and listened to the sound of my drum.

I sit down and I am striking my drum.
Even the water creatures[3] rise out[4] of the water and listen to my drum
and more, Atwosskonikess[5] stops chopping and he listens to my drum.

I sit down and I beat my drum and the great sea serpent Aputamkon[6]
he also comes out, he listens to my drum.

Lightnings, thunders, winds, storm clouds,
Atwosskonikess, whirlwind, water creatures, Cipelahq;
they begin to come to me, following[7] the sound of my drum.

---

1. wiqtahan: lit., hooking them in.
2. mecikiskak: lit., bad weather
3. lumpeqinuwok: lit., creatures that live under water.
4. moskapasuwok: lit., they start coming out.
5. Prince says this is "an invisible being who roams the forest armed with a stone hatchet with which he occasionally fells trees with a single blow" (1901:386,n4). David Francis says the word means "cater-pillar" or "inch-worm." Wayne Newell suggests it is an earth creature that is coming out like the water creatures in the previous line.
6. David Francis says the name means "his face is turned inside out," i.e., is concave. Prince says this is a "bugaboo" with long red hair that lived under the water, invoked to frighten children (ibid.).
7. "mace petapasuwok naciciksotomoniya": literally, "they start walking over here, they change direction [to] listen to it."

Example 2. Welcome Dance Songs, 1995 Sipayik Indian Day. Sung by Blanche Sockabasin and Wayne A. Newell. Author's recording.

First Song

Drum

Voice

A li ya ha_____ A li ya qa nu te, A li ya ha_____ A li ya qa nu te,

Repeated 3 times, then once transposed beginning on G.

A li ya ha_____ A li ya qa nu te_____

Second Song

Qe he wa ne hu, Qe he wa ne hu. Qe wa ne he he qe yu wa ne,

The whole song repeated twice

Qe wa ne he he qe yu wa ne.

Third Song

Repeated 3 times

Qe he ya he Qe ya he Qe ya he ya he ya he_____ He qe ya he.

Example 3. Qanute Song, fast type, 1995 Sipayik Indian Day.
Sung by Little Eagles Drum. Author's recording.

Example 4. Greeting Dance: First (Slow) Section, 1995 Sipayik Indian Day. Sung by Blanche Sockabasin and Wayne A. Newell. Author's recording.

He qa nu te   He qa nu te   Qa nu te,

Final: End

He qa nu te   He qa nu te   Qa nu te,

He - e qa nu te   Qa nu te.

Last phrase repeated ad lib.
The whole song repeated as necessary to accompany the dance.

Example 4. Greeting Dance: Second Section, 1995 Sipayik Indian Day.
Sung by Blanche Sockabasin and Wayne A. Newell. Author's recording.

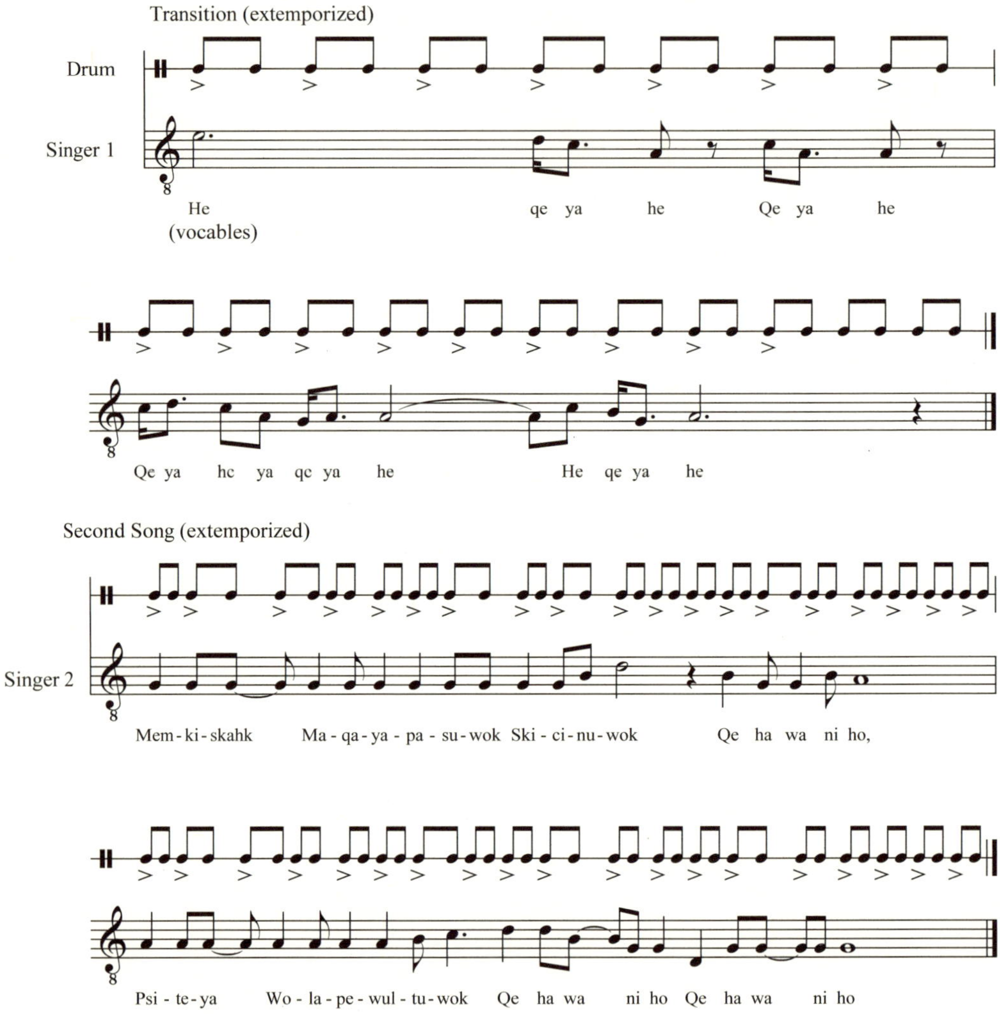

Translation: Today all the Native people are gathered
         Qe ha wa ni ho
         Everyone looks good
         Qe ha wa ni ho, qe ha wa ni ho

Example 5. Greeting Chant, "Skawehe." Singer unknown.
Penn Museum, F. Speck (ATM EC 10" 453.5063).

"Then came the hand shaking referred to in the account of the ceremony.
'Welcome to you, my good people. I am glad to meet with you who are coming to visit us.
Much do I rejoice that you have come to visit us, my kinfolk.'
Here the Greeting Song was repeated several times and the address was continued."
(Speck 1997:294)

Example 5. (*continued*)

He ka   qa nu ta___   He ka qa nu te,

Qan ha   li ya ho   Qan ha___ li ya he,   Qan ha   li ya ho_____ He ka qa nu te,

He ka   qa nu ta___   He ka qa nu te,

Qan ha   li   ya ho   Qan ha___ li ya he,   He ka   qa nu te_____ He ka qa nu te.

"Much do I rejoice that you have come to visit us."

Example 6. Greeting Chants, Comparison of Melodic Material.
(notated in pitch collection of A minor)

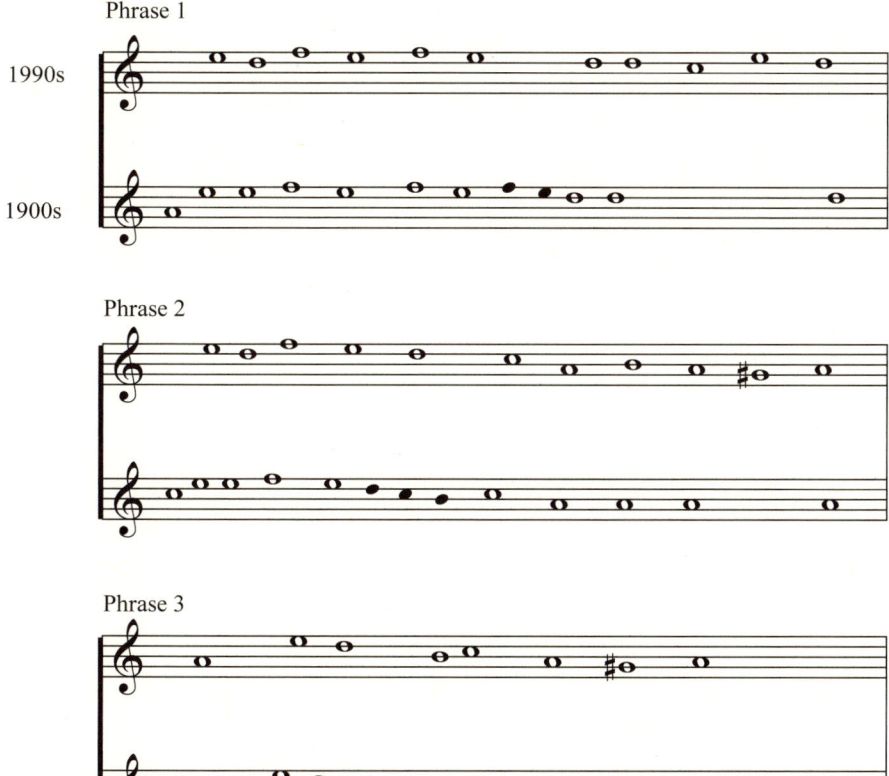

Example 7. Election Dance Songs. Sipayik, November 1994.
Sung by Wayne A. Newell. Author's recording.

[A rattle was shaken up and down regularly on the eighth-note following the drum throughout.]

He qa nu te, He qa nu te, qa nu te, He qa nu te, He qa nu te, qa nu te,

He _ qa nu te, qa nu te   te   He qa nu te _____ he li ya qa nu te,

(a second singer in spontaneous polyphony)

He qa nu te, He li ya qa nu te, he li ya qa nu te, He _ li ya ha qa nu te,

Ho ho ya he _ ho ho ya he _ ho ho ya he

"If you want a symbol for Unity..."
Then repeated from 2nd ending to *
& while accelerating beat to double speed:
"Now that everybody's greeted each other ..."

Example 7. (*continued*)

Second Song

Ho!   Psi-te-wen — Wo-la-kuk Sak' maw kan   Qe ha wa ni hu

Qe ha wa ni hu   Qe ha wa ni hu   Qe ha wa ni hu

Ka - kaw-teh - k'mu-sic   Keh-t'-lu - seh - ta - ken   Psi-te-wen! Psi-te-wen!

Qe ha wa ni hu,   Qe ha wa ni hu,   Qe ha wa ni hu

Translation: Ho! Everyone, a good Sakom dance, Qe ha wa ni hu.
Dance faster, Step backwards, Everyone! Everyone! Qe ha wa ni hu.

Example 8. Greeting Song for Elections, no date.
Sung by Peter Dana.Waponahki Museum recording.

Greeting

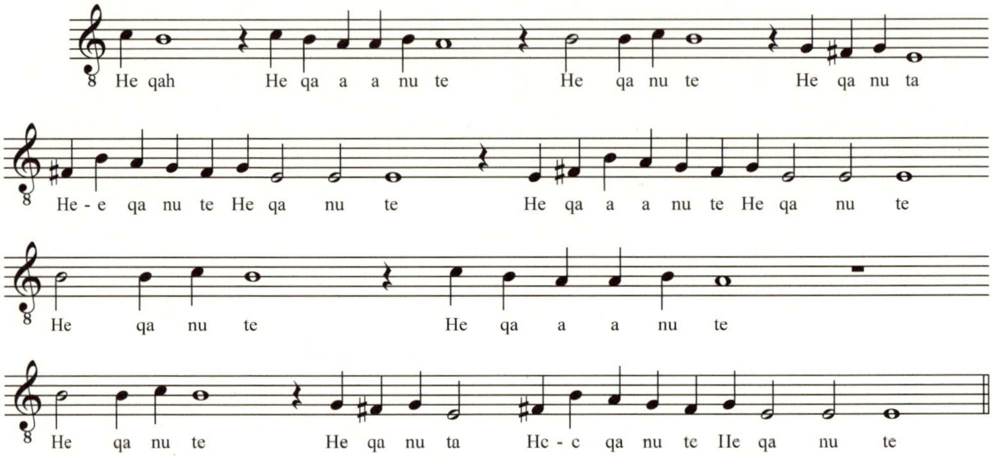
He qah He qa a a nu te He qa nu te He qa nu ta
He - e qa nu te He qa nu te He qa a a nu te He qa nu te
He qa nu te He qa a a nu te
He qa nu te He qa nu ta He - e qa nu te He qa nu te

"At this point then, the greeting is then returned, from the visiting chief, on behalf of his Tribe."

Return Greeting

He qa nu te He qa a a nu te He qa nu te qa nu ta
He - e qa nu te he qa nu ta He - e qa ne te - e he qa nu ta
He qa nu te A li ya qa nu te He qa nu te

(remainder obscured)

Example 9. Peace Pipe Ceremony Dance Songs, 1995 Sipayik Indian Day.
Sung by Blanche Sockabasin. Author's recording.

Refrain

Drum

Voice

'Sa - mi Mo-to-we - yu,   'Sa - mi Mo-to-we - yu.

Verse 1

Nil te Nka son We - ci - yu - ki,   Nil te Nka-son We - ci - yu - ki.

Verse 2

'Tma-k'na-toq Mu-sa Pu-tu-wa - t'mon,   'Tma-'kna-toq Mu-sa Pu-tu-wa - t'mon.

Refrain: It's a shame. Verse 1: We are close cousins. Verse 2: He doesn't blow through the pipe stem.

Second Song   repeated as necessary

Qey   hey a he   qe ya he   qe ya he ya he ya he_____ he qe ya he

203

Example 9. (*continued*)

Third song, Verse 1

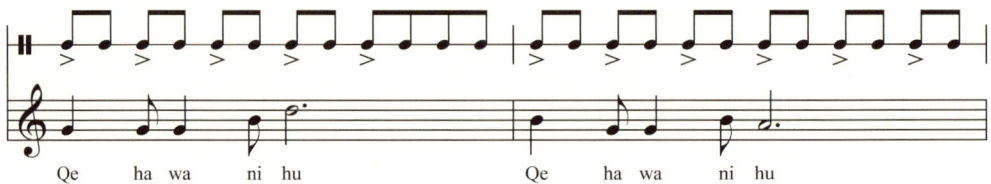

Verse 2

Translation:
Verse1: Vocables
Verse 2: Dance faster Qehawanihu <Very nice!>
There were two other extemporized verses containing personal jokes
that the singers did not want transcribed.

Example 10. Maliseet War Dance. Sung by Frank Sappier. Canadian Museum of Civilization, Archives William Hubbs Mechling, 1911, 8:123(a).

The lyrics are all vocables. K is always unvoiced here.

Example 11. Marriage Ceremony Dance, 1994 Sipayik Indian Day.
Sung by Blanche Sockabasin. Author's recording

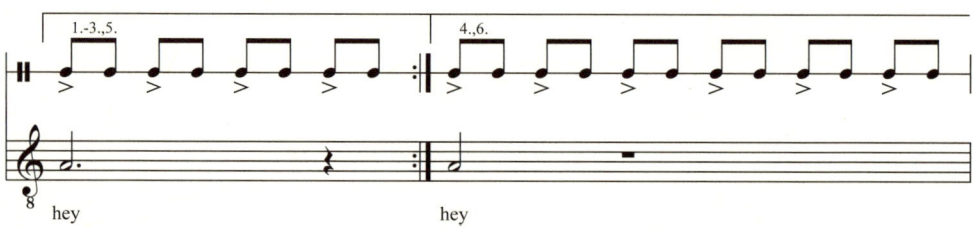

Part 1. The bride's and groom's parties dance out to meet each other.
Fourth and sixth repetitions have extensions of drum beats only.
Here, the verse is repeated 7 times. The singer varies the length and placement
of the verses to suit the accompanying action.
Part 2 (2nd song). The Bride's and Groom's parties form squadrons and dance.

Example 11. (*continued*)

Qey hay wa ne ho, Qey hay wa ne ho, Qey hay wa ne ho. Ka-kaw-tehk-muh-sic

Mo - teh san - sis-kan, Et' - ci wo-la - pe-wi - ce - e-ka, Qey hay wa ne ho,

Qey hay wa ne ho. Ka-kaw-tehk-muh-sic Mo - teh-san - sis-kan,

Ka - kaw-tehk - muh-sic Qey ha wa ne ho, Qey ha wa ne ho.

The Bride's and Groom's parties dance together to symbolize their unity.
Translation: qey hay we ne ho (vocables) Dance faster, children(?), very handsome they are!

207

Example 12. Tuhtuwas Dance Song. Sung by Joseph A. Nicholas.

Translation: Have it dance sideways, the little pine tip.

Example 13. Passamaquoddy Snake Dance Song, 1994 Sipayik Indian Day. Sung by Blanche Sockabasin. Author's recording.

Translation: (Vocables...) Dance faster / The snake dance / Let it dance around in a circle / (Vocables)

Example 14. Snake Dance Song. Sung by Noel Josephs.
Fewkes Collection, Cylinder 10. Courtesy of Waponahki Museum, Sipayik.

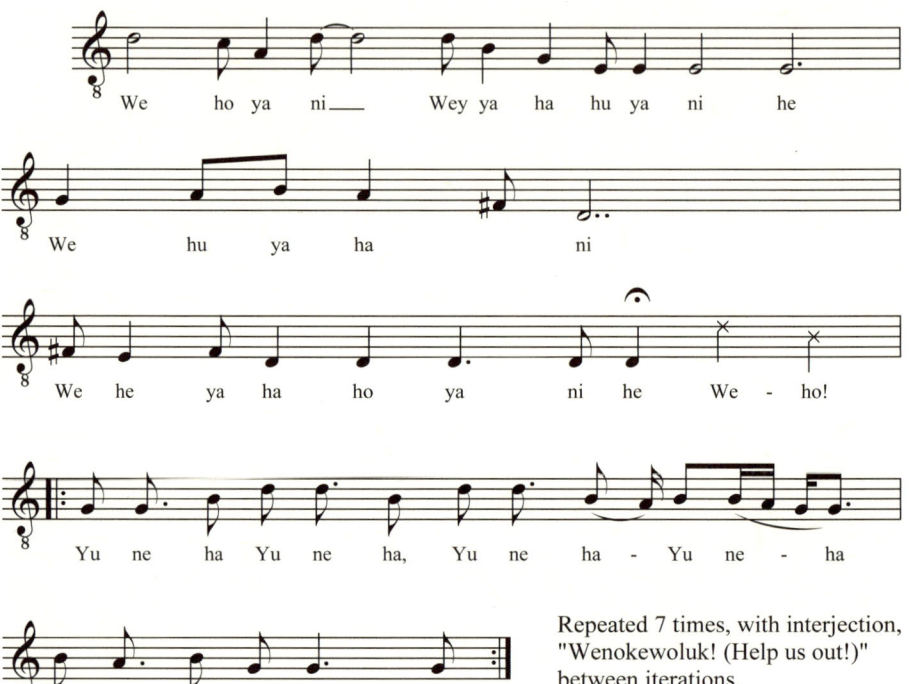

We ho ya ni___ Wey ya ha hu ya ni he

We hu ya ha ni

We he ya ha ho ya ni he We - ho!

Yu ne ha Yu ne ha, Yu ne ha - Yu ne - ha

Yu ne ha Yu ne ha.

Repeated 7 times, with interjection,
"Wenokewoluk! (Help us out!)"
between iterations.

Example 15. Snake Dance Song. Singer unknown.
Penn Museum, F. Speck (ATM EC 10" 453.5046).

Yu ne ha yu ne, Yu ne ha yu ne

Yu ne ha yu ne, Yu ne ha yu ne

(recording off track) Yu ne ha yu ne

Yu ne ha yu ne, Yu ne ha yu ne

Yu ne ha yu ne, Yu ne ha yu ne

(end)

Yu ne ha yu ne, Yu ne ha yu ne

Yu ne ha yu ne, Yu ne ha yu ne

Last phrase repeated
3 or 4 times, then
from the sign 7 times
concluding at end of line 6.

Example 16. Maliseet Snake Dance Song. Singer unknown. Canadian Museum of Civilization, Archives, William Hubbs Mechling 1911, 8:121(a).

Part One
Drumming: irregular
Singing: intermittent, repeating the phrase several times, with interjections. Indistinct text.

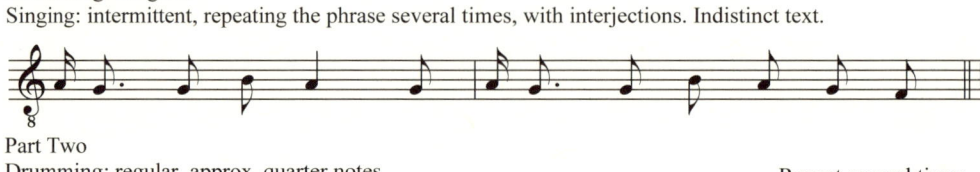

Part Two
Drumming: regular, approx. quarter notes.
Singing: independent of drumming.

Repeat several times, with interjections.

Ha ye he ha ye he, Ha ye he ha ye he, Ha ye he ha ye he, Ha ye he ho.

Part Three.
Drumming continues.

(etc.)

indistinct text, intermitent, with spoken interjections

17. Maliseet Snake Dance Song. Sung by Jim Paul. Canadian Museum of Civilization, Archives, William Hubbs Mechling 1911, 8:121(a).

Part 1
Drumming: eighth notes, evenly

(recording skips)

vocables He wa he   e ka ya ne he   Wa he

Part 2
Drumming continued

We he ya we e he ya We he ya We he ya, We he ya we e he ya We he ya We he ya

Sung 2 times, return to Part 1

We he ya we e he ya We he ya— we he ya We he ya we e he ya We he ya——we he ya

212

Example 18. Maliseet Snake Dance Song. Sung by Jim Paul. Canadian Museum of Civilization, Archives, William Hubbs Mechling 1911, 8:121(a).

213

Example 19. Maliseet Snake Dance Song. Sung by Frank Sappier. Canadian Museum of Civilization, Archives, William Hubbs Mechling 1911, 8:121(a).

Drumming: evenly in eighth notes

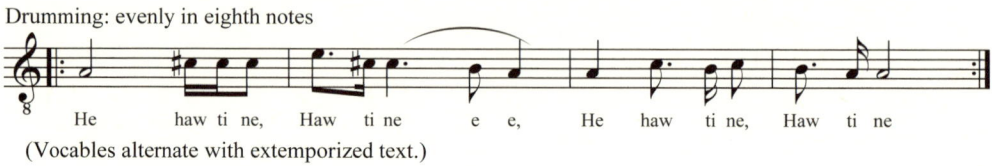

He haw ti ne, Haw ti ne e e, He haw ti ne, Haw ti ne

(Vocables alternate with extemporized text.)

Example 20. Mte'skmuey (Snake Dance Song) excerpt. Kitpu Singers. From Denny Family, Mi'kmaq Chants.

Drum

Voice

(phonetic) Ha do pa da ha i yo ha i ye Ha do pa da ha i yo ha i ye

Lead Chorus (etc.)

Example 21. *Baylo Baylo* Songs. From *Songs of the Passamaquoddy.*

1. Sung by Delia Mitchell

Ku wa ssi lic tu si___ sol Ku wa ssi lic tu si___ sol.

Let the baby sleep, Let the baby sleep.

2. Sung by Wayne Newell

Hun gun gin gee hun gun gee we je ke je gin gee hun gung ging

(nonsense words, phonetic)

Example 22. "Mahqankahtik" verse 1. Sung by David A. Francis.

Mah - qan - ka - tik Ktolu - ta nen, Nuh - kome - qotek - on kni - ma - nen.

Vocable chorus added

Uh pi ye wi he ye, Uh pi ye he wi he ye

Translation: "To the maple sugar place we went, a dried codfish skin we took along to eat.
[Again and again, the paddle dips in] wi-he-ye"

Example 23. "Liwisu." Sung by Joseph A. Nicholas.

[Nu - wel Nu - wel] Li - wi - su Ni - ta - peh - sis We - la - qik

Translation: "Noel Noel He is named, My little friend from last night"

215

Example 24. "Qonasqamki Monihkuk." Sung by Joseph A. Nicholas.

Drum

Voice

Qo nas - qam-ki Monih-kuk   We - ci - ma - ce-hay,

Qey hay wa ni hu   Qey hay wa ni   Qe hay wa ni hu.

Qo nas - qam ki Monih-kuk   We - ci ma - ce-hay,

Qey hay wa ni hu   Qey hay wa ni   Qey hay wa ni hu, Qey hay wa ni   Qey ha' wa ni hu.

Translation: St. Andrews Island They left (vocables)

25. "Qayuwa," 1994 Sipayik Indian Day. Sung by Delia Mitchell.
Author's recording

M'tah - k'mi-kuk,   I - t'muk Qa - ya-wa,___   Si - pa-yik   I - t'muk Qa - yu-wa.___

At Motahkomikuk, they said they are angry   At Sipayik, they said they are angry

216

Example 26. "Waponahkiyik." Sung by Joseph A. Nicholas.

Wa - pa - po-ni - hik, Wi - wo-nu - qe - pi - ya - ne

Wo - pa - po-ni - hik, Wo-la - sih - ka-wo-tul - ti - ne

A - li - a - he - ya, A - li - ya - qa - nu-te

Wa - pa - po-ni - hik Wo - na - kul - ti - ne

Wa - pa - po-ni - hik Wi - wo-nih - teh-ko-muh - ti-ne

A - li - ya - he - ya A - li - ya - qa - nu-te. (etc.)

Translation: Wabanaki people, let us all greet each other. Wabanaki people, let us all treat each other well. Wabanaki People, let us all dance. Wabanaki people, let us all move in a circle.

Example 27. "Nil te nkason weciyuki" verses 1–2. Sung by Joseph A. Nicholas.

Translation: We are close cousins (repeat). It's a shame, it's a shame.
It's no wonder they are talking about it (repeat). It's a shame, it's a shame.

Example 28. "Musa Kotusomihkoc Puktewick" verse 1.
Sung by Joseph A. Nicholas.

Translation: Don't drink alcohol, Don't drink alcohol.
           It's a shame, It's a shame.

Notes

1. Identity, History, Tradition

1. Some native speakers shorten *Peskotomuhkatiyik* to *Pestomuhkatiyik*.

2. *Skicin* is the modern form. The *w* prefix is an old nominative form, according to Elder David A. Francis. Fannie Hardy Eckstorm says "the Passamaquoddies call themselves Skidjim, Men (that is, Indians) the same word as Etchemin" (1941:xxvi). We can assume that the old *w* prefix gave the sound Europeans reproduced with *e-*.

3. *Etchemin* is the conventional spelling. Champlain and other early French writers spelled it *Etechemin*.

4. The translation is disputed: Ruth Holmes Whitehead gives "don't speak like us" (quoted in Bourque 1989).

5. The Sipayik website is http://www.wabanaki.com. The Indian Township website is http://www.passamaquoddy.com. Links can be found there to information about the Schoodic Band and the Joint Tribal Council.

6. Harald Prins (1999) offers the "conjecture" that the Wabanaki Confederacy was already a formal alliance in 1680, before the "Grande Paix de Montréal" was signed in 1701, in which delegates of the nations now known as Wabanaki participated.

7. The Maine Indian land claims case set a precedent for acknowledging Native sovereignty and land rights in the United States. It is formally known as *Joint Tribal Council of the Passamaquoddy Tribe v. Morton* (often *Passamaquoddy v. Morton*). Rogers C. B. Morton was the secretary of the interior when the case was brought to the federal level. It was headed for the United States Supreme Court when it was settled in December 1980, one of the last acts of the Carter administration.

8. First Nations is the equivalent of Native Americans. It is the legal designation for Native communities used in Canada and is preferred here because it emphasizes that they were the first inhabitants of North America to organize as political entities.

9. This section accords with Bruce Bourque's argument that "historical sources from the late seventeenth and early eighteenth centuries reveal that the ethnic divisions described by the early French were basically accurate. Champlain's labels, *Abenaki, Etchemin*, and *Souriquois*, remained current into the 1670s despite numerous epidemics and internecine warfare; only the term *Almouchiquois* was dropped almost immediately after Champlain left the Gulf of Maine." (Bourque 1989:273–74) As the rest of this section makes clear, I

agree with Bourque, A. H. Morrison, and others that territorial occupation was not stable until perhaps the middle of the nineteenth century.

10. Eckstorm presents this argument and abundant evidentiary details in *Indian Place-Names of the Penobscot Valley and the Maine Coast*. She also argues that the presence of Mi'kmaq people is evidenced by Mi'kmaq place names as far southwest as Monhegan Island but declines to speculate as to what they were doing there and for how long (1941:xxvii).

11. Bourque notes changes in the historical record concerning ethnic groups: "As the linguistically oriented French perspective on ethnicity disappeared from the historical record of western Acadia, a very different, geographically oriented English one replaced it." (1989:273).

12. William Fenton considers the Iroquois league to be the "symbolic system" and the Iroquois Confederacy to be "the effective political institution" (1998:4)

13. The term "Teaching" is defined in the preface. Paraphrasing both Ojibwa and Passamaquoddy consultants: The Ancestors of both lived in Waponahkik. When the coming of Europeans and the trauma it would bring were foreseen by their spiritual leaders, some elected to stay and deal with the white men, but a large group decided to migrate west, along the rivers and Great Lakes; as they went, they followed beads deposited in the water by a *megis* shellfish. The website of the Passamaquoddy Tribe at Sipayik gives a version of this Teaching: http://www.wabanaki.com/migration.

14. The term "Anishena'abeg" ("the people" or "original people") includes Ojibway nations in Canada as well as Ojibwa, Ojibwe, and Chippewa nations in the United States. Their language, Ojibwe, is also in the Alonquian family.

15. This was originally a control devised by Euro-Americans to limit their treaty obligations; it has been adopted by Native communities out of necessity to control limited resources. But many Native people find it nontraditional or otherwise offensive to enforce, and some anthropologists see it as a way of "mathematically legislating people out of existence" (A. H. Morrison, personal communication), because traditionally, outsiders were incorporated into the community by many processes, including adoption and marriage. Historically, exogamy was a form of alliance, and marriage is one of the protocols recorded in the Wampum Records.

16. See Eckstorm 1980 [1945]:140–80 for different perspectives, with analysis. In several articles Vincent O. Erickson (especially 1982 and 1985) has analyzed aspects of the conflict.

17. An example of Native proficiency is the Thomas Kyrie manuscript in the collections of the New Brunswick Museum, St. John, N.B. It is a scrap of paper with Maliseet language prayers on one side and a Kyrie chant notated on the other, signed Etienne Thomas (Tomah). See Erickson 1980 for an analysis of who the writer might have been and Spinney 2006 on the context for making such notations.

18. The missionization of North America and the responses of Native peoples, including their indigenization of Christianity, are part of a vast interdisciplinary field of scholarship that continues to generate a large body of literature. The focus of my study dictates limited consideration and references. Readers may wish to consult a general introduction to the subject such as Rollings (2004).

19. The suppression of the Society of Jesus was the result of political conflicts in Europe and the Americas. It began in Portugal and spread; the dates are usually given as 1750–83 (see chapter 2).

20. See Spinney 2006 for a detailed analysis.

21. An illuminating analysis of the relationship between the Missions Étrangères and the French Court is contained in Koren 1962.

22. Before crossing the Delaware River on December 24, 1776, General Washington dictated a letter to the "Brothers of Passamaquodia" imploring their alliance. The settlement at Sipayik, one of their traditional shoreline outposts, resulted from the colonists' request that they watch Passamaquoddy Bay for English naval activity. Sopiel Selmore is supposed to have shot across the bow of an English warship during one encounter (N. Smith 1990:337–44).

23. The State of Maine was obliged under the treaty obligations it had inherited from Massachusetts to provide continual funding for the church buildings, but the account into which funds from the sale of lands and timber was supposed to be deposited was found to exist in name only. This was one of the complaints that led to the Maine Indian land claims in *Passamaquoddy v. Morton.*

24. The churches involved included many denominations and there were also non-denominational schools. Prime Minister Stephen Harper apologized to former students, their families, and their communities on behalf of the government of Canada on June 11, 2008. See http://www.ainc-inac.gc.ca/rqpi.

25. The terms "retrieved traditions" and "adopted traditions" are taken from Prins 1994:383–94.

26. Mary Philbrick was Chief of the Aroostook Band of Mi'kmaq when they won recognition from the United States federal government.

27. The best source describing their role in war parties is Maillard's letter (1758), even though it is corrupted (see chapter 2).

28. Julie Cruikshank (2005) has dealt extensively with the differences between the oral traditions of the Canadian Arctic and scientific records. Her work is exemplary in offering rich combinations of different kinds of evidence.

29. "Christians ask us to accept that there is a history, that there is a central event making the rest of the history intelligible, and that because there is a central event , there must necessarily be a history. The logic is clearly a precursor of Catch-22" (Deloria 2003:120).

30. An example from within the Wabanaki context is the controversy over the group IRATE (Indigenous Resistance Against Tribal Exploitation). Led by members of the Penobscot community, the group protested against the participation in Native-designated activities such as ceremonies of persons without what they deemed sufficient blood quantum—even though outsiders had been included historically. IRATE also targeted individuals who taught Native cultural arts to non-Natives and the multicultural programs that sponsored such classes, circulating a "blacklist" during the 1990s. The Native community in Maine was divided over IRATE's activities, reflected by the denial of its request for recognition as a Penobscot Tribal organization in 1995.

31. This saying has been attributed to a veritable cast of characters, from the eighteenth century to the twenty-first.

32. On phenomenology of music, see Lochhead 1982.

33. I use "mimesis" in its perhaps older sense of sympathetic magic, where representation accesses the power of that which is represented; I am not implying any cross-cultural imitation of the exotic as in recent studies of interactions between Native Americans and Europeans such as Greenblatt 1991.

34. Aesthetics has roots in a long tradition of Western philosophy. A survey is beyond the scope of this study, but readers may wish to consult the valuable anthology *Music and Aesthetics in the Eighteenth and Early Nineteenth Centuries*, edited by Peter Le Huray and James Day (1981). In European cultures, social strata were linked to qualities of the beautiful—or grotesque—and represented by style features of music, dance, and speech. This was a generative principle in seventeenth-century English courtly masques, a precursor genre to opera, in which themes of social hierarchy, including colonized and marginalized groups, were explored. Several masques of Ben Jonson exemplified these themes (*The Irish Masque*; *Gypsies Metamorphosed*), as did Shakespeare's play *The Tempest*, which drew inspiration from reports of Bermuda (Tomlinson 2007:2).

35. In recent musicological debates, "aesthetic" has been used by those wishing to remove music from its social context, limit its meanings to self-referentiality, and make it an object of contemplation in itself. See, for example, Pieter van den Toorn's frequent invocation of the term in his attack on the so-called new musicology (1991). That is obviously not the intent of its application here, as my analysis of Passamaquoddy song and dance style proceeds from performances that are explicitly situated in their social contexts.

36. Bourdieu's findings carried negative implications for the culture under analysis; my findings do not.

37. These terms are now seldom used but were central to the theories of Ruth Benedict and Gregory Bateson, who wrote: "the concepts, ethos and eidos, which I am suggesting may be regarded as subdivisions of her [Benedict's] more general concept, *Configuration*. The eidos of a culture is an expression of the standardised cognitive aspects of the individuals, while the ethos is the corresponding expression of their standardised affective aspects" (1958:33; original emphasis).

38. A formative example for Turner occurred when a young Ndembu man wished to accede to the power held by his uncle, and so publicly refused him a customary honor (1986:75).

2. Sources

1. J. D. Prince published another version in 1921. Several written versions are now available: Leavitt and Francis 1990 includes several, and the website of the Passamaquoddy Tribe at Sipayik includes two others transcribed from Sopiel Selmore: http://www.wabanaki.com.

2. As previously noted, this kind of consolidation has frustrated attempts for federal recognition, since populations were not stable during the eighteenth century.

3. Wampum belts have been displayed in more private contexts at the Sipayik Indian Day and are used at meetings of the Confederacy. Belts have also been incorporated into public speeches made by leaders at the Abenaki ceremonial day in Swanton, Vermont.

4. For a summary of contacts in northeastern North America, see Hoffman (1955:9–41); initial contact sources for Maine are discussed in Bourque (2001, 103–27).

5. William T. Vollmann's *The Ice Shirt* is a recent attempt to bring these sources together in narrative that is itself mythohistorical. He writes: "My aim . . . has been to create a 'Symbolic History'—that is to say, an account of origins and metamorphoses which is often untrue based on the literal facts as we know them, but whose untruths further a deeper sense of truth.—Did the Norsemen, for instance, really come to the New World bearing ice

in their hearts?—Well, of course they did not. But if we look upon the Vinland episode as a precursor of the infamies there, of course they did" (Vollmann 1990:[397]).

6. A popular idea in New Age circles is that the cultures of the Norsemen and Native Americans are related. Nineteenth-century writers theorized about cultural influences on Native Americans from these Norse visitors. But current scholarship posits that what parallels there are between these cultures may be due more to similar geographic and environmental factors. Charles Leland argued for the origin of the Northeast Algonquian legends in Norse sagas (Leland 1884:9); but as Mrs. W. Wallace Brown argued in an unpublished manuscript, the influence could as easily have gone the other way (Calais Free Library mss).

7. A. H. Morrison notes "Ca. 1250, Pope Innocent IV...had stated that 'lordship, possession, and jurisdiction can belong to infidels licitly and without sin, for these things were made not only for the faithful but for every rational creature.' However, most Europeans during the Age of Discovery tended to honor this theoretical precedent negatively, in practice" (1992:2 n1).

8. The details in parentheses appear in the margins of the Cèllere Codex; see Wroth 1970:141. Hoffmann (1961:105–12) argued that these and other marginalia in this manuscript are in Verrazzano's hand.

9. Hakluyt was involved in translating and publishing many accounts; his own major collection is *The principal navigations, voiages, traffiques and discoveries of the English nation, made by sea or over-land, to the remote and farthest distant quarters of the earth* (1589). Purchas included material from Hakluyt's manuscripts in his *Hakluytus Posthumus, or, Purchas his Pilgrimes* (1624–25). There have been many subsequent editions of both works.

10. Native people have been celebrated dance musicians in the Northeast. Examples are the Mi'kmaq fiddler Noel Jack Tomer and Passamaquoddy bandleader Bennie Francis.

11. In a personal communication A. H. Morrison clarifies that this expedition was jointly sponsored by Catholics and Protestants, and that it was the last such. The Protestant sponsors had suggested kidnapping Native people as a means of getting exclusive knowledge of the area. The idea of a Catholic colony was dropped after the "gunpowder plot" of November 5, 1605, that was pinned on Guy Fawkes.

12. Champlain's Caribbean voyage is disputed, and likewise his account of it; details in it do not accord with other accounts, among other issues. See Marcel Trudel's brief summary of the problems in the *Dictionary of Canadian Biography*, s.v. Champlain, Samuel de, online at http://www.biographi.ca/EN.

13. On the Americas he continually cites Jean de Léry and Laudonniere.

14. Fixed-*do* solmization means that the pitch D is always *re*, even if it is the tonic; in movable-*do* solmization the tonic is always *do* regardless of what pitch it is. This argument assumes that Lescarbot had perfect pitch, which cannot be proved. Gabriel Sagard borrowed two of Lescarbot's melodies and presented them as Huron songs in his *Histoire* (1939 [1636]). Sagard also transposed them to another key, set them into European meter, and added three harmony parts and some melody pitches to make the harmonies work out. See Robert Stevenson's discussion of the history of these melodies in European music literature (1973:14–16).

15. On the French ballets, see Balthasar de Beaujoyeulx, *Le ballet-comique* ([1581] 1981). On the English masques, see Peter Walls, *Music in the English Courtly masque, 1604–1640* (1996). See also the discussion of aesthetics in chapter 1, above.

16. The 1914 Champlain Society edition of Lescarbot includes the songs from the third edition, with new academic harmonizations designed to show the tonal implications of the melodies. This created a conflict with the Champlain Society's subsequent edition of Sagard's *The Long Voyage to the Country of the Hurons* (1939), which incorporates much of the *Histoire* (1636). In its edition of *The Long Voyage* the Champlain Society reprinted Sagard's renditions of Lescarbot's songs as "Huron Music." The "Canadian" dance song melody given by Marin Mersenne (*Harmonie Universelle*, 1636) is not one of Lescarbot's; Jean-Jacques Rousseau included a mistranslated version of Mersenne's "Canadian" song in his *Dictionnairie de Musique* (1768).

17. The terms "ethnographic, ethnographer," etc., were not used until the nineteenth century; however, following Hodgen's example of calling the late medieval writers' methods "anthropology," many scholars have accepted such accounts as ethnographic although the term is anachronistic (e.g., Bohlman 1991). In any case, I treat these early sources as ethnographic; they have been so treated in other studies of Native American cultures, even if not so named.

18. Richelieu was not a member of any religious order, but his assistant, Le Clerc du Tremblay, was a Capuchin.

19. The term syncretism is also used in nondenominational religious studies and anthropology to denote the process when Native forms or functions are fulfilled with borrowed means, or vice versa.

20. Lescarbot accused Biard of being the informant; Biard accused a local *Sakom* (see A. H. Morrison 1994).

21. Copies I consulted were at Houghton Library, Harvard University, and online at http://www.canadiana.org/eco.php. This sort of sectarian tract was a feature of eighteenth-century English public life.

22. It was first published in its entirety in the periodical *Les Soirees Canadiennes* 1863, and portions in English translation are quoted in Whitehead 1991.

23. Léry's official capacity in this expedition is disputed, but his account ([1580] 1990) of his voyage and the Native peoples he encountered has become one of the classic texts of early ethnography and influenced Marc Lescarbot's description of the Etchemin and Souriquois, as discussed above.

24. Richelieu gained power in 1616 when he was appointed a secretary of state; he went into exile with Marie de Medici, was restored to favor in 1622, and became prime minister in 1624. He was thus in a controlling position in the French court from 1624 to 1642.

25. These letters are collected in *An Historical Account of the... Christian Indians in New England in... 1675, 1676, 1677*; originals are at the Massachusetts Historical Society, Boston.

26. The English publication of Maillard's letter (1758), discussed above, is another example: marginal comments and footnotes added by the editor make explicit the subtext that both groups are equally unenlightened, oppressed with superstition, and obsessed with violence.

27. This idea is treated in greater detail in Spinney 2006 and K. Morrison 1974.

28. The Wabanaki Bilingual Education Program at Indian Township used Colonel Allen's records as the basis for exploring these decisions in the textbook *Tokej, Qatop Qenoq Sipkiw* (For now, but not for long) by Robert M. Leavitt and Wayne A. Newell (1974). Allen's journals were edited and published by Frederic Kidder (1867).

29. Father Demillier's manuscript prayerbook is in the collection of the Maine Historical Society in Portland, Maine.

30. His contemporary John Gilmary Shea explosed many of these problems; Fanny Hardy Eckstorm pointed out more in several publications.

31. Described in the preface to his *Ahiamihewintuhangan (The Prayer Song)* 1858. See Spinney 2006 and Morrison (Spinney) 1996 for an analysis of his transcriptions.

32. Whitehead's (1988) bibliography of Mi'kmaq legends in publication provides a representative sampling of these sources.

33. Speck gave the dates of his Penobscot research as 1907 to 1912, the winters of 1913 and 1914, and a return trip in 1935. The early years overlap with his research in Maliseet communities.

34. A. H. Morrison has treated thoroughly in several papers the subject of Wabanaki land occupation, and Speck's interpretation of it (1978, 1980, 1995).

35. It is possible that Mechling also quarreled with Speck over who should have the rights to recordings that Mechling had made, some with Speck and some on his own. It seems likely that the Penobscot recordings were left with Speck, while Mechling secured the Maliseet and Mi'kmaq records. If he believed that Speck would make some claim on the material, this belief would explain why he never published his monograph. Mechling's materials on music were apparently deposited at the National Museum with the other results of his fieldwork. During his many years of research, Nicholas N. Smith was able to work with part of Mechling's materials.

36. See Eckstorm 1924 for details on the river drivers, who drove the logs down streams and rivers from the woods to the mills.

3. Overview of Passamaquoddy Songs

1. James Clifford calls such terms "translation terms" in a 1990 paper quoted by Mark Slobin (1992:3).

2. An analogy may be drawn from this concept of a song I am calling "immanent" to the grammatical structure of the language. Passamaquoddy verbs use one prefix, meaning demonstrated action, for the equivalent of both the English past tense and the conditional "can, is able to do."Here as in the songs, past experience is integral to comprehending the present discourse.

3. These comments are based on data gathered informally by several of my classes over the last ten years. Each student is assigned to find out how subjects define the term "song." The communicative functions of music in European cultures have been and continue to be well studied, with musicologists recently joined by semioticians, psychologists, biologists, and other specialists.

4. This exclamation is not lexical but signals the ending of the song.

5. Pentatonic means five different pitch classes; sexatonic, six; septatonic, seven. Anhemitonic means there are no half-steps. A half-step is the smallest difference between pitches in the tonal system of common Western practice; it is the difference between *mi* and *fa* in the *do-re-mi* scale.

6. Strophic means that the same melody underlies all the verses of text.

7. Antiphony is a performance technique in which one singer or group sings a phrase and another singer or group sings the next phrase.

8. An interval is the difference between one pitch and another, as octave, minor third, etc.

9. The tonic pitch is the pitch around which the melody is oriented.

10. Earlier studies referred to vocables as "meaningless," but nonlexical is more correct, as these syllables often convey information about the song form.

11. Consequent phrases answer or balance previous phrases. An example is the song that goes *Apolahcihqe, Qey-hu-wa-ne-he* ("He is coming back," qey-hu-wa-ne-he) said by some to refer to Koluskap.

12. The Wabanaki songs from Natalie Curtis's *The Indians' Book* were most vexing. Curtis was a musical prodigy with an acute ear, but her field methodology was problematic. She used her own phonetic system without supplying a key; and as she did not spend much time in the Native communities in Maine, her transcriptions do not reflect the lexical structure of the languages. Furthermore, she does not seem to have checked her transcriptions with anyone other than the singers she got them from, so that idiosyncratic features of pronunciation such as lisps are reproduced. She did not use recording equipment, but transcribed by ear in one session.

13. Stichic and strophic are the two major forms of poetry in Europe. Stichic is the bardic form that takes the line as its structuring unit; strophic is structured in verses. Stichic song forms set text to stock melodic formulas, whereas stropic song forms set text to a repeated, independently structured, melody.

14. The vocal tone and drum beat of intertribal singing creates an energetic sound that is familiar to fans of punk rock (such as the author). There are parallels with other rock styles as well.

15. See chapter 4 for discussion of the specific musicological meaning of the terms "drum" and "idiophone."

16. Honor Beats are a series of drum beats accented and played twice as slowly to signal dancers and audience members to make an honoring gesture. Honor Beats distinguish Honor Songs in the intertribal performance style; any song can be an Honor Song if offered properly. Honor Beats are placed between or at the start of the repeat of the second section of a song. See Browner 2000 for a discussion of Honor Beat placement in Northern and Southern Plains intertribal songs.

17. Speck Collection, cylinder 5066b. See chapter 8 on social dancing for further commentary.

18. Leland included several examples in his collection *Algonquian Legends*: a shaman took seven steps through the ground up to his ankles, "just as if it had been light snow"; a *Mikumwess* danced into hard ground, plowing it up (Leland 1884:341, 88).

19. Neptune would have traveled by dreaming. Grand Manan Island (*Mananok* in Passamaquoddy) is sometimes linked with the Isle of Man (*Mannin* in Manx) by members of the New Age subculture. The link is apparently imaginative; though the two islands are suggestively positioned on opposite sides of the Atlantic there are no records of any contact between Waponahkiyik and Manx. It is possible that individuals could have crossed the ocean physically by design or accident.

4. Musical Instruments

1. The missionary LeClercq observed this of the Gaspesians (1691 [1910]:103–6).

2. See Browner 1997; Levine 2002; and Pisani 2006 for discussion of the different uses mainstream composers have made of Native songs.

3. Further evidence that it is the sound of an instrument that is spiritually powerful is found in Nicholas Denys's description of his argument with a Gaspesian (Mi'kmaq) man about life after death. Denys convinced the man to dig up a grave into which goods had been placed for the deceased to take to the next life. Denys's aim was to prove that the goods were not assumed but simply rotting. But the Gaspesian, banging on a buried kettle, indicated that the rusted kettle "no longer says a word because its spirit has abandoned it" and gone with the spirit of the deceased to whom it was given (Denys [1672] 1908:440).

4. Nicholas N. Smith (personal communication) recounted that one of the Penobscot singers he recorded in the 1950s beat out his accompaniments on a copy of Frank Speck's book *Penobscot Man*. The reflexivity in this action delighted Smith.

5. There is no Passamaquoddy word corresponding precisely to the term "sacred." It seems to be a Western European cognitive category used by Peskotomuhkatiyik to convey conveniently their concept of the Drum's power, as explained below.

6. Shaman (shamanism, shamanic, etc.) is a term dreived from Eurasian culture. It is used by anthropologists to denote "part-time religious specialists who establish and maintain personalistic relations with specific spirit beings through the use of controlled and culturally scripted altered states of consciousness (ASC). Shamans employ powers derived from spirits to heal sickness, to guide the dead to their final destinations, to influence animals and forces of nature in a way that benefits their communities, to initiate assaults on enemies, and to protect their own communities from external aggression" (D. Jorelemon 2002).

7. The text is chanted, not sung, in Mark Hedden's film *Song of the Drum: The Petroglyphs of Maine* (Gerber and Heddon 2004). By executive order of Maine's Governor John Baldacci on February 27, 2007, the Passamaquoddy Tribe was given joint custody of the Machias Bay petroglyphs, a site associated with shamanic activity. Although it is difficult to decode their precise meaning, at least one of the petroglyphs depicts dancing and one may depict drumming.

8. As these people were under the leadership of Bessabez, they were probably Etchemin, but Bessabez led an alliance of bands that included Abenaki as well. See Eckstorm [1945] 1980:76.

9. Ruth Holmes Whitehead (1991) translates the Mi'kmaq equivalent of *ktahant* as "Power," capitalized, and generations of anthropologists have used this translation. See especially Ruth Murray Underhill, *Singing for Power* (1938). The name of the highest mountain in Waponahkik is derived from *ktahant*: it is anglicized as Mount Katahdin.

10. Speck (1926) believed that the Naskapi and Wabanaki were ethnically and culturally related.

11. See Vennum 1982 for a description and analysis of the Dance Drum and its ceremonies. A succint introduction to the powwow Drum is contained in the educational video *Into the Circle* (1992). Because it is a ceremonial instrument, it is capitalized here.

12. Ritzenthaler's fieldnotes were unpublished. According to Vennum the information in them dates from around 1940.

13. Rob Coyne is a pseudonym. Native Gatherings were held concurrently with Indian Days during the 1990s.

14. Richard Keezer is a well-known artist; the imaginative conception behind this example provides just a glimpse of his talents.

15. *Mihkomuwehsisok* are small supernatural beings that reside in the woods; they are often solitary. Like the fairies of Irish folklore and the trolls of Finnish folklore, they can sometimes help human beings but can do great harm if angered. Unlike the Irish, Peskotomuhkatiyik do not have elaborate protocols for keeping them happy.

16. Nakai is of mixed heritage, including Navajo, and plays several kinds of flutes in various contemporary and traditional styles. Many of his compositions and improvisations are based on traditional songs from Native cultural repertories.

17. *Dreamwalk*, Klarity Multimedia: www.klaritymusic.com.

18. My interpretation of what I was told concurs with the classification of unconscious power given by Mary Douglas (1966:98) but not entirely with her complete analysis, since she goes on to argue that unconscious power is generally treated as evil, whereas in the Wabanaki case, women's unconscious power is not evil, only dangerous if not contained.

19. My data about women's power, and my conclusions, contradict those of many previous scholars, but I have no reason to doubt my consultants' statements. Many factors could account for the differences: my own gender versus that of previous researchers; changing attitudes toward discussing bodily functions with outsiders, both within the Passamaquoddy community and in American society generally; and changing attitudes toward women in both cultural contexts.

20. My historical knowledge was solicited by some of the women drummers, but I stayed out of the formal discussions.

21. There have been several outstanding exceptions. The Red Dawn Drum from Sipayik was largely directed by women, and between 1993 and 1995 the majority of the group's membership was women. The Bear Claw singers from Wagmatcook Mi'kmaq Reserve, active in the 1990s, was an all-women group of teenagers and young adults, led by an older (middle-aged) woman. In 1994, efforts to start a women's Drum group in the Aroostook Mi'kmaq community surrounding Presque Isle, Maine, were frustrated. Mary Philbrook, former chief of the Aroostook Band of Mi'kmaqs who achieved prominence during their suit for U.S. Federal recognition, was a supporter of the effort. But there was opposition based on the belief that women should not drum, even in private. Philbrook has maintained drumming as part of teaching her girls about their tradition (*Wabanaki: A New Dawn*, 19:36).

22. Talking Circles are nonconfrontational discussion groups with a protocol that the name itself implies: participants sit in a circle, and each has a chance to speak in turn; everything said is held confidential. One need not speak if one does not wish to.

23. The latter facility had several reorganizations between its opening in 1994 and 2003. It was originally a facility for youth transitioning back into the community from outside experience such as treatment and incarceration.

24. The cannon was donated to a metal drive during World War II. A humorous anecdote about the custom of firing the cannon was related by Joseph A. Nicholas, who recalled that a limousine driver working one summer on Campobello Island had decided to drive to Eastport on his Sunday off; mistaking his car for the bishop's, those watching on the reservation had the cannon fired, and a procession went out to greet him. According to Nicholas, the surprised driver declared that a black man had never received such a welcome anywhere.

5. Welcoming Ceremonies

1. At several public gatherings and powwows I have attended, including the Bar Harbor Annual Native American Day and the Maine Native American Appreciation Day, the ceremonies were not used. These occasions were open to the public and included large numbers of participants who would not have known how to perform the dances. Powwows

in the Northeast tend to fall into two categories: public, concerned with teaching outsiders; and private, focused on concerns of the Native community.

2. See the Passamaquoddy pronunciation guide, table 1, for the pronunciation of *qanute*: *gwah nooo day*. The meaning of the term is discussed in the analysis section of this chapter.

3. My interpretation contradicts that of Nicholas N. Smith, who in a 1995 paper analyzed the ceremonies observed by Cartier and Biard as part of a historical Trading Dance and implied that trade was so necessary for survival that it dictated alliance structures. His supporting evidence for the primary importance of trade in Wabanaki cultures is drawn from a Northwest culture based on an economy entirely different from that of the Wabanaki peoples. Smith's larger point that the nineteenth- and twentieth-century Trading Dances functioned to reinforce social bonds within Native communities is excellent; but I do not agree with his conflation of sixteenth- and seventeenth-century interactions between Native communities and outsiders with these later, internal practices. Trading with Europeans in early seventeenth-century encounters arguably was not a necessity for Waponahkiyik. The insults given to Verrazzano when he presented poor-quality goods to a group of men on the coast of Maine in the early sixteenth century (Wroth 1970:141), and incidents in which Europeans resorted to violence to get furs, suggest that Native traders were discriminating in their dealings with Europeans (Bourque 2001:126). European goods were prestige items in Native communities (Prins 1996:59). Great cultural changes occurred rapidly; by the mid-seventeenth century, access to European trade goods had altered the political economy of the Northeast.

4. The presence, and reception, of representatives from Venezuela at the 2008 Wabanaki Confederacy meeting suggests that this idea is still prevalent; at the time, the Venezuelan-owned oil company Citgo had a special agreement to supply heating oil to some of the constituent First Nations.

5. Anthropologists have paid a great deal of attention to the functions of gift-giving, both cross-culturally (e.g., Mauss [1925] 1967) and in specific cultures. A full analysis of Wabanaki gift-giving is beyond the scope of this study.

6. Recent evidence that the Powhatan, also Eastern Algonquians, conducted warfare in similarly symbolic fashion has been presented by Frederic Gleach (1993, 1994).

7. See Havard 2001 for a detailed analysis of the Treaty of Montreal. The advent of European colonial interests in Wabanaki territories was at first more an intrusion on the existing indigenous situation than a determining factor.

8. An overview of Wabanaki indigenization of Catholic practices is the subject of my article, "Medeolinuwok, Music, and Missionaries in Maine" (Spinney 2006).

9. *Portland Press Herald*, undated clippings in University of Maine at Machias, Merrill Library, vertical file. The original photographs were lost in a fire at the *Press Herald* building.

10. Smudging is a religious ceremony used in many Native contexts. At a powwow, it is typically used to prepare dancers, singers, drums, and other participants. Sweetgrass and other medicines are slowly burned, usually in a large shell, and the smoke is brushed, usually with an eagle feather, over the participant while praying.

11. Ethnomusicologists and anthropologists generally call this the Stomp Dance step, although in many cases the motion is light and graceful. The step is used in the Cherokee Stomp Dance.

231

12. Curtis used her own phonetic system, and as she did not spend much time in the Native communities in Maine, her system does not reflect the structure of their languages. Furthermore, she does not seem to have checked her transcriptions with anyone other than the singers she got them from, so that individual features of pronunciation such as lisps are reproduced. She did not use recording equipment, but transcribed by ear in one sitting.

13. Iroquois examples are found in Fenton (1942b:18, 20, 25, 29); and Kurath (1964:121, 193, 201, 259). The word is prominent in a Maliseet Lonesome Song recorded by J. D. Prince (1898, 1914) and also by Natalie Curtis ([1907] 1968:27). This song represents a man singing of greeting his beloved as he comes down river in a canoe. Mechling's recordings do not contain any songs identified as Welcome or Greeting Songs.

14. My consultants were unable to identify John Salis.

15. Manuscripts of several songs from *The Indians' Book* were given to the Maine State Museum in 2003; thanks to Dr. Bruce Bourque I was able to examine them. These manuscripts look like fair copies, the final handwritten copy made after any number of drafts (this term was codified by researchers studying the compositional processes of composers such as Beethoven); however, there are some deviations from the published versions. Most notably, the song labeled "Penobscot Song of Greeting II" is labeled "Passamaquoddy Song of Greeting" in the manuscript. It has a different second phrase, rising to D flat instead of B flat; and the second bar of the third phrase has only three eighth notes where the published version has four. Whether these are a copyist's mistake or represent the original information is undetermined. Research into the provenance of the manuscripts has not turned up proof that they are in Curtis's hand. The music paper is commercial, widely available, and difficult to date. Letters are shaped differently than they appear in the published book. This could be her own hand or that of an assistant, or an erroneous diplomatic copy made from her published book by someone with an interest in the songs. A diplomatic copy is one that attempts to reproduce the original, rather than to transcribe it into conventional notation—here, someone attempting to make his handwritten copy conform to Curtis's published text. *The Indians' Book* broke new ground in presenting handwritten transcriptions rather than typeset ones; Curtis insisted that this showed the phrasing of the music more accurately (Curtis [1923] 1968:xii). Her use of meter signatures, however, does not correspond with her notation in several of the Wabanaki examples.

16. The transcriptions are numbered independently of the recordings, but can be correlated by close listening. The provenance and functional designations on the recordings do not always match those ascribed to the transcriptions. PR 18 described as sung by the host chief to visitors on page 294 of the book is labeled "Skawahe (Old Style Greeting Dance)" in the cylinder collection. PR 72 the second example of the "formal Penobscot Greeting Song" is labeled "Maliseet, Wedding Dance" in the cylinder collection.

17. Penobscot Elders told researcher Nicholas Smith that Speck had not known how to handle the cylinder recorder and had been shown up by his student assistant, William Hubbs Mechling. Smith believes that Mechling left Speck's tutelage after this (Smith, personal communication). Mechling was working for the Canadian Geological Survey between 1910 and 1913, recording songs with Mi'kmaq and Maliseet singers in Canada. His dissertation based on this material was completed at Harvard in 1917. Mechling's recordings are mostly excellent; most of Speck's suffer from overmodulation and distortion.

18. Melismatic means that more than one tone is sung to a syllable. In the transcriptions, this is indicated by a dash extending from one syllable under several notes.

19. This expedition is discussed in chapter 2.

20. This is one of two International Park facilities in Passamaquoddy Bay shared by the United States and Canada. The other is the Roosevelt estate on Campobello Island.

21. An informational pamphlet publicizing the recognition issue was distributed at various heritage sites in the area during the summer of 2004.

6. Ceremonies of Peace and War

1. "Tribal" is used here in no derogatory sense but only to designate a specific type of social organization. In the context of changing patterns of warfare over the course of Western history, the current emphasis on sanctions and United Nations resolutions could signal a return to ritual displays of power after the most lethal century of warfare in human history.

2. See especially I. Brown 2006 and Turnbaugh 1979.

3. For a summary, see Paper 1988.

4. Blakeslee 1981 argues for an origin in the Plains culture area as early as the thirteenth century.

5. See Ruth Whitehead's summary in Bourque (2001:306–9); plates VI, XV, and catalogue description in Paper (1988:133); and discussion in Willoughby ([1935] 1973:181–90).

6. Such duality seems to be a theme in Passamaquoddy aesthetics. A similar principle is also used by Passamaquoddy artist Richard Keezer to decorate shakers such as illustration 4. See also Morrison and Ezzo 1985.

7. The catalogue of pipes in museum collections in Paper (1988:121–40) indicates pipes associated with treaties.

8. Paper (1988:1–3) includes a concise description of an intertribal pipe ceremony.

9. *Mihkomuwehsisok* are analogous to the Irish *Sí* (fairies): supernatural beings who do not always choose to be seen by human beings, who sometimes bless and sometimes are malevolent toward humans. See chapter 4, note 15.

10. Melvyn Francis died in a tragic winter traffic accident in 2006. The 2006 Sipayik Indian Days were dedicated to his memory, and the commemorative T-shirt is an image of *Sakom* Francis offering the Pipe in this ceremony.

11. By pointing out the similarity, I do not mean to imply a Catholic basis for the Peace Pipe Ceremony. See discussion of the Calumet Dance, below. I am simply following the lead of my consultants. Many Catholic and Wabanaki ceremonies share a similar underlying aesthetic as well as some procedures. See my analysis of Wabanaki Catholic practice (Spinney 2006).

12. In the passage cited, Lescarbot says, "Some [men] have girdles made of matachias [wampum] which they use only when they wish to set themselves out." John Josselyn noted in his general observations about the First Nations of New England that wampum was used to adorn leaders ([1674] 1988:101). The ceremonial use of wampum is discussed in more detail in chapter 7, on the Marriage Dance.

13. Several illustrations of Native leaders with calumets and with wampum are included in the first edition of Havard, *La Grande Paix de Montréal de 1701* (Recherches Amérindiennes au Québec, 1992).

14. The evidence is that Passamaquoddy people played flutes privately for charming a beloved or other personal uses (see chapter 3).

15. Cylinders 9, 20, 23, 34, and 38; cylinder 6 is broken. 34 appears to be a Mi'kmaq song, and 9 ends with the exclamation proper to Wedding Dance Songs: "Matamaliye!"

16. Cylinder 5048 is labeled Maliseet, 5109 and 5111 are labeled Micmac [*sic*], 5069 and 5097 (which is broken) are labeled Penobscot.

17. William Neptune told Nicholas Smith in 1953 that the press were always invited, but never came (Smith, personal communication). Three photos from the *Portland Press Herald* document the installation of the Penobscot *Sakom* by visiting Passamaquoddy delegates in the 1940s and 1950s. I found these undated, uncatalogued photos in the Vertical File at Merrill Library, University of Maine at Machias; the originals were lost in a fire at the *Press Herald* building in Portland.

18. They were held in November 1994; in January 2007 (following the October 2006 election). January installations were the custom when Nicholas Smith was documenting them in the mid-1950s (personal communication).

19. This is Williamson's spelling. The name is usually spelled Attean, and is derived from the French *Etienne* (Stephen).

20. This group was not a formal choir that met regularly for rehearsals but was composed of parishioners who volunteered consistently and were contacted by the priest when needed. During my fieldwork at Sipayik I was welcomed into it. Blessed Kateri Tekakwitha (1656–1680), "the Lily of the Mohawks," is venerated by many Native North American Catholics. She was beatified in 1980 but has not yet been confirmed a saint.

21. Although several Wabanaki individuals have made careers in Nashville and on the country circuit, this band had no personal connection to the tribe.

22. This song is used often for dances of all kinds, with the phrase, *kakawtehkomuhsic*, which means "dance faster." Commonly used dance melodies are discussed in the concluding chapter as a significant feature of Passamaquoddy performance style.

23. There is no date on the recording, but it is estimated to be from the 1960s.

24. In an unpublished paper, "Views of Repatriation—from the Ground," I discussed the Passamaquoddy community's process of absorbing the 1890 Fewkes recordings, to which they gained access in 1980 after the cylinders were salvaged.

7. The Marriage Ceremony and Social Dances

1. Traditional (capitalized) is a term Native people used to indicate connection to the past. Scholars may debate the linkage as previously discussed, or refine it using terms such as neotraditional, borrowed tradition, etc. In this case, there is a difference between a contemporary Traditional wedding and historical practices.

2. Frank Speck (1919a) reported that wampum belts and collars made for purposes of the Wabanaki Confederacy had been repurposed as marriage wampum, but this does not negate that fact that originally, strings were woven with cues for the marriage protocols. It only emphasizes the connection between marriage ceremonies and political protocols.

3. Speck 1919a contains photographs of several strings.

4. Maillard's description of marriage among the Mi'kmaq (and Maliseets) "in their unconverted state" says that the "juggler" (i.e., a tribal religious leader) "pronounced" the couple married (1758:53, 57). It is possible that even after conversion, during the yearly periods when clergy were absent, this function could have been performed by a Native leader. We know that Wabanaki community leaders did fulfill the functions of clergy, sometimes officially sanctioned by the church as deacons (Erickson 1980, 1985; Milliea 1989). This practice continues today, with men in the Native communities of the Diocese of Maine consecrated as deacons and able to perform marriages within the Catholic Church.

5. The concept of "song families" or "tune families" is commonly applied to European folk music. See Bayard 1950 for a full explication.

6. "Traditional" is a self-designation by which an individual means that she follows Native teachings. These may include contemporary ideas as well as her specific tribal heritage. See note 1 above.

7. The different powwow dance genres are discussed in detail in many excellent studies ranging from the scholarly (Browner 2002) to surveys designed for elementary schools (Burton 1993).

8. This is a feature of Ghost Dance song texts (Vander 1997:332–34) and of many Navajo ceremonial song texts (Witherspoon 1977:34). The *Tuhtuwas* Dance does not share the ritual function of those song genres, however.

9. This transcription in Speck's text is not linked with a cylinder number but may have been taken from cylinder 5066, track b, which has a similar melody. The recording is designated a "Micmac Dance," a comical men's freestyle dance (one of four songs Speck recorded for the "Micmac Dance"). See chapter 3 for a hypothesis of why a comical dance might have been identified with Mi'kmaq dancers.

10. I am grateful to Nicholas Smith for granting me access to his master tapes.

11. Most of the material in this section was previously published in the Papers of the Thirtieth Algonquian Conference (Spinney 1999).

12. The Two-Step is a popular powwow dance for couples.

13. The transcriptions in Fewkes's article were done by Simeon P. Cheney, who also transcribed bird songs and seems to have had an excellent ear. See his *Wood Notes Wild* (1892). Because Fewkes's recordings of the Snake Dance songs were the first field recordings made, they are famous in academic circles. A Snake Dance song sung by Noel Josephs was included in the Spottswood (1978) collection of American folksongs put out by the Library of Congress in the 1970s. The error in the published transcription is not noted in the literature.

14. Hagar's findings were reaffirmed by Trudy Sable.

15. This cylinder in the Speck collection is now broken.

16. On the piano this matches the following sequence of white keys: C, D, F, G, A with D as tonic. In cylinder 8 the actual tonic is G; In cylinder 13 it is F#; In cylinder 25 it is E.

17. During his lifetime, Andrew Dana was ambivalent about granting public access to his recordings, so no transcription is given here.

18. Sable also speculates on this point, referring to the Adena mounds in Ohio from ca. 3000 to 4000 years before the present (1997:331).

19. Accounts range from the period of early contacts to the present day. Recall Martin Pring's description of Native men dancing to European music on board his ship in 1603 (chapter 2). These days, pop bands and DJs are hired to perform after ceremonial dances at the *Sakomawkan* and other occasions.

20. None of my consultants could remember precisely when.

8. Aethetics and Survival

1. Densmore (1926:72) noted the importance of these "private" song genres in the transmission of Native American traditions.

2. Historical documents dating as far back as the seventeenth century indicate that

early spring has always been the hardest time of year. Trade with Europeans strained the natural resources of the Maritimes, making survival difficult (Denys 1908 [1672]:446).

3. An example occurred when one of the Passamaquoddy Drum groups was invited to a university some hours distant for Earth Day. After arrival, they were unhappy with the situation, and when asked to sing a song at the formal luncheon for invited speakers, they sang a well known one in the 49 Song intertribal genre about Mickey Mouse. While the lyrics may have been obvious, the whole 49 Song genre makes fun of Anglo-American cultural institutions: country music songs, one-eyed Fords, the obsession with infidelity, etc.

4. This technique is common in medieval and Renaissance European music manuscripts, and it is from this context that the term *contrafactum* comes. It was used extensively in the creation of Protestant hymns.

5. Context is also an important component in the meaning of ceremonies, as discussed in the Introduction with reference to Vine Deloria's argument in *God Is Red* (2003).

6. Incompatibilities between administrative structures and traditional values are discussed in chapter 1.

7. The Passamaquoddy language is generally classified as nonconfigurational and polysynthetic. See Bruening 2001.

8. See Szabo and Bode 1974 for other examples. See Rees-Miller 1996 on the morphology of loan word lexemes in Algonquian languages.

9. Benedict (1932, 1934) used the term *ethos*, which was later refined by Gregory Bateson into *ethos* and *eidos*, with *ethos* being "the system of emotional attitudes" of a cultural system and *eidos* referring to its cognitive aspects (Bateson 1958:220).

10, More ornate decorations of collars, lapels and hems were preferred. See Ruth Whitehead's discussion of dress and illustrations in Bourque 2001:258–69.

11. By that time they were also being performed in similar contexts at other reservations, including St. Francis (Ôdanak), Quebec, and Indian Island, Maine.

References

AFSC (American Friends Service Committee). 1989. *The Wabanakis of Maine and the Maritimes: A Resource Book about Penobscot, Passamaquoddy, Maliseet, Micmac, and Abenaki Indians.* Bath, ME: American Friends Service Committee.

Alger, Abby Langdon. 1897. *In Indian Tents: Stories Told by Penobscot, Passamaquoddy and Micmac Indians to Abby L. Alger.* Boston: Roberts Brothers.

Allan, John. 1867. *Military Operations in Eastern Maine and Nova Scotia During the Revolution: Chiefly Compiled from the Journals and Letters of Colonel John Allan with Notes and a Memoir of Col. John Allan by Frederic Kidder.* Albany [N.Y.]: J. Munsell.

AMS (Ann Morrison Spinney). Ethnographic Fieldnotes, various dates.

Augustine, Donna, George Paul, James Augustine, et al. 1994. *Traditional Voices from the Eastern Door* (cassette). Vols. 1–2. Available from James Augustine, Big Cove, N.B., Canada.

Axtell, James. 1979. "Ethnohistory: An Historian's Viewpoint." *Ethnohistory* 26/1:1–13.

Bateson, Gregory. [1936] 1958. *Naven.* 2d ed. Stanford, CA: Stanford University Press.

———. 1978. "Towards a Theory of Cultural Coherence: Comment." *Anthropological Quarterly* 51/1:77–78.

Bayard, Samuel P. 1950. "Prolegomena to a Study of the Principal Melodic Families of British-American Folk Song." *Journal of American Folklore* 63/247:1–44.

Beaujoyeulx, Balthasar de. [1581] 1981. *Le ballet-comique.* Facsimile, with an introduction by Margaret M. McGowan. *Medieval and Renaissance Texts and Studies*, vol. 6; *Renaissance Triumphs and Magnificences*, n.s.1. Binghamton, NY: Center for Medieval & Early Renaissance Studies.

Benedict, Ruth. 1932. "Configurations of culture in North America." *American Anthropologist*, n.s., 34/1:1–27.

———. 1934. *Patterns of Culture.* New York: Mariner Books, 2005.

Biard, Pierre. [1611] 1896. "Lettre au R. P. Christophe Baltazar, Provincial de France, à Paris; Port Royal, June 10." In *The Jesuit Relations and Allied Documents: Travels and Explorations of the Jesuit Missionaries in New France 1610–1791*, edited by Rueben Gold Thwaites, 1:139–183. Cleveland: Burrows.

———. [1612] 1896. "Lettre au R. P. Provincial à Paris; Port Royal, January 31." In *The Jesuit Relations and Allied Documents: Travels and Explorations of the Jesuit Missionaries in New France 1610–1791*, edited by Rueben Gold Thwaites, 2:3–56. Cleveland: Burrows.

———. [1616] 1896. *Relation de la Novvelle France, de se Terres, Natvrel du Pais, & de ses Habitans*. In *The Jesuit Relations and Allied Documents: Travels and Explorations of the Jesuit Missionaries in New France 1610–1791*, edited by Rueben Gold Thwaites, 3:21–283, 4:7–165. Cleveland: Burrows.

Blakeslee, Donald J. 1981. "The Origin and Spread of the Calumet Ceremony." *American Antiquity* 46/4:759–68.

Bock, Philip K. 1966. *The Micmac Indians of Restigouche: History and Contemporary Description*. National Museum of Canada, Bulletin 213, Anthropological Series 77. Ottawa.

Bohlman, Philip V. 1991. "Representation and Cultural Critique in the History of Ethnomusicology." In *Comparative Musicology and Anthropology of Music: Essays on the History of Ethnomusicology*, edited by Bruno Nettl and Philip V. Bohlman. Chicago: University of Chicago Press.

Bourdieu , Pierre. 1977. *Outline of a Theory of Practice*. Translated by Richard Nice. Cambridge Studies in Social Anthropology, 16. Cambridge: Cambridge University Press.

———. [1979] 1984. *Distinction: A Social Critique of the Judgement of Taste*. Translated by Richard Nice. Cambridge, MA: Harvard University Press.

Bourque, Bruce. 1989. "Ethnicity on the Maritime Peninsula." *Ethnohistory* 36/3:257–84.

———. 2001. *Twelve Thousand Years: American Indians in Maine*. Lincoln: University of Nebraska Press.

Brasser, Theodore J. 1978. "Early Indian-European Contacts." In *Handbook of North American Indians*, edited by William C. Sturtevant, 15, *Northeast*, edited by Bruce G. Trigger, 78–88. Washington, DC: Smithsonian Institution.

Brown, Ian W. 2006. "The Calumet Ceremony in the Southeast as Observed Archeologically." In *Powhatan's Mantle: Indians in the Colonial Southeast*, edited by Gregory A. Waselkov, Peter H. Wood, and Tom Hatley. Rev. ed., 371–419. Lincoln: University of Nebraska Press.

Brown, Mrs. W. Wallace. 1888. "Some Indoor and Outdoor Games of the Wabanaki Indians." *Transactions of the Royal Society of Canada*, section 2:41–46.

———. 1892. " 'Chief-making' among the Passamaquoddy Indians." *Journal of American Folk-lore* 5/16:57–59.

Browner, Tara. 1997. "Breathing the Indian Spirit: Thoughts on Musical Borrowing and the 'Indianist' Movement in American Music." *American Music* 15/3:265–84.

Browner, Tara. 2000. Making and Singing Pow–wow Songs: Text, Form, and the Significance of Culture–based Analysis. *Ethnomusicology* 44/2:214–33.

———. 2002. *Heartbeat of the People: Music and Dance of the Northern Pow-wow*. Urbana: University of Illinois Press.

Bruening, Benjamin. 2001. "Constraints on Dependencies in Passamaquoddy." In *Actes du Trente-Deuxième Congrès des Algonquinistes*, edited by John D. Nichols. Winnipeg: University of Manitoba.

Burrage, Henry S., ed. 1967 [1906]. *Early English and French Voyages (Chiefly from Hakluyt), 1534–1608*. In *Original Narratives of Early American History*, general editor J. F. Jameson. New York: Barnes and Noble.

Burton, Bryan. 1993. *Moving within the Circle: Contemporary Native American Music and Dance*. Danbury, CT: World Music Press.

Cadieux, Lorenzo, ed. 1973. *Lettres des Nouvelles Missions du Canada, 1843–1852*. Montreal: Editions Bellarmin

Calloway, Colin. 1990. *The Abenakis of Western Vermont, 1600–1800: War, Migration, and the Survival of an Indian People*. Norman: University of Oklahoma Press.

Cartier, Jacques. 1924. *The Voyages of Jacques Cartier*. Publications of the Public Archives of Canada, no. 11. Ottawa: F. Acland.

Cavanaugh, Beverly Diamond. 1989. "Music and Gender in the Sub-Arctic Algonquian Area." In *Women in North American Indian Music: Six Essays*, edited by Richard Keeling, 55–66. Bloomington, IN: Society for Ethnomusicology, Special Series no. 6.

Ceci, Lynn. 1990. "Squanto and the Pilgrims: On Planting Corn 'in the Manner of the Indians.'" In *The Invented Indian: Cultural Fictions and Government Policies*, edited by James Clifton. New Brunswick, NJ: Transaction.

Champlain, Samuel de. 1922 [1603]. *Of Savages*. In *The Works of Samuel de Champlain, in Six Volumes*, edited by H. P. Biggar. vol. 1:1599–1607. Translated and edited by H. H. Langton and W. F. Ganong, 83–189. Toronto: Champlain Society.

Cheney, Simeon P. 1892. *Wood Notes Wild: Notations of Bird Music*. Boston: Lee and Shepard.

Clifford, James. 1990. "Traveling Selves, Traveling Others." Paper presented at the conference, Cultural Studies Now and in the Future, April 5–9, University of Illinois at Urbana Champaign. Quoted in Slobin (1992).

Clifton, James. 1990. *The Invented Indian: Cultural Fictions and Government Policies*. New Brunswick, NJ: Transaction.

Cruikshank, Julie. Do Glaciers Listen?: "Local Knowledge, Colonial Encounters, & Social Imagination" Seattle: University of Washington Press.

Curtis (Burlin), Natalie. [1923] 1968. *The Indians' Book*. 2d ed. New York: Harper; New York: Dover.

Davenport, Linda Gilbert. 1977. "Music among the Contemporary Penobscot Indians." Masters thesis, University of Illinois, Urbana-Champaign.

Deloria, Vine. 2003. *God Is Red*. 30th Anniversary Edition. Golden, CO: Fulcrum.

Demillier, Edmund Louis. n.d. [Prayerbook, manuscript.] Maine Historical Society, Portland, ME, Eugene Vetromile Papers.

Denny Family Singers. *Mi'kmaq Chants*. Kewniq Recordings Productions, SRC505. Audiocassette.

Densmore, Frances. 1926. *The American Indians and Their Music*. New York: Woman's Press.

Denys, Nicholas. [1672] 1908. *The Description and Natural History of the Coasts of North America (Acadia)*. Translated and edited by William F. Ganong. Publications of the Champlain Society, no. 2. Toronto: Champlain Society.

Diamond, Beverly, M. Sam Cronk, and Fanziska von Rosen. 1994. *Visions of Sound: Musical Instruments of First Nations Communities in Northeastern America*. Chicago: University of Chicago Press.

Douglas, Mary. 1966. *Purity and Danger: An Analysis of Concepts of Pollution and Taboo*. New York: Praeger.

———. 1968. "Pollution." *International Encyclopedia of the Social Sciences*, edited by David L. Sills, 12:336–41. Reprinted in *Reader in Comparative Religion: An Anthropological Approach*, 3rd ed, edited by William Lessa and Evon Vogt, 196–202. New York: Harper & Row, 1972.

Drake, James. 1999. *King Philip's War: Civil War in New England, 1675–1676*. Amherst: University of Massachusetts Press.

Duffy, Patrick 1994. "Conflicts in Heritage and Tourism." In *Culture, Tourism, and Development: The Case of Ireland*, edited by Ullrich Kockel, 77–86. Liverpool: Liverpool University Press.

Duggan, Betty. 1997. "Tourism, Cultural Authenticity, and the Native Crafts Cooperative: The Eastern Cherokee Experience." In *Tourism and Culture: An Applied Perspective*, edited by Erve Chambers, 31–57. Albany: State University of New York Press.

Eckstorm, Fannie Hardy. 1924. *The Penobscot Man*. Boston: Houghton Mifflin.

———. 1939. "Who Was Paugus?" *New England Quarterly* 12/2:203–26.

———. 1941. *Indian Place-Names of the Penobscot Valley and the Maine Coast*. University of Maine Studies, 2nd ser., 55. Orono: University of Maine at Orono Press.

———. [1945] 1980. *Old John Neptune and Other Maine Shamans*. Portland, ME: The Southworth-Anthoensen Press. Reprint: Orono: University of Maine at Orono Press.

Erickson, Vincent O. 1978. "The Micmac Buoin: Three Centuries of Cultural and Semantic Change." *Man in the Northeast* 15–16:3–41.

———. 1980. "The Thomas *Kyrie* Manuscript." In *Papers of the Tenth Algonquian Conference, 1979*, edited by William Cowan, 79–91. Ottawa: Carleton University.

———. 1982. "Economic Factors and the Development of Factionalism among the Passamaquoddy in the Early 19th Century." In *Papers of the Thirteenth Algonquian Conference, 1981*, edited by William Cowan, 169–78. Ottawa: Carleton University.

———. 1985. "Passamaquoddies and Protestants: Deacon Sockabason and the Reverend Kellogg of the Society for Propagating the Gospel." *Man in the Northeast* 29:87–107.

Feit, Harvey. 1991. "The Construction of Algonquian Hunting Territories." In *Colonial Situations: Essays on the Contextualization of Ethnographic Knowledge*, edited by George W. Stocking Jr., 109–33. *History of Anthropology*, Vol. 7. Madison: University of Wisconsin Press.

Fenton, William N. 1942a. *Songs from the Iroquois Longhouse: Folk Music of the United States*. Washington, DC: The Library of Congress.

———. 1942b. *Songs from the Iroquois Longhouse: Program Notes for an Album of American Indian Music from the Eastern Woodlands*. Washington, DC: Smithsonian Institution.

———. 1998. *The Great Law and the Longhouse*. Norman: University of Oklahoma Press.

Fewkes, Jesse Walter. 1890a. "A Contribution to Passamaquoddy Folk-Lore." *Journal of American Folk-lore* 3/11:257–80.

———. 1890b. [Passamaquoddy Recordings, wax cylinders]. Audiocassette copies, Waponahki Museum, Perry, ME, general collection.

Fischer, David Hackett. 1989. *Albion's Seed: Four British Folkways in America*. New York: Oxford University Press.

French, Edward. "Inauguration Ceremony Held for Sipayik Leaders." *Quoddy Tides*, January 26, 2007, 25.

Frisbie, Charlotte. 1989. "Gender and Navajo Music: Unanswered Questions." In *Women in North American Indian Music: Six Essays*, edited by Richard Keeling, 22–38. Bloomington, IN: Society for Ethnomusicology, Special Series, No. 6.

Gerber, Ray, and Mark Hedden. 2004. *Song of the Drum: The Petroglyphs of Maine*. DVD. Brunswick, ME: Acadia Productions.

Gleach, Frederic W. 1993. "The Powhatan Aesthetic of War: A Work in Progress." In *Papers of the Twenty-fourth Algonquian Conference*, edited by William Cowan, 119–211. Ottawa: Carleton University.

————. 1994. "Pocahontas and Captain John Smith Revisited." In *Actes du 25 Congrès des Algonquinistes*, edited by William Cowan, 167–86. Ottawa: Carleton University.

Graettinger, Diana. "Pleasant Point Governor Inaugurated." *Bangor Daily News*, January 22, 2007, B1, B4.

Greenblatt, Stephen. 1991. *Marvelous Possessions: The Wonder of the New World*. Chicago: University of Chicago Press.

Grumet, Robert S. 1996. *Northeastern Indian Lives, 1632–1816*. Amherst: University of Massachusetts Press.

Gyles, John. 1736. *Memoirs of Odd Adventures, Strange Deliverances, &c in the Captivity of John Gyles, Esq. . . .* Boston: S. Kneeland and T. Green; Facsimile, Early American Imprints, 1st Series No. 4021.

Haefeli, Evan, and Kevin Sweeney. 1994. "Wattanummon's World: Personal and Tribal Identity in the Algonquian Diaspora c. 1660–1712." In *Actes du Vingt-cinquième Congrès des Algonquinistes*, edited by William Cowan, 212–24. Ottawa: Carleton University.

Hagar, Stansbury T. 1895. "Micmac Customs and Traditions." *American Anthropologist* 8:31–42.

Hall, Robert L. 1997. *An Archeology of the Soul: North American Indian Belief and Ritual*. Urbana: University of Illinois Press.

Havard, Gilles. 2001. *The Great Peace of Montreal of 1701: French-Native Diplomacy in the Seventeenth Century*. Montreal: McGill-Queen's University Press.

Heriot, George. [1807] 1971. *Travels Through the Canadas, Containing a Description of the Picturesque Scenery on Some of the Rivers and Lakes; With an Account of the Productions, Commerce, and Inhabitants of those Provinces*. Rutland, VT: Charles E. Tuttle.

Heth, Charlotte. 1982. "Can Ethnohistory Help the Ethnomusicologist?" *American Indian Culture and Research Journal* 6/1:63–78.

————. 1985. *Songs of the Eastern Indians from Medicine Spring and Allegheny*. Recorded Anthology of American Music. New World Records, NW 337.

Hobsbawm, Eric, and Terrance Ranger. 1983. *The Invention of Tradition*. Cambridge: Cambridge University Press.

Hodgen, Margaret T. 1964. *Early Anthropology in the Sixteenth and Seventeenth Centuries*. Philadelphia: University of Pennsylvania Press.

Hoffman, Bernard G. 1955. "The Historical Ethnography of the Micmac of the Sixteenth and Seventeenth Centuries." Ph.D. dissertation, University of California at Berkeley.

Hoffmann, Bernard G. 1961. *Cabot to Cartier: Sources for a Historical Ethnography of Northeastern North America 1497–1550*. Toronto: University of Toronto Press.

Hughes–Freeland, F. 2001. "Performance: Anthropological Aspects." In *International Encyclopedia of the Social and Behavioral Sciences*, edited by Neil J. Smelser and Paul B. Baltes, 11231–11236. Oxford: Pergamon. http://www.sciencedirect.com/science/article/B7MRM–4MT09VJ–2CY/2/53087a8965589ec6a8c4bb9648b3750d.

Ignace de Paris. [1653] 1883. "Lettre du Rev. Père Ignace, Capucin, Senlis, ce 6e Aoust." In *Collection de manuscrits et autre documents historiques relatifs a la Nouvelle France*, pages 136–139. Québec: A. Cote.

————. [1656] 1905. "Lettre du Père Ignace sur l'Acadie." In *Rapport sur les Archives Canadiennes, Document de la session*, 18:3–11.

Into the Circle: An Introduction to Native American Powwows. DVD. 1992. Full Circle Communications.

The Jesuit Relations and Allied Documents: Travels and Explorations of the Jesuit Missionaries in New France 1610–1797. 1896–1901. 73 vols. Edited by Reuben Gold Thwaites. Cleveland: Burrows.

Josselyn, John. [1674] 1988. "The Second Voyage" In *A Critical Edition of Two Voyage to New-England,* edited by Paul J. Lindholdt, 27–147. Hanover: University Press of New England.

Kaeppler, Adrienne. 2001. "Dance and the Concept of Style." *Yearbook for Traditional Music* 33:49–63.

———. 2007. "Ethnochoreology." *Grove Music Online,* edited by L. Macy. http://www.grovemusic.com.

Kauder, Charles Christian. 1866. *Buch das Gut, enthaltend den Katechismus, Betrachtung, Gesang.* Vienna: Staatsdruckerei.

Keeling, Richard, ed. 1989. *Women in North American Indian Music: Six Essays.* Society for Ethnomusicology, Special Series No. 6.

Kemper, S. 2001. "Practice: Anthropological Aspects." *International Encyclopedia of the Social Sciences.*

Kenny, Kevin. 2000. *The American Irish: A History.* New York: Longman/Pearson.

Kidder, Frederic. 1867. *Military Operations in Eastern Maine and Nova Scotia during the Revolution, Chiefly Compiled from the Journals and Letters of Colonel John Allan, with Notes and a Memoir of Col. John Allan.* Albany: Joel Munsell; reprint, New York: Kraus, 1971.

Klein, Laura F., and Lillian A. Ackerman. 1995. *Women and Power in Native North America.* Norman: University of Oklahoma Press.

Kostyk, Dennis, and David Westphal. 1995. *Wabanaki: A New Dawn.* Hallowell, ME: Maine Indian Tribal–State Commission.

Koren, Henry J. 1962. *Knaves or Knights? A History of the Spiritan Missionaries in Acadia and North America, 1732–1839.* Duquesnes Studies, Spiritan Series, 4. Pittsburgh: Duquesne University Press.

Kurath, Gertrude. 1956. "Antiphonal Songs of Eastern Woodland Indians." *The Musical Quarterly* 42/2:520–26.

———. 1964. *Iroquois Music and Dance: Ceremonial Arts of Two Seneca Longhouses.* Smithsonian Institution Bureau of American Ethnology, Bulletin 187. Washington, DC: U.S. Government Printing Office.

Lalement, Jerome. [1647] 1896. "Relation of 1647." In *The Jesuit Relations and Allied Documents,* edited by Rueben Gold Thwaites. Vols. 30–32. Cleveland: Burrows Brothers.

———. [1662] 1896. "Relation of 1661–62." In *The Jesuit Relations and Allied Documents,* Edited by Rueben Gold Thwaites. Vol. 47. Cleveland: Burrows Brothers.

Leavitt, Robert M., and David A. Francis, eds. 1990. *Wapapi Akonutomakonol: The Wampum Records; Wabanaki Traditional Laws.* Fredericton: Micmac-Maliseet Institute, University of New Brunswick.

Leavitt, Robert M., and Wayne A. Newell. 1974. *Tokec, Katop Qenoq Sipkiw (For now, but not for long).* Title VII ESEA. Indian Township, ME: Wabanaki Bilingual Education Program.

LeClercq, Chretien. 1910 [1691]. *New Relation of Gaspesia, with the Customs and Religion of the Gaspesian Indians.* Translated and edited by William F. Ganong. Publications of the Champlain Society, no. 5. Toronto: Champlain Society.

Leger, (Sister) Mary Celeste. 1929. *The Catholic Indian Missions in Maine (1611–1820).*

Vol. 8 of *Studies in American Church History*. Washington, DC: Catholic University of America.

Le Huray, Peter and James Day. 1981. *Music and Aesthetics in the Eighteenth and Early-Nineteenth Centuries*. New York: Cambridge University Press.

Le Jeune, Paul. [1634] 1896. "Relation de ce qui s'est passé en La Nouvelle France, en l'année 1634, Maison de N. Dame de Anges, en Nouvelle France, August 7." In *The Jesuit Relations and Allied Documents*, edited by Rueben Gold Thwaites. 6:91–317; 7:5–235. Cleveland: Burrows Brothers.

Leland, Charles Godfrey. 1884. *The Algonquin Legends of New England*. Boston: Houghton Mifflin.

Leland, Charles Godfrey, and John Dynely Prince. 1902. *Kulóskap the Master and Other Algonkin Poems*. New York: Funk & Wagnalls.

Lepore, Jill. 1998. *The Name of War: King Philip's War and the Origins of American Identity*. New York: Knopf.

Léry, Jean de. [1580] 1990. *History of a Voyage to the Land of Brazil, Otherwise Called America*. Translated by Janet Whatley. Berkeley: University of California Press.

———. [1585] 1941. *Viagem à terra do Brasil*. Translated by Sérgio Milliet. Sao Paulo: Livrario Martins.

Lescarbot, Marc. [1607] 1914. *La Défaite des Sauvages Armouchiquois*. In Lescarbot, *History of New France*. Vol. 3. Translated by W. L. Grant. Publications of the Champlain Society, no. 11.

———. [1618] 1968. *History of New France*. 3 vols. Translated by W. L. Grant. Publications of the Champlain Society, nos. 1, 7, 11.

LeSueur, Jacques. 1952. "History of the Calumet and of the Dance." *Contributions from the Museum of the American Indian, Heye Foundation* 12/5.

Levine, Victoria Lindsay. 2002. *Writing American Indian Music: Historic Transcriptions, Notations, and Arrangements*. Recent Researches in American Music, vol. 44; Music of the United States of America, vol. 11. Middleton, WI: A-R Editions.

Lochhead, Judy. 1982. "The Temporal Structure of Recent Music: A Phenomenological Investigation." Ph.D. dissertation, State University of New York at Stony Brook.

Lucey, William Leo, S.J. 1957. *The Catholic Church in Maine*. Francistown, NH: Marshall Jones.

MacCannell, Dean. 1984. "Reconstructed Ethnicity: Tourism and Cultural Identity in Third World Communities." *Annals of Tourism Research* 11:375–91.

Maillard, Abbé. 1758. *An Account of the customs and manners of the Mickmakis and Maricheets, Savage Nations…from an original French manuscript-letter, never published… to which are annexed, several pieces, relative to the savages, to Nova Scotia and to North-America in General*. London: Printed for S. Hooper and A. Morley.

———. 1863. "Lettre de M. L'Abbe Maillard…à Madame de Drucourt." *Les Soirees Canadiennes* 3. Quebec: Brousseau.

Maine Indian Tribal-State Commission. 1995. *Wabanaki: A New Dawn*. Videorecording. Produced by Dennis Kostyk and David Westphal. Hallowell, ME.

Mauss, Marcel. 1967 1925. *The Gift: Forms and Functions of Exchange in Archaic Societies*. Translated by Ian Cunnison. New York: Norton.

McAllester, David P. 1952. "Penobscot and Passamaquoddy Songs, Recorded at Indian Island, Maine." Northeast Archives of Folklore and Oral History, University of Maine at Orono, NA 857 [Tape].

McBride, Bunny. 1995. *Molly Spotted Elk: A Penobscot in Paris*. Norman: University of Oklahoma Press.

———. 1999. *Women of the Dawn*. Lincoln: University of Nebraska Press.

Mechling, William Hubbs. 1911. "Malicite and Micmac Songs, 1911." Canadian Museum of Civilization, Hull, PQ Collection III-E-1.

———. 1912. "On Micmac and Maliseet Work, 1911." In Canada, Department of Mines, Geological Survey Branch, *Summary Report of the Anthropological Division for the Calendar Years 1910 and 1911.*Ottawa: Government Printing Bureau.

———. 1914. "On Micmac and Maliseet Work." In Canada Department of Mines, Geological Survey Branch, *Summary Report of the Anthropological Division.* Ottawa: Government Printing Bureau.

———. 1917. "The Social and Religious Life of the Malecite and Micmacs." Ph.D. dissertation, Harvard University.

———. 1958–59. The Malecite Indians, with Notes on the Micmacs" *Anthropologica* 7–8.

Mersenne, Marin. [1636] 1965. *Harmonie universelle, contenant la théorie et la pratique de la musique*. Facsimile. Paris: Centre national de la recherche scientifique.

Milliea, Mildred. 1989. "Micmac Catholicism in My Community / Miigemeoei Alsotmagan Nemetgig." In *Actes du Vingtième Congrès des Algonquinistes*, edited by William Cowan. Ottawa: Carleton University.

Morrison, Alvin H. 1975. "Membertou's Raid on the Chouacoet 'Almouchiquois': The Micmac Sack of Saco in 1607." In *Papers of the Sixth Algonquian Conference*, 1974, edited by William Cowan, 141–58. National Museum of Man, Mercury Series. Canadian Ethnology Service, Paper no. 23. Ottawa: National Museums of Canada.

———. 1976. "Dawnland Directors: Status and Role of 17th Century Wabanaki Relationships." *Papers of the Seventh Anglonquian Conference, 1975*, edited by William Cowan, 495–517. Ottawa: Carleton University Press.

———. 1978. "Penobscot Country: Disagreement over Who Lived There in the 17th Century Needs Resolving—if Possible." *Papers of the Ninth Algonquian Conference*, 47–57. Worcester, MA.

———. 1980. "Frank G. Speck and Maine Ethnohistory." *Papers of the Eleventh Algonquian Conference*, 8–18.

———. 1982. "The Spirit of the Law versus the Storm Spirit: A Wabanaki Case." *Papers of the Thirteenth Algonquian Conference, 1981*, edited by William Cowan, 306–17. Ottawa: Carleton University.

———. 1992. "Indian Land-Deeds in the Northeast: Some Ethnohistorical Basics. *Papers of the Twenty-third Algonquian Conference*, 298–309. Ottawa: Carleton University.

———. 1994. "Case of the Slandered (?) Sagamore: Ouagimou of the St. Croix River." In *Papers of the Twenty-fifth Algonquian Conference*, 332–46. Ottawa: Carleton University.

———. 1995. "Anglo-Wabanaki Relations 1605–1630. *Papers of the Twenty-Sixth Algonquian Conference*, 291–305. Ottawa: Carleton University.

Morrison, Alvin H., and David Ezzo. 1985. "Dawnland Dualism in Northeastern Regional Context." *Papers of the Sixteenth Algonquian Conference*, 131–49. Ottawa: Carleton University.

Morrison (Spinney), Ann. 1996a. "Christians, Kyries, and Kci Niwesq." *European Review of Native American Studies*. 10/2:15–21.

———. 1996b. "Views of Repatriation—from the Ground." Paper presented at the annual meeting of the Society for Ethnomusicology, Toronto.

————. 1997. "Music that Moves between Worlds: Passamaquoddy Songs in the Cultural History of the Northeast." Ph.D. dissertation, Harvard University.

Morrison, Kenneth. 1974. "Baptism and Alliance: the Symbolic Mediations of Religious Syncretism." *Ethnohistory* 37/4:416–37.

Needham, Rodney. 1967. Percussion and Transition. *Man* 2:606–14, reprinted in *Reader in Comparative Religion: An Anthropological Approach*, 3rd ed., edited by William Lessa and Evon Vogt, 391–98. New York: Harper and Row, 1972.

Nettl, Bruno. 1989. *Blackfoot Musical Thought*. Kent, OH: Kent State University Press.

Nettl, Bruno, et al. 2001. *Excursions in World Music*. 3rd ed. Upper Saddle River, NJ: Prentice-Hall.

Nicolar, Joseph. 2007 [1893]. *The Life and Traditions of the Red Man*. Edited by Annette Kolodny. Durham, NC: Duke University Press.

Nordstrom, C. R. 2001. "War: Anthropological Aspects." In *International Encyclopedia of the Social and Behavioral Sciences*, edited by Neil J. Smelser and Paul B. Baltes, 16350–16354. Oxford: Pergamon. Available at http://www.sciencedirect.com.

Paper, Jordan. 1988. *Offering Smoke: The Sacred Pipe and Native American Religion*. Moscow: University of Idaho Press.

Peers, Laura. 1999. " 'Playing Ourselves': First Nations and Native American Interpreters at Living History Sites." *Public Historian* 21/4:39–59.

Picard, Michel, and Diana Darling. 1996. *Bali: Cultural Tourism and Touristic Culture*. Singapore: Archipelago.

Pisani, Michael. 2005. *Imagining Native America in Music*. New Haven: Yale University Press.

Plane, Ann Marie. 1996. "Putting a Face on Colonization: Factionalism and Gender Politics in the Life History of Awashunkes, the 'Squaw Sachem' of Saconet." In Robert S. Grumet, *Northwestern Indian Lives, 1632–1816* (Amherst: University of Massachusetts Press, 1996), 140–65.

Pote, William. 1896. *The Journal of Captain William Pote, Jr., During his Captivity in the French and Indian War from May, 1745, to August, 1747*. New York: Dodd, Mead.

Prince, John Dyneley. 1898. "Some Passamaquoddy Documents." *Annals of the New York Academy of Sciences* 11/15:369–77.

————. 1901. "Notes on Passamaquoddy Literature." *Annals of the New York Academy of Science*, 13:295–302.

————. 1921. *Passamaquoddy Texts*. In *Publications of the American Ethnological Society*, vol. 10. New York: G. E. Stechert.

Prince, John Dyneley. 1914. "The Morphology of the Passamaquoddy Language of Maine." *Proceedings of the American Philosophical Society*, 53/213:92–117.

Prins, Harald E. R. 1994. "Neo–Traditions in Native Communities: Sweat Lodge and Sun Dance among the Micmac Today." *Papers of the Twenty-fifth Algonquian Conference*, edited by William Cowan, 383–94. Ottawa: Carleton University Press.

————. 1996. *The Mi'kmaq: Resistance, Accommodation and Cultural Survival*. Case Studies in Cultural Anthropology. Orlando, FL: Harcourt Brace.

————. 1999. "Storm Clouds over Wabanakiak: Confederacy Diplomacy until Dummer's Treaty (1727)." Online at http://www.wabanaki.com/Harald_Prins.htm.

Quoddy Tides. Unsigned news articles, various dates. Eastport, ME.

Râle, Sebastian. 1722. Letter from Father Sébastien Rasles, Missionary of the Society of Jesus in New France, to Monsieur his Nephew, Nanrantsouak, October 15. In *The Jesuit*

Relations and Allied Documents, edited by Reuben Gold Thwaites, 67:84–119. Cleveland: Burrows.

[Râle] Rasles, Sebastian. 1691–1724. [Dictionary of the Abenaki Indian Language.] Manuscript. Houghton Library, Harvard University, Cambridge, MA.

Rand, Silas. 1850. *A Short Statement of Facts relating to the History, Manners, Customs, Language, and Literature of the Micmac Tribe of Indians in Nova Scotia and P.E. Island*. Halifax: J. Bowes.

———. 1894. *Legends of the Micmacs*. New York: Longmans, Green.

Rees-Miller, Janie. 1996. "Morphological Adaptation of English Loanwords in Algonquian." *International Journal of American Linguistics* 62/2:196–202.

Rhodes, Willard. 1987. "Program Notes to *Indian Songs of Today*." In *Music of the American Indian*, vol. 3. Washington, DC: Library of Congress.

Rollings, Willard Hughes. 2004. "Indians and Christianity" In *A Companion to American Indian History*, edited by Philip J. Deloria and Neal Salisbury. Oxford: Blackwell Reference Online, http://www.blackwellreference.com.

Romagne, James. 1834. *The Indian Prayer Book: Compiled and Arranged for the Benefit of the Penobscot and Passamaquoddy Tribes*. Boston: H. L. Devereux.

Rosier, James. 1605. *A True Relation of the Most Prosperous Voyage Made This Present Yeere 1605, by Captaine George Waymouth, in the Discovery of the Land of Virginia...* London: George Bishop; Early English Books Online, http://eebo.chadwick.com.

Rousseau, Jean–Jacques. [1768] 1969. *Dictionnaire de musique*. Facsimilie. Hildesheim, G. Olms; New York, Johnson Reprint Corp.

Sable, Trudy. 1998. "Multiple Layers of Meaning in the Mi'kmaw Serpent Dance." *Papers of the Twenty-Eighth Algonquian Conference*, edited by David H. Pentland. Winnipeg: University of Manitoba.

Sagard, Gabriel. [1636] 1939. *Histoire du Canada et voyages que les freres mineurs recollects y ont faicts pour la conversion des infidelles. Divisez en quatre livres. Où est... traicté des choses principales arrivées dans le pays deupis l'an 1615 jusques à la prise qui en a esté faicte par les Anglois*. Paris: C. Sonnius. Translated as *The Long Journey to the Country of the Hurons* by George McKinnon Wrong and H. H. Langton. Toronto: Champlain Society.

Schmidt, David L., and Murdena Marshall. 1995. *Mi'kmaq Hieroglyphic Prayers: Readings in North America's First Indigenous Script*. Halifax: Nimbus.

Seeger, Charles. 1977. *Studies in Musicology, 1935–1975*. Berkeley: University of California Press.

Shea, John Gilmary. 1855. *History of the Catholic missions among the Indian Tribes of the United States, 1529–1854*. New York: Edward Dunigan.

Siebert, Frank. 1941. Review of *Penobscot Man*. By Frank G. Speck. *American Anthropologist*, n.s. 43:278–80.

Slobin, Mark. 1992. "Micromusics of the West: A Comparative Approach." *Ethnomusicology* 36/1:1–87.

Smith, Nicholas N. 1955. "Wabanaki Dances." *Bulletin of the Massachusetts Archeological Society* 16/2:29–37.

———. 1957. "Smoking Habits of the Wabanaki." *Bulletin of the Massachusetts Archaeological Society*, 18/4:76–77

———. 1962. "St. Francis Indian Dances." *Ethnomusicology* 6/1:15–18.

————. 1959. "Wabanaki Songs and Dances Recorded between 1951 and 1959." Canadian Museum of Civilization, Hull, PQ, Collection III-E-2.

————. 1990. "The Long Shot: Fact and Tradition." *Papers of the Twenty-First Alogonquian Conference, 1989*, 337–44. Ottawa: Carleton University.

Sockabasin, Allen. 2007. *An Upriver Passamaquoddy*. Gardiner, ME: Tilbury House.

Socobasin, Mary Ellen. 1979. *Maliyan*. Indian Township, ME: Wabanaki Bilingual Education Program.

Soctomah, Donald. 2002. *Passamaquoddy at the Turn of the Century 1890–1920: Tribal Life and Times in Maine and New Brunswick*. Indian Township, ME: Passamaquoddy Tribe of Indian Township.

————. 2003. *Hard Times at Passamaquoddy, 1921–1950: Tribal Life and Times in Maine and New Brunswick*. Indian Township, ME: Passamaquoddy Tribe of Indian Township.

Speck, Frank G. 1911. "Songs, Various Native American Groups, 1905–1911." Indiana University, Archives of Traditional Music (ATM), Collection 60-018-F.

————. 1915a. "The Family Hunting Band as the Basis of Algonkian Social Organization." *American Anthropologist* 17:289–305.

————. 1915b. "The Eastern Algonkian Wabanaki Confederacy." *American Anthropologist*, n.s. 17:492–508.

————. 1919a. "The Functions of Wampum among the Eastern Algonquian." *Memoirs of the American Anthropological Association* 6/1:3–71.

————. 1919b. Penobscot Shamanism. *Memoirs of the American Anthropological Association*, 6/4:237–88.

————. 1926. "Culture Problems in Northeastern North America." *Proceedings of the American Philosophical Society* 65/4:272–311.

————. 1928. "Wawenock Myth Texts from Maine." *43rd Annual Report of the Bureau of American Ethnology for the Years 1925–26*. Washington, D.C.

———— [1940] 1997. *Penobscot Man: The Life History of a Forest Tribe in Maine*. Philadelphia: University of Pennsylvania Press; Reprint, Orono: University of Maine Press.

Spinney, Ann Morrison. 1999. "Dance Songs and Questions of Intercultural Influence in Wabanaki Ceremonial Life." *Papers of the Thirtieth Algonquian Conference, 1999*, edited by David H. Pentland, 334–50. Winnipeg: University of Manitoba.

————. 1995. Sipayik 30th Annual Indian Day, 1995. Cassette tape. Waponahki Museum, Perry, ME, general collection.

————. 2006. "Medeolinuwok, Music, and Missionaries in Maine." In *Music in American Religious Experience*, edited by Philip V. Bohlman, Edith L. Blumhofer, and Maria M. Chow, 57–82. New York: Oxford University Press.

Spottswood, Richard K., ed. 1978. *Folk Music in America,* Vol. 15, *Religious Music*. Washington, DC: Library of Congress.

Stevenson, Robert. 1973. "Written Sources for Indian Music until 1882." *Ethnomusicology* 17/1:1–40, 3:399–439.

Szabo, Laslo, and Carl Bode. 1974. "English Loanwords in Malecite." *American Speech* 49/3–4:235–40.

Taussig, Michael. 1993. *Mimesis and Alterity: A Particular History of the Senses*. New York: Routledge.

Thoreau, Henry David. [1864] 1972. *The Maine Woods*. Edited by Joseph Moldenhauer. Princeton: Princeton University Press.

Titon, Jeff, et al. 2002. *Worlds of Music: An Introduction to the Music of the World's Peoples.* 4th ed. Belmont, CA: Schirmer/Thomson Learning/Wadsworth Group.

Tomer, Noel "Jack." n.d. Interview with Jeff McKeen. Northeast Archives of Folklore and Oral History, University of Maine at Orono, NA 2028.

Tomlinson, Gary. 2007. *The Singing of the New World.* New York: Cambridge University Press.

Trudel, Marcel. 2000. "Champlain, Samuel de." In *Dictionary of Canadian Biography On-line*, http://www.biographi.ca/EN. Toronto: University of Toronto.

———. 1966. *Le Comptoir, 1604–1627. Histoire de la Nouvelle-France.* Montreal: Fides.

Turnbaugh, William A. 1979. "Calumet Ceremonies as a Nativistic Response." *American Antiquity* 44/4:685–91.

Turner, Victor. 1986. *The Anthropology of Performance.* New York: PAJ Publications (a division of *Performing Arts Journal.*)

Underhill, Ruth Murray. 1938. *Singing for Power.* Berkeley: University of California Press.

Van Den Toorn, Pieter. 1991. "Politics, Feminism, and Music Theory." *Journal of Musicology* 9/3:275–99.

Vander, Judith. 1997. *Shoshone Ghost Dance Religion: Poetry, Songs, and Great Basin Context.* Urbana: University of Illinois Press.

Vecsey, Christopher. 1986. The Story and Structure of the Iroquois Confederacy. *Journal of the American Academy of Religion* 54/1:79–106.

Vennum, Thomas. 1982. *The Ojibwa Dance Drum: Its History and Construction.* Smithsonian Folklife Studies, no. 2. Washington, DC.

———. 1989. "The Changing Role of Women in Ojibway Music History." In *Women in North American Indian Music: Six Essays*, edited by Richard Keeling, 13–21. Society for Ethnomusicology, Special Series no. 6.

Vetromile, Eugene. 1858. *Ahiamihewintuhangan: The Prayer Song.* New York: E. Dunigan.

———. 1866. *The Abenakis and Their History.* New York: James B. Kirker.

Vollmann, William T. 1990. *Seven Dreams: A Book of North American Landscapes.* Vol. 1, *The Ice-Shirt.* New York: Viking.

Walker, Willard. 1973. "Gabriel Tomah's Journal: A Report." Manuscript, Archives of St. Joseph's Convent, Sisters of Mercy, Portland, ME.

Walls, Peter. 1996. *Music in the English Courtly Masque, 1604–1640.* New York: Oxford University Press.

Wallis, Wilson D., and Ruth Sawtell Wallis. 1955. *The Micmac Indians of Eastern Canada.* Minneapolis: University of Minnesota Press.

West, Patricia. 1998. *The Enduring Seminoles: From Alligator Wrestling to Ecotourism.* Gainesville: University Press of Florida.

White, Richard. 1991. The Middle Ground: Indians, Empires, and Republics in the Great Lakes Region, 1650–1815. New York: Cambridge University Press.

Whitehead, Ruth Holmes. 1988. *Stories from the Six Worlds: Micmac Legends.* Halifax: Nimbus.

———. 1991. *The Old Man Told Us: Excerpts from Micmac History 1500–1950.* Halifax, NS: Nimbus.

———. 2001. "Appendix: The Traditional Material Culture of the Native Peoples of Maine." In *Twelve Thousand Years: American Indians in Maine*, by Bruce Bourque, 249–309. (Lincoln: University of Nebraska Press).

Whitehead, Ruth Holmes, and Harold McGee. 1983. *The Micmac: How Their Ancestors Lived Five Hundred Years Ago.* Halifax, NS: Nimbus.

Williams, Roger. [1643] 1973. *A Key into the Language of America.* Edited by John J. Teunissen and Evelyn Hinz. Detroit: Wayne State University Press.

Williamson, William D. 1832. *History of the State of Maine, from Its First Discovery, A.D. 1602, to the Separation, A. D. 1820, Inclusive.* 2 vols. Facsimile reprint. Freeport, ME: Cumberland Press.

Willoughby, Charles C. 1973 [1935]. *Antiquities of the New England Indians with Notes on the Ancient Cultures of the Adjacent Territory.* Cambridge, MA: Peabody Museum of American Archaeology and Ethnology, Harvard University; reprint with Introduction by Stephen Williams (New York: AMS Press).

Witherspoon, Gary. 1977. *Language and Art in the Navajo Universe.* Ann Arbor: University of Michigan Press.

Wroth, Lawrence C. 1970. *The Voyages of Giovanni da Verrazzano, 1524–1528.* New Haven: Yale University Press.

Wzokhilain, Peter Paul. 1830. *Wobanaki kimzowi awighian* [Wabanaki prayerbook]. Boston: Crocker and Brewster.

Index